The cast and crew of It's a Wonderful Life *assembled for a photograph at the "wrap picnic" Frank Capra and Jimmy Stewart threw on August 4, 1946. As a joke, Capra and Stewart managed to appear in the picture twice (taking advantage of the sequential method necessary to produce this kind of extended horizontal photograph). On the left-hand side of the photograph, shown at the front of this book, they are on the extreme left; on the right-hand side, which is reproduced at the back of the book, they appear again, on the extreme right.*

THE
It's a Wonderful Life
BOOK

THE
It's a Wonder
BOOK

ful Life

by Jeanine Basinger

In Collaboration with the Trustees
of the Frank Capra Archives

Interviews by Leonard Maltin

PAVILION
MICHAEL JOSEPH

THIS IS A BORZOI BOOK
PUBLISHED BY ALFRED A. KNOPF, INC.

Grateful acknowledgment is made to the following for permission to reprint previously
published material:

The New Yorker Magazine, Inc.: "Wonderful" from The Talk of the Town, *The New
Yorker,* January 15, 1979. Copyright © 1979 by The New Yorker Magazine, Inc.
Reprinted by permission.

The Wall Street Journal: "A Christmas Movie's Wonderful Life," by John McDonough,
originally published in *The Wall Street Journal,* December 19, 1984. Reprinted by
permission of the author.

Library of Congress Cataloging-in-Publication Data

The "It's a wonderful life" book.

Includes the final script of the motion picture (by F. Goodrich,
A. Hackett, and F. Capra).
1. It's a wonderful life (Motion picture)   I. Basinger, Jeanine.
II. Maltin, Leonard.   III. Goodrich, Frances. It's a wonderful life.
IV. Frank Capra Archives
(Wesleyan University, Middletown, Conn.). Trustees.
PN1997.I7583.I87   1986   791.43′72   86-7313
ISBN 0-394-55605-4   ISBN 0-394-74719-4 (pbk.)

Manufactured in the United States of America

FIRST EDITION

For Frank and Lu

Contents

From Frank Capra

It's a Wonderful Life sums up my philosophy of filmmaking. First, to exalt the *worth* of the individual. Second, to champion *man* — plead his causes, protest any degradation of his dignity, spirit, or divinity. And third, to dramatize the viability of the individual — as in the theme of the film itself.

I wanted *It's a Wonderful Life* to say what Walt Whitman said to every man, woman, and babe in the world: "The sum of all known reverences I add up in you, whoever you are. . . ." I wanted it to reflect the compelling words of Fra Giovanni of nearly five centuries ago: "The gloom of the world is but a shadow. Behind it, yet within reach, is joy. There is a radiance and glory in the darkness, could we but see, and to see we have only to look. I beseech you to look!"

Today, people tell me *It's a Wonderful Life* is a classic, the kind of great film that "they don't make anymore," or even that "can never be made again." I say classics and great films are still to come. They will be made by the youth of today, and loving and praising the old films ought not to stop our belief that good ones are still to come.

In the meantime, I'm glad people want to keep on looking at *It's a Wonderful Life*. I hope they'll keep on looking at it and loving it long after I'm gone. I think they probably will. For myself, I can only say . . . it was my kind of film for my kind of people.

From the Capra Archives

The Frank Capra Archives at Wesleyan University contain a wealth of material covering all aspects of Capra's remarkable career. Of all these, none are more informative or entertaining than those which concern *It's a Wonderful Life*: production memos, press releases, telegrams, reviews, newspaper clippings, and letters from all around the world.

In reading through the letters, we noticed at once how often people not only praised Capra and thanked him for the film but also made suggestions about new projects to be based on it: radio plays, Broadway plays, musical productions from opera to musical comedy, television series, both daytime and nighttime, and, of course, the inevitable remakes and sequels. Some of these suggestions actually led to new productions, such as Marlo Thomas's 1977 television movie, "It Happened One Christmas," in which she played Mary Bailey in a feminized version of George's story. Other projects have been inspired by *It's a Wonderful Life*: David Thomson's use of characters from the film in his remarkable book *Suspects*; the Billy Joel video "You're Only Human." Of all these ideas, however, none was mentioned more often than a book in celebration of the film. After the Capra papers came to Wesleyan, many people suggested creating such a book to benefit the Archives, among them Raymond Carney, Jeffrey Lane, Charles Maland, Charles Wolfe, and Galen Guy Quick. It seems as if people not only wanted to watch reruns of the original film, they also wanted to possess parts of it — photos, clippings, anecdotes, scripts. This book is a result of those letters. We thank everyone who gave us the idea. We also thank Knopf and Bob Gottlieb for helping us with it.

This book tells the story of the production of *It's a Wonderful Life,* as it appears in the Frank Capra Archives. Some of the material is from his scrapbooks and advertising materials, some from his diaries, some from production files and notes, and some from correspondence and interviews. All photos, stills, and souvenirs are from his personal collection. Other archives, other files, may contain contradictory material; like all the great Hollywood films, *It's a Wonderful Life* is surrounded by press agentry and planted stories as well as by legendary tales that embellish the facts.

This book has been a labor of love and friendship, in the true spirit of *It's a Wonderful Life*. In July 1985 we gathered together at the Archives in Middletown, Connecticut, to go through all the material on *It's a Wonderful Life*. The times we shared together, working, discussing, cooking, eating, and, of course, laughing, will always be for us a part of the movie's total spell. The book is a collaboration of friends, not only among the Trustees, but also with Leonard and Alice Maltin, Steve Ross, John and Savannah Basinger, Bob Gottlieb, Audrey Kupferberg, and Angie Berger. We also wish to thank James Stewart, Donna Reed, Joe Biroc, the UCLA Archives, John Hall and David Chierichetti at the RKO Archives, Steven Spielberg, Dustin Hoffman, John T. McDonough, Joe McBride, the Academy of Motion Picture Arts and Sciences, and, for his support of the Archives, Colin Campbell of Wesleyan University. This book is for everyone who loves *It's a Wonderful Life* as much as we do.

Jeanine Basinger, *Curator*

Trustees: Bruce Corwin, Daniel Edelman, John Goldsmith, Patricia Manney, Toni Ross, Leah Schmidt, Alicia Springer, *and* Richard Teller

THE
It's a Wonderful Life
BOOK

The Many Lives of
IT'S A WONDERFUL LIFE

O n September 1, 1945, Charles Koerner, then the head of RKO Radio Pictures, sold Frank Capra a property. Koerner was glad to get rid of it, even though his company would end up distributing the resulting film. For a lowly $10,000, he unloaded a story that had been on the shelves of RKO for some time, a property that allegedly was first bought at the suggestion of Cary Grant. Both Grant and RKO thought it might be a suitable vehicle for the popular star, but, try as they might, no one seemed able to turn the oddball story into a treatment that could work well on screen. Koerner sold Capra and his new company, Liberty Films, the rights to the property, all the original material, and three complete versions of a script for it, attempted by such diverse talents as Marc Connelly, Dalton Trumbo, and Clifford Odets. At the time, it didn't seem like a very important deal. In fact, it was more than two weeks (on September 16) until the *Motion Picture Daily* carried a terse and very precise announcement of the transaction: "Liberty Films has announced 'The Greatest Gift,' an original by Philip Van Doren Stern, as its first production. Frank Capra will produce and direct."

Not a very illustrious beginning for what would ultimately become one of the most beloved films in the history of movies — Frank Capra's *It's a Wonderful Life*.

In the fall of 1945, Frank Capra had just returned to Hollywood from his World War II service in the Office of War Information. He hadn't made a commercial feature for the duration of the war, and he was anxious to return to work — anxious, and a bit frightened. He had changed. The world had changed. Could he still work the old magic that had made him one of the most successful and respected of all Hollywood directors? Capra told *New York Times* reporter Thomas M. Pryor: "It's frightening to go back to Hollywood after four years . . . wondering whether you've gone rusty or lost

touch. I keep telling myself how wonderful it would be just to sneak out somewhere and make a couple of quickie westerns first — just to get the feel of things again."

The Wesleyan Cinema Archives include the records of Frank Capra's World War II service to his country — his scripts and plans for the remarkable "Why We Fight" series, his citation for the Distinguished Service Medal, his pictures of himself with Churchill, his letters from George Marshall. There are also photographs of the victims of Nazi atrocities, part of the material Capra needed to produce the motion pictures that his citation hailed as "a remarkable series . . . which graphically presented the causes leading up to the present war and the responsibility of the Axis powers for the tragic consequences." When Capra came back to Hollywood after the war, he brought the atrocity material with him; it represented the new darkness in his vision of the world. His work had always had its darker side — the political corruption of *Meet John Doe* and *Mr. Smith Goes to Washington* — but his natural optimism and humor had always carried the day. It would continue to do so, but in the immediate postwar period, Capra was looking for a story that could express some of what he had been feeling during World War II, and yet still remain "a Frank Capra comedy." In his autobiography, Capra wrote that he faced "a loneliness that was laced with the fear of failure." As he would tell Walter Karp for *Esquire* magazine in 1981, after the war Capra wondered, "Perhaps I had put too much faith in the human race — you know, in the pictures I had made. Maybe they were too much as things should be. I began to think that maybe I really was a Pollyanna."

When Frank Capra came across the Van Doren Stern property, he felt it might be right for his first postwar film. Although the war had sobered him, he still valued laughter, and he felt he was the right

The Liberty Films Corporation partners. LEFT TO RIGHT, Frank Capra, William Wyler, George Stevens, Samuel Briskin.

man to give the story its required Dickensian blend of humor and pathos. Above all, he saw that he could turn "The Greatest Gift" into a perfect starring vehicle for James Stewart. Capra, with his unerring instinct for understanding how to create powerful, involving movies, was unafraid of the theme of suicide and of the protagonist's moments of despair. He commented to interviewers and to co-workers: "Sometimes a greater lesson can be read into a bad example than a good one."

Capra saw at once the problems screenwriters had encountered with Van Doren Stern's story. It was thinly developed, containing only one idea (although that remained the central idea of the completed film) — a man given a chance to see what the world would have been like if he had never lived. The problem was what to stress. The fantasy? The despair? The social milieu that shaped the character?

Capra knew that to weave fantasy and reality together effectively would be difficult—to interest

an audience in a potential suicide for two hours would require some humor, but not so much humor that the viewers wouldn't take his impending death seriously. It demanded a delicate balance of real and unreal, dark and light, that had defeated the earlier scriptwriters, who found themselves able to create only one side or the other.

Unlike some directors who returned from World War II and floundered at first, Capra, always an organized man, was ready to go. On April 10, 1945, even before he had officially returned to civilian life, Capra had formed Liberty Films Corporation in partnership with Samuel Briskin. (Later, on July 6, William Wyler would join Liberty as the third partner, and George Stevens would become the fourth on January 5, 1946.) When the announcement of the purchase of "The Greatest Gift" appeared in the trades on September 16, 1945, Capra had already assigned husband-and-wife screenwriters Albert Hackett and Frances Goodrich the task of helping him create a completely

4

new script. Capra's notes and files indicate that while they worked, he hustled around town and did what producers do — set about assembling the best cast and crew he could possibly put together.

From the beginning, he wanted only one actor for the leading role — James Stewart. On October 10, 1945, he talked to Stewart, and Capra's notebook on the production reads: "Wasserman [Stewart's agent] present in Briskin's apartment. As I tell story, it evaporates into thin air. Tell Stewart to forget it. Wasserman dying. Jimmy doesn't want to hear story."

Although Capra's notes say nothing else about the matter, legend has created its own versions of this celebrated encounter. In his autobiography, Capra himself created a colorful, detailed version of it — a sort of miniature Frank Capra movie with himself as Mr. Smith. (When Stewart tells the story, *he* plays Mr. Smith; Capra is more William Demarest.) Stewart told reporters in May 1946,

"I'd decided some time before coming back to Hollywood that if I could, I'd make my first picture with Capra. Looking back over the pictures I'd done before going away, I felt that the two previous ones I'd made under his direction had been, to me at least, the most satisfying." Then, added Stewart, Capra called him up and said, "I've got a script for you to read." Stewart said he went to pick it up, read it, and called Capra the next morning, saying, "This is it. When do we start?"

Capra says that as he told the story in Briskin's apartment, it sounded "dumber and dumber — talking angels, heavenly voices — What was I saying?" but that Stewart finally said that if Capra was directing, he'd take a chance on it. Whatever happened, and whenever it happened, the fact is that on November 5, 1945, James Stewart signed with Liberty Films to play the lead in Capra's "Greatest Gift" project, which had been newly titled *It's a Wonderful Life*. A clause was written into his

Liberty Films, Capra's longtime dream of artistic independence, becomes a legal reality.

contract forbidding any publicity exploitation of his exemplary war record. Stewart explained his choice of his first postwar film role with a simple public statement: "I don't pick stories. I pick directors."

On November 16, Capra wrote: "I try to interest Jean Arthur in girl part. Go to NY to talk to her. She refuses. She has promised Garson Kanin to go into his play." Wonderful though she was, Arthur was perhaps too sophisticated and also perhaps already too old for the part. Choosing her might have made the film slightly less romantic, more cerebral and sophisticated. Mary would have had to be more independent, more critical of George, more of a force in helping him make choices. If Jean Arthur had said yes, *It's a Wonderful Life* would not be the same film, and her own postwar career might have been very different. Her Garson Kanin play — *Born Yesterday* — did not work out for her, and she made only a few more movies.

With his first choice eliminated, Capra then prepared a detailed list of possible casting suggestions for all the roles in *It's a Wonderful Life,* some of which are intriguing as well as surprising.

Interestingly, this list contains no suggestions for the role of Clarence. (How do you cast an angel, particularly an *incompetent* one?) Henry Travers, who immortalized the role and defined forever the cinematic concept of Angel Second Class, is listed as a possible choice for several other parts, among them George Bailey's father (a role finally given to Samuel S. Hinds), the drunken druggist (H. B. Warner), and Uncle Billy (Thomas Mitchell).

But there is something about Travers, in his voice and in his face, that gives him a mysterious quality: as cheerful and believable as the old man down the street who putters in his garden every day, and yet fey and magical too. In the end, Henry Travers alone could give us Clarence, because he brought the totally believable together with the incredibly imaginary in just the proper mixture, and because his marvelous "otherness" is essentially benign.

Looking over Capra's lists, it can be seen what a great many people he considered for even the most minor roles. One of Capra's strong points as a director was his attention to detail. He wanted the

most memorable face he could find in even the tiniest role, and he wanted each of those actors to understand his character in a much larger sense. "Be somebody," he told bit players. "If you're walking down the street, where are you going and why?"

To picture any of the *It's a Wonderful Life* roles played by anyone other than the person finally cast is almost impossible. To look at Capra's list of other choices and weigh them against the final ones is to see his incredible skill in casting. If Claude Rains had been Potter . . . or Louis Calhern . . . or Raymond Massey . . . Potter would have been a more sophisticated and urbane character. Capra's final choice of Lionel Barrymore created a proper villain in the dastardly-landlord tradition, but it also created an appropriately *small-town* villain. Potter belongs in Bedford Falls. His horizons are greedy but limited.

One of Capra's biggest headaches was the casting of George's wife, Mary Bailey. When Jean Arthur turned him down, he decided to reconsider the character and look for a lesser-known actress. Publicity agents for RKO coaxed Hedda Hopper into promoting RKO favorite Ginger Rogers for the role. Rogers and Stewart had starred together earlier with great success in George Stevens's *Vivacious Lady,* so Hopper wrote in her March 13, 1946 column: "How would you like to see Jimmy Stewart and Ginger Rogers in another picture together? Well, you'll probably be doing just that. Frank Capra wants Ginger for the role opposite Jimmy in *It's a Wonderful Life.* She's reading the script right now."

Capra's files, however, do not indicate that he ever sent Rogers the script or even considered her for the role. In fact, on March 15, two days after Hopper's story appeared, he signed fresh-faced Donna Reed for the part, and records indicate that he had made up his mind to borrow her from MGM as early as January 30. Reed wanted the part, but Metro held out, refusing to lend her to Capra unless she signed a new seven-year contract with MGM. Since she had nearly two years to go on her current one, she was naturally reluctant. But by March 15 the deal was made, and Reed was asked to report the following week for her costume and makeup tests. It was Donna Reed's first assignment away from her home lot, and Metro bosses were

OVERLEAF: *Capra's lists of possible actors for each of the characters in the film, with last-minute thoughts (including the notion of W. C. Fields as Uncle Billy!) added in his own hand.*

IT'S A WONDERFUL LIFE

GEORGE

James Stewart

MARY

Olivia DeHaviland
Martha Scott
Ann Dvorak
~~Jean~~ *(struck through)*

HERBERT POTTER

Dan Duryea	- Stanley Ridges
Henry Hull	- Victor Jory
Charles Bickford	- Walter Abel
Lee Tracy	- Leon Ames
Thomas Mitchell	- Raymond Massey
Ray Collins	- Richard Gaines
Louis Calhern	- Edgar Barrier
George Colouris	- Edward Arnold
Charles Dingle	- George Bancroft
Gene Lockhart	- Charles Halton

Edgar Buchanan — Albert Dekker
Otto Kruger — Tommy Gomez
Claude Rains — Vincent Price
Charles Coburn

UNCLE BILLY

Barry Fitzgerald
Walter Brennan
Donald Meek
Leon Errol - x
Dudley Digges
Frank Morgan - x
Ernest Truex
Henry Travers
Porter Hall
Grant Mitchell
James Bell   *my tel*
Tom Tully   *Tommy Fitzgerald*
Cecil Kellaway
Roman Bohnen   *Vic Moore*
Charles Ruggles
Eddie Horton
Hugh Herbert
Roland Young
Adolphe Menjou
W.C. Fields

OLD MAN GOWER

Donald Meek
Harry Davenport
Charles Grapewin
Irving Bacon
John Qualen
Erskine Sanford
Samuel Hinds
Percy Kilbride
Henry Travers
Happy Cheshire
Phillip Merivale
E. J. Ballantyne
Charles Halton
Jimmy Conlin.
Jean Hersholt
Guy Kibbee
Reggie Owen.

chekov

PETER BAILEY (FATHER)

Henry Travers
Russell Hicks
Thurston Hall
Tom Tully
Moroni Olsen
Sam Hinds

VIOLET BICK

Ann Doran
Iris Adrian
Claire Carleton
Veda Ann Borg
Bernadine Hayes
Doris Merrick
Betty Lawford
Isabel Jewel
Jean Porter
Myrna Dell

AUNT LAURA

Mildred Natwick
Olive Blakeny
Spring Byington
Jean Adair
Mildred Dunnock
Florence Bates
Margalo Gillmore
Patricia Collinge
Mary Boland
Barbara O'Neil
Mary Nash.
Isobel Elsom

ANN (COOK)

Jane Darwell
Sara Allgood
Clara Blandioi
Una O'Connor
Hattie McDaniel
Helen Broderick
Irene Ryan
Ruth Donnelly
Connie Gilchrist

Hattie McDaniel

ERNIE (TAXI DRIVER)
William Demarest
Frank Jenks
Walter Sande ———————
Frank McHugh
Walter Catlett
John Ireland
Red (Charles) Marshall
Wally Ford
Don Barclay
Allan Carney
Eddie Brophy

Steve Brodie

BERT (MOTORCYCLE COP)
John Alexander
Walter Sande ———
Irving Bacon
James Burke
Wally Brown
Barton MacLane
Sam Levene
Ward Bond
Bob Mitchum

AUGUST FRIEHOFER
John Qualen
Steve Geray
Geo Cleveland

SAM WAINWRIGHT
Gordon Oliver
John Howard
Van Heflin
Dean Jagger
Gene Raymond
Kent Smith
Phil Warren
Alan Joslyn
Bill Goodwin

MARIA MARTINI (WIFE)

GUISEPPE MARTINI
Frank Puglie
William Edmunds
Nestor Paiva
Chef Milani
Bob Vignola
Louis Alberni
Fortunio Bononova
— Ed Cianelli
Joe Calleia

MOTHER BAILEY
Ann Revere
Selena Royle
Kathleen Lockhart
Mary Nash
Mary Young

HEAVEN - JOSEPH
Wilcoxson
Maurice Evans
Fritz Leiber
John Carradine
Michael Chekhov

OFFICIAL
Trowbridge

CLARENCE

MISS SACKLEY
Anita Bolster
Constance Purdy

RUTH DAKIN

DR. CAMPBELL - Loan Board
Henry Kalker
Harry Tyler
Charles Williams
Eddie Laughton

MRS. HATCH (Mary's Mother)

MARTY HATCH

INGIE (Town Girl)
Stock

very pleased to have her opposite Stewart in a Capra film. They participated in a large publicity buildup for her, culminating in a *Life* magazine cover story in the June 10, 1946 issue.

The casting of Donna Reed as Mary Bailey provided a very specific direction to the film. She sweetens the film, in the finest sense of the word. As a young woman, she is surely one of the loveliest American girls anyone could imagine. (In real life, she had grown up as an Iowa farm girl.) Her innocence and purity represent the pull that Bedford Falls and all its inhabitants would exert on George, what keeps him *home,* year after year after year. Since the point of the film is that this was a wonderful thing, beautiful Donna Reed represents both Stewart's reward and the proof that he made the right choice.

THE It's a Wonderful Life PLAYERS.
BACK ROW, LEFT TO RIGHT: *Charles Williams, Mary Treen, Sarah Edwards, Beulah Bondi, Ward Bond, Thomas Mitchell, James Stewart, Donna Reed, Frank Capra, H. B. Warner, Frank Faylen, Todd Karns, Bill Edmunds.* FRONT ROW, LEFT TO RIGHT: *Harry Holman, Jimmy Hawkins, Carol Coomes, Lionel Barrymore, Larry Simms, Karolyn Grimes, Gloria Grahame.*

The Cast

Donna Reed

as Mary Bailey

James Stewart

as George Bailey

HENRY TRAVERS
as Clarence, the Angel

THOMAS MITCHELL
as Uncle Billy

Lionel Barrymore
as Mr. Potter
and Gloria Grahame *as Violet*

Ward Bond as Bert

Frank Faylen as Ernie

Beulah Bondi as Mrs. Bailey

Bobbie Anderson as young George

Of course, it is impossible to imagine anyone but Jimmy Stewart in the part of George Bailey, and, in many ways, people think of it as *his* film. There is no doubt that his performance is practically perfect, and his personal qualities deepen the role. Stewart's persona is not the "gosh darn, gee whiz" thing many people assume. He can be remarkably complex and ambiguous — a quality that directors as different as Capra, Alfred Hitchcock, and Anthony Mann all observed and put to use in very different films. Capra used Stewart's tension, his underlying anger and indignation, to create a man with an outraged sense of justice in *Mr. Smith Goes to Washington,* one with a modern outlook on social equality in *You Can't Take It with You,* and one with a deep personal frustration because of dreams gone astray in *It's a Wonderful Life.* Hitchcock used him as an obsessive in both *Rear Window* and *Vertigo,* and Anthony Mann used his capacity for anger to create a hero hell bent on revenge in a series of excellent westerns. Hitchcock and Mann, however, worked out of what Capra had seen and developed in Stewart, and no director ever understood him better.

Slowly, the final cast was signed and the trades carried the announcements:

April 1. Lionel Barrymore borrowed from MGM to play Potter. ("It's a great villain," Capra wrote. "People seeing him will ask themselves whether they have any of the qualities he portrays and will shun even the faintest traces of them.")

April 4. H. B. Warner signed to play the drunken druggist. (This was a highly unusual choice. Ever since he had played Christ in Cecil B. De Mille's *King of Kings* in 1927, Warner had been offered mostly dignified roles. "Twenty years ago," Warner told reporters, "De Mille typed me and I've been typed ever since. Lost hundreds of jobs. C. B. will die when he sees me playing a bum in Capra's new picture, but I'm delighted. I'm playing the damndest, dirtiest bum you ever saw, a proper drunk. . . . Thanks to Capra, who used a little imagination.")

April 5. Samuel S. Hinds to play George's father. ("He looks like a father. He's so perfect he looks like *two* fathers," Capra once told a film class.)

According to newspaper accounts of 1946, Stewart himself helped in the casting of Gloria Grahame as the town "bad girl," Violet. In describing the girl he wanted, Capra told Stewart, "She has to be sultry! She must be beautiful, too, because she'll be vying with Donna Reed for your love. But she can't be a big-town siren. She's got to have a small-town goodness about her." (According to Capra, Stewart had replied, "I see. She's a good girl, but willing to be bad for the right guy.")

With shooting set to begin, Capra still had not found the actress he wanted for the part. According to press releases, Stewart volunteered to keep his eyes open (at that time, he was quite a notorious young bachelor about town). As newspapers of the day tell it, Stewart paid a call on his friend Bill Grady, head casting director at MGM, where Stewart had first become a star. Told that Grady was in the projection room looking at some screen tests, Stewart went in to join him. Grady was looking at footage of Gloria Grahame, who had played bit parts in such MGM films as *Without Love,* starring Hepburn and Tracy. When Stewart saw Grahame on screen, he felt she would be perfect as Violet, and he borrowed the test to show Capra. (Capra's autobiography says he himself walked in on Grady, and today Stewart also says it was Capra.) Capra took one look, said, "That's a good bad girl if I ever saw one," and Grahame got the part, one of her first big breaks in film.

With Grahame the last of the casting was completed, and production records on casting close out with Capra's hiring of two midgets, Charlotte Sullivan and Henry Stone, to act as stand-ins for the children playing Stewart and Reed's offspring. (Since children were subject to both school calls and state child welfare and labor laws, the midgets were a time-saving, money-saving Hollywood expediency.)*

One final note on casting: last but not least, Jimmy the Raven. Jim first worked for Frank Capra in *You Can't Take It With You* in 1938. Since that time, he had played a role in every picture Capra had shot in Hollywood. Alas, there was no part for a raven in the original shooting script of *It's a Wonderful Life.* Nevertheless, one day in July, Jimmy the Raven appeared on the set in the company of

* See Appendixes for complete cast list and bit part and extra budget.

his trainer, Curley Twifford. Before too long, the intrepid bird was sitting on Thomas Mitchell's desk in the Building and Loan set during shooting breaks, and, in true show business legend, Capra wrote him into the script as a permanent living desk ornament. Not content with a mere fly-on, Jimmy, the old pro, padded his role whenever possible. You can't keep a good raven down. In a moment of madness, Capra wrote a dramatic scene for Jimmy: "Potter pecked by Uncle Billy's crow and has to be rushed to drug store." But sanity prevailed, and the scene was never shot. It remains only as one of Capra's handwritten notes on his estimating script.

Capra's files indicate that after Goodrich, Hackett, and he finished their script in January 1946, it was scheduled to undergo "polishing" by Jo Swerling. At the same time, the New York *Herald* of February 18, 1946, carried the news item that Dorothy Parker had changed her plans to return to New York in order to remain in Hollywood to "polish" the screenplay for *It's a Wonderful Life.* No written records of Parker's alleged polishing job, or of any payment for work done by her, exist in Frank Capra's files. Swerling was given the on-screen credit "additional scenes by" for his contributions, which are marked as "Swerling-Capra" and dated April 18, 1946, in Capra's personal copy of the estimating script.

Capra had worked closely with Goodrich and Hackett, and he receives screen credit — "Screenplay by Frances Goodrich, Albert Hackett and Frank Capra" — but no specific records of this collaboration are in the files. His contributions can be seen by comparing the final script and his own estimating script. As to the three original versions by Connelly, Trumbo, and Odets, Capra told Richard Glatzer in a 1973 interview that he kept in "a couple of scenes from the Odets script." When pressed as to which ones, he replied, "Well, the relationship between the boy and the drugstore man."*

On March 15, Capra announced a ninety-day schedule for *It's a Wonderful Life,* and Capra's autobiography affixes the official starting date as April 8, 1946.† The original budget was set at

$1,700,000. (After sixty days, it would be re-estimated at $2,300,000.) A few days earlier, Capra had told the Los Angeles *Times* drama editor, Edwin Schallert:

> People are numb after the catastrophic events of the past 10 or 15 years. I would not attempt to reach them mentally through a picture, only emotionally. Anything of a mental sort, anything apart from the purely human will have to be incidental. Improving the individual and bringing a more hopeful outlook on life to him is the only way that you can improve the nation, and ultimately the world. It is the individual that must be built up in his beliefs, his hopes and his aspirations and then as a matter of course you will find the new world we all talk about developing in the larger way. I think first that we must entertain in pictures . . . and then convey our message, whatever it may be, but achieve this quite incidentally.

As Capra worked over the script he was about to shoot — tightening, writing new dialogue, changing characterizations, eliminating scenes in some places, adding needed action in others — he prepared a list of notes, his handwritten comments on everything from sound and gag ideas to the philosophy that underlies the film. The list shows some of his thoughts, his ideas, his questions, and provides remarkable insight into Capra's mind and method.

He jots down funny lines as he thinks of them and notes recurring bits of business that might be used to delineate characters. He questions how a major character, like George, is linked to a minor character, like Annie, the cook in the Bailey home. He makes sure there are *reasons* why characters do things, such as Ernie looking for George at night at the Building and Loan. He quotes Thoreau and waxes poetic ("I'm going to taste of eternity"). He reflects on the different sounds rain makes in summer and winter, on leaves or bare limbs (no sound at all if the limbs are of pine trees). No detail is too small to be worked on, polished, perfected. In college, Capra had been trained as a scientist, and his keen sense of observation and attention to detail is reflected in his notes.

---

* See pages 103–107 for a discussion of the early scripts.
† See Appendix D for shooting schedule.

[Handwritten facsimile of the notes below]

1. "To inform the quality of the day." Thoreau

2. Lord's prayer at end —
   Uncle Billy or Mary pray alone. Mass prayer only if parson or priest present to lead.

3. Xmas song at end.
   Should be merry.

4. Mary at Library at end —
   Timing bad at 11:30 p.m. Could be Xmas party or decorating job to be finished that night.

5. Mrs. Hatch at end —
   Not taken care of.

6. "Excuse me!" "Excuse me!" "What's the matter?" "I burped."
   Use for Little Tommy and George.

7. "Hey, fellas, whatcha doing?" "Just breathing."

(8) [handwritten: George matches nickels with some one. Running gag.]

(9) [handwritten: The differences between sound of rain in summer and winter. Rain on leaves makes a different sound than rain on bare limbs. But not in a grove of pines.]

(10) [handwritten: The quest of man has no limitations. I'm going to taste of eternity.]

(11) [handwritten: Like three colors of an icicle in the sun.

(Possible forword)
There's a reason in the world for even a blade of grass.

—

How does George affect luggage man's life?

—

How does George affect Annie?

—]

8. George matches nickels with someone. Running gag.

9. The differences between sound of rain in summer and winter. Rain on leaves makes a different sound than rain on bare limbs. But not in a grove of pines.

10. The quest of man has no limitations. I'm going to taste of eternity.

11. Like three colors of an icicle in the sun.
(Possible forword)
There's a reason in the world for even a blade of grass.
———

How does George affect luggage man's life?
———

How does George affect Annie?
———

Ernie has hunch he would find George at Bldg and Loan at night. Evidently George has worked many nights.

Violet more during unborn sequence. Make more violent and vicious. Being beaten up, or arrested.

Bailey Sr. & Uncle Billy in re offices. "must build a door in between."

Ed and Miss Brackett. Running romance. Ed love-sick but Miss Brackett dreams and moons only of movie stars. Ed cant compete

---

Franklin. Still flies kites in heaven.
Still reads Sat. Eve. Post.

Ernie has hunch he would find George at Bldg and Loan at *night*. Evidently George has worked many nights.

Violet more during unborn sequence. Make more violent and vicious. Being beaten up, or arrested.

Bailey, Sr. & Uncle Billy in re offices "must build a door in between."

Ed and Miss Brackett. Running romance. Ed love-sick but Miss Brackett dreams and moons only of movie stars. Ed can't compete.

Franklin. Still flies kites in heaven.
Still reads Sat. Eve Post.

Ed + Miss Brackett — always saying it's their last
week.

Violet — beauty shop operator — men hanging around — she
leaves them for George — when George leaves she whistles
and men come running.

George and Clarence.
George.
"I was a 4·F. ~~——~~ In my case it
didn't stand for four freedoms, it meant
four failures. failure as a husband,
father, business — failure as a human
being. I wish I'd never been born."

Violet
She ~~——~~ doesn't count sheep to go to
sleep, she counts men.

Ed + Miss Brackett — always saying it's their last week.

Violet — beauty shop operator — men hanging around — she leaves them for George — when George leaves she whistles and men come running.

George and Clarence.
George:
"I was a 4–F. In my case it didn't stand for four freedoms — it meant four failures. Failure as a husband, father, business — failure as a human being — I wish I'd never been born."

Violet
She doesn't count sheep to go to sleep, she counts *men*.

Prior to the start of shooting, two months were spent at RKO's Encino Ranch, constructing "Bedford Falls," one of the longest sets that had ever been made for an American movie. The main street was 300 yards long — three whole city blocks — including a tree-lined center parkway, 75 stores and buildings, a bank with a marble front, a rubber tile floor, and real cashier's cages, a post office, and a library. The set was built in separate sections, and when it was put together, it covered over four acres. The separate sections were the downtown business section on Main Street, a factory district, a large residential area, and a slum section. The main street of Bedford Falls would be seen in all four seasons. Twenty full-grown oak trees were transplanted to the street. All the shots for spring and summer were made while the trees bloomed. For autumn, crews knocked the leaves off for filming, and for the winter scenes, the limbs of the trees were sprayed with fifty tons of white plaster.

"The largest special effects crew ever assembled," according to a press release, worked three weeks to create the snowstorm that takes place the night of George's contemplated suicide. Capra had always loved special effects, and his background in chemical engineering had helped him to produce

many unusual effects for his films, including the use of a real ice house for the snow scenes in *Lost Horizon* and the innovative use of convection currents, an aquarium, and sodium bubbles to create the illusion of ocean depths in his underwater rescue story, *Submarine.* (He was also a master at nighttime shooting; and in filming the night scenes of *It's a Wonderful Life,* he used enough electricity to illuminate a city with a population of five thousand.) For *It's a Wonderful Life,* Capra wanted snow that looked real. For years, movies had used gypsum and cornflakes to create snow — the gypsum for snow on the ground, and white-coated cornflakes dropped between the players and the camera to simulate falling flakes. Because cornflakes were noisy — plenty of crunch and crackle — close-ups had to be shot without sound and voices dubbed in later. Capra wanted a snow effect that would allow him to record live dialogue.

Special effects man Russell Shearman, working with his RKO staff, evolved a new snow technique which mixed foamite (the chemical mix used in fire extinguishers) with soap and water. When this was forced out of large pipes under high pressure, the mixture resembled a ribbon of pure white fluff. Blown through wind machines, that same ribbon of fluff took on the consistency and shape of real snowflakes. And while the cornflakes could be dropped only at one speed, the rhythm of the wind machine could be varied. The foamite snow could therefore look soft and fluffy, like a whirling storm, or as wild as a raging blizzard. "Tastes swell, too," Jimmy Stewart would later tell a publicist. "The only trouble is you have to work fast with it. If I take too long, what with the soap and the water, I'm apt to find myself frothing at the mouth."

Altogether, the winter scenes used 300 tons of plaster — 250 of it to build up snow banks, 50 to spray in the snow mixture. Window sills were covered with gypsum. Snow paths and rutted car tracks were made out of 3,000 tons of shaved ice. *It's a Wonderful Life* would ultimately use more snow than any motion picture since *Lost Horizon.* The special effects crew spent three weeks getting ready to create the snowstorm. Their job was to cover all four acres of Bedford Falls with snow. Besides the 3,000 tons of shaved ice, the 300 tons of gypsum, and the 300 tons of plaster, they used 6,000 gallons of chemicals for the new film snow which replaced the trusty crunchy white cornflakes.

The day they began to shoot the snowstorm, it was 84°F, and by noon it was in the 90s. The "snow," however, remained hard and cold-looking. Everyone stood around to watch, despite the heat. Reporters were brought in, to give the always desirable extra bit of publicity: "Refreshing!" wrote Walter Hackett of the Lansing, Michigan *State Journal* on June 30, 1946.

Out of the nozzles, ejected under very high pressure came the purest of driven snow, all made from chemicals. When used as a ground covering, the new snow looked properly slushy, as though it had been walked through, driven over, and then had lain around town awhile. When shot through the air, it looked like perfect falling, fluffy snowflakes. It was no problem to work with, being odorless and harmless to clothes, paint, wood, and people, to follow Hollywood's usual order of economic priority. (Capra once turned to a companion during a screening of *It's a Wonderful Life* and confessed, "I am in love with weather. Movie weather,

I mean.") At the 1948 Oscar ceremony, Russell Shearman, Marty Martin, Jack Lannon, and the RKO Radio Studio Special Effects Department would receive a Motion Picture Academy Class III Certificate of Honorable Mention "for the development of a new method of simulating falling snow on motion picture sets."

In early April, Capra sent a copy of his estimating script to his editor, William Hornbeck, asking Hornbeck to review all potential legal, censorship, continuity, and credibility problems. Capra totally trusted Hornbeck, the distinguished film editor who had worked with him on the "Why We Fight" series and who would edit such famous Hollywood films as *Shane* and *A Place in the Sun* as well as *It's a Wonderful Life*. Capra and Hornbeck became lifelong friends, and in his will, William Hornbeck left his own papers and memorabilia to the Capra Archives at Wesleyan. Hornbeck went through the script with RKO's legal department, and the following interdepartment communication ensued:

FORM E-3 10M 1-46 A.P.

RKO RADIO PICTURES, Inc.
RADIO STUDIOS
Inter-Department Communication

Date........8 APRIL 1946..........

Subject...."IT'S A WONDERFUL LIFE"

To...MR. WILLIAM HORNBECK..........

From.........WILLIAM GORDON..........

Herewith a resume of our conference anent the Estimating Script of IT'S A WONDERFUL LIFE, Part I and II to page 143, dated March 20, and First Draft pink script, pages 164 to the end, dated January 14:

ok Sc. 18   Policy &   It is recommended that the word "Streamliner"
                Foreign   be used instead of "Twentieth Century."

         Sc. 40   Legal   It is recommended that a fictitious name be
                               chosen instead of "The National Geographic
Get clearance for   Magazine" now described. If this magazine
"National Geographic"   is to be retained, it will be necessary to procure
                               a clearance from the copyright owner, who may
                               require that the illustrations described be from
                               the actual magazine. Should you decide to select
                               a fictitious name, we will be glad to clear its
                               availability for you. If you decide to retain
                               "The National Geographic" please advise so that
                               we may request the Legal Department to prepare
                               the necessary forms.

ok Sc. 62   PCA   It will be necessary to delete the word
                               "impotent" as used on page 38.

ok Sc. 65   Policy   It is recommended that the various references
                & Legal   to Cornell be omitted and some expression such
                            as State or State University be substituted.
                            If you decide to retain Cornell, we will make
                            every effort to quickly check whether they have
                            any alumni named Sam Wainwright and Harry Bailey
                            who would fit the period now described.

         Sc. 70   Legal   Since you advise us that the swimming pool-
                               under-a-floor is actually the invention of a
will furnish   real person, our crediting a character with
                               this idea probably requires a legal clearance.
                               Please furnish us the name of the patentee, so
                               that we may proceed further.

         Sc. 107   Legal   Reference is made to Tommy Manville. Such use
                               will require a legal clearance. By a copy of
                               this memorandum we are asking the Legal Department
ok   to prepare the necessary forms and procure their
                               execution.

*The "Hornbeck Memo": The RKO legal department worries about the phrase
"Those Rockefellers" and declares the words "lousy" and "impotent" unacceptable.*

RKO RADIO PICTURES, Inc.
RADIO STUDIOS
Inter-Department Communication

To...... MR. HORNBECK

From..... WM. GORDON   Date.... 4/8/46

-2-   Subject....."IT'S A WONDERFUL LIFE"
                                                          (cont'd)

Sc. 112   PCA

The underlined word in the expression "My answer is _nuts_ to you" is on the Association's banned list.

Sc. 114   Legal

Reference is made to "Those Rockefellers." Such use will require a legal clearance. By a copy of this memorandum we are asking the Legal Department to prepare the necessary forms and procure their execution.

Sc. 116   Legal

This scene describes a phonograph playing a musical selection and in front of the phonograph a sign reading, "Guy Lombardo." If this is to be retained, we would have to secure Mr. Lombardo's permission for the use of his name and also a clearance concerning the selection played. Please advise.

**Sc. 125   Policy
et seq.**

It is urgently recommended that the name Lester Reineman be changed to one which is not descriptive of any particular race or religion.

Sc. 132   Foreign

This scene contains four instances of the Martinis crossing themselves. This type of action is invariably deleted in Great Britain. It is recommended that you protect yourselves accordingly.

Sc. 134   Policy

While it is well understood that no offense whatsoever is intended with the expression "garlic eaters" it is yet recommended that it be revised because of the possibility that some people will take offense.

Sc. 135   PCA

The expression "pulling the chain" must be deleted.

Sc. 135   PCA

The underlined word in the line, "I hate the _dang_ place," must be changed.

**Sc. 138   Policy
& Legal**

We will attempt to procure a clearance from the White House for the impersonation of the President in the photograph.

Sc. 177   PCA

The word "lousy" as used here is unacceptable.

FORM E-3 10M 1-46 A.P.

RKO RADIO PICTURES, Inc.
RADIO STUDIOS
Inter-Department Communication

Date .... 4/8/46 ....

To ...... MR. HORNBECK ......

Subject ...... "IT'S A WONDERFUL LIFE" ...... (Cont'd)

From ...... WM. GORDON ......   -3-

The following refers to your Pink Script dated January 14, pages 167 to the end:

dc P. 167	PCA	The two uses of the word "impotent" are unacceptable.
OK P. 172	PCA	The word "jerk" is unacceptable.
7 P. 179	PCA	The underlined word in the expression, "I wish to <u>God</u> I'd never been born!" is unacceptable. the word "heaven" can be substituted for the underlined word.
ok P. 212	Foreign	The British Board of Censors invariably deletes any quotation from the Lord's Prayer. Quoted herewith is an excerpt from British regulations re religious ceremonies:

"There is a standing objection to the Lord's prayer, and it is invariably deleted, whether spoken by a Minister or a Layman, in church or out of church, reverently or not - treatment has nothing to do with it - it must come out."

Should you so request, we will attempt to obtain a substitute prayer which will be universally acceptable. In any event, if you retain the Lord's Prayer, it will be necessary to shoot an alternate protection for Great Britain.

Further reference is made to our discussion re the Breen letter of March 29:

We are in agreement that the comments concerning the action and dialogue on pages 34-35-36-37-38-55-58-65-71-72-78-82-88 and 95 will be observed. We further agree that the reference to "gin" on pages 38 and 39 will be retained; that the drinking of cocktails in the scenes on page 64 will be deleted, but that Uncle Billy will still be shown tipsy; Uncle Billy will take a nip on page 86.

With reference to Mr. Breen's letter of March 6, covering the latter portion of the script, the comments re pages 160-167-169-172-174-178-179-180-195 and 201 will be observed. I will discuss with the PCA reader the criticism of the characterization of Violet as a street-walker and I will report to you further.

WG/s

cc: Mr. Frank Capra (2)
Mr. Sam Briskin

cc: Mr. N. Peter Rathvon
Mr. Sid Lipsitch

The detail with which Hollywood produced motion pictures is clearly demonstrated here. Every aspect of the production was gone over with a fine-tooth comb before shooting to avoid potential problems with lawsuits. Note the item on scene 70, in which the studio attempts to avoid a lawsuit by finding out exactly who patented the idea of a swimming pool under the floor ("will furnish," Capra has written on the memo). (While RKO anticipated the real inventor of the pool suing, they did *not* anticipate what really happened: no one believed such a pool could exist. Capra received many letters about it, and the famous film critic James Agee, who disliked the film, said in his *Nation* review, "The high-school dance floor coming apart over a swimming pool is a sample of cooking-up that no movie has beaten for a long time.")

The Hornbeck-Gordon memo also indicates prior correspondence about potential censorship problems with *It's a Wonderful Life*. (No copies of such a correspondence exist in Capra's files.) It's difficult today to imagine what anyone would want to censor in *It's a Wonderful Life*. Nevertheless, the script had to be reviewed, and such words as "jerk," "impotent," "dang," and "lousy" had to be removed. Scenes with people "drinking cocktails" and referring to "gin" had to be watched. The Motion Picture Association of America's Production Code was well known for some of its bizarre restrictions. It became famous for its edict "The following subjects must be treated with discretion, restraint, and within the careful limits of good taste." The list of "subjects" included bedroom scenes, hangings, and electrocutions. Today people may wonder how the scene in which Stewart sits on a double bed with Donna Reed reclining in it passed review. Many people have the mistaken notion that any combination of two people and a double bed was taboo. In *It's a Wonderful Life,* Stewart and Reed play a married couple, and Stewart is not in the bed with her, just sitting on it. The Production Code obviously found this "within the careful limits of good taste."

Considering the restrictions of the Code, many viewers have been surprised that in *It's a Wonderful Life* Capra got away with letting Lionel Barrymore go unpunished after stealing the eight thousand dollars from Stewart. The Code definitely stipulated that criminals must be punished for their crimes. But Capra stoutly decreed that he would leave the punishment — in fact, the entire matter — to the audience's imagination, and this seems to have sufficed. (Over the years, Capra's private correspondence indicates that more people wrote him about this than any other single element in the film.)

As shooting began, the efficient RKO publicity mill transformed perfectly ordinary happenings on the set into the kind of anecdotes and events that could appear in the press, thus keeping the director, the stars, and the impending film on the public's mind. For instance, the case of the dozing electrician. According to newspaper accounts, as Capra and his crew filmed the scene in which Thomas Mitchell, as a drunken Uncle Billy, lurched off-screen and down the street singing, a half-asleep worker accidentally knocked over a stack of props. The sound was immediately recorded, of course, and it sounded as if Mitchell had collided full-force with a marauding herd of mobile garbage cans. The frightened electrician expected to be fired; but instead, Capra, delighted with the effect, gave him a ten-dollar reward for "improving sound and characterization." (The stuff auteurs are made of!) The next day, this item appeared in many newspapers around the country, among them the July 19, 1946, Toledo, Ohio *Blade*. Whether this really happened or was simply the product of a publicist's imagination, it helped to keep people thinking about Frank Capra's new film.

The Philadelphia *Record* reported that no award-winning pedigreed dog was wanted for *It's a Wonderful Life*. Instead, Capra sent someone to the Los Angeles dog pound to hire a "proper pooch, a dog of the streets, an All-American immigrant hound." Later, in January 1947, after the film's release, the *Record* would report that the three-year-old French sheepdog that got the part, named Shag, was an overnight discovery now much in demand for dog roles as a result of his big performance in *It's a Wonderful Life*. (Whatever happened to Shag?)

The Walnut, Illinois *Leader* deplored the waste of good pies in making the film: "Considering the high price of bakery goods, it's disconcerting to learn that eight pies were wasted on the set of *It's a Wonderful Life,* for a scene in which Todd Karns [playing Harry] had to walk while balancing a pie on his head." (This story may be a perfect definition of a slow news day.) Actually, production notes in-

RKO salutes surrealism. The publicity department creates believable, real-life situations that show off the natural rapport between their two stars.

Donna Reed, LEFT, *a good girl.*
Gloria Grahame, RIGHT,
not such a good girl.

Left, Jimmy studies his script in front of his two-door trailer, while Donna waves to…somebody…from the passenger seat of what must be a '47 De Chirico.

Jimmy poses proudly in front of an RKO Utrillo, ABOVE, *while Donna demonstrates how to care for really fine art.*

dicate that this problem was solved by property man Lou Hafeby, who "deflated the pie tin and inserted two pins on each side for balance." The ninth pie stayed on. However, how one "deflates" a pie tin — or just *what* the two pies were affixed to on Karns's head — is never explained.

Some of the publicity gimmicks were solid items based on the day's production problems. For instance, when a white tablecloth in the family dinner scene caused too much glare, the prop man commandeered all fountain pens on the set and sprayed the cloth blue in ten minutes' time, reducing the shine, saving the scene, and allowing the production to continue. The next day, July 11, the Seattle *Star* dutifully reported the news.

Capra's absentminded habit of forgetting his shooting script when arriving on the set was turned into a publicity puff. The *Independent* in New York City picked up the item: "We've heard some prominent directors say, 'I shoot even the commas and exclamation marks.' Capra, without his shooting script, lets the scene work itself out as it goes. Reckon the answer to this contradiction is that Capra's genius doesn't need the script to prop it up. Lesser men must depend on mechanical aid. Too bad there aren't more Capras and fewer scripts."

Everything connected with Donna Reed or Jimmy Stewart was covered in the papers — some of it generally accurate, some of it downright ludicrous. Stewart's parents lending Capra a real-life snapshot of Stewart at six months of age to put on the set was transformed into a charming story of Stewart's amazed reaction at the sight of himself in diapers. Reed's considerable ability to throw a baseball straight and hard — learned with her brothers back on the Iowa farm — became a story about how, in a now-famous scene, she broke the window in the old house with true aim and heft. (Capra had allegedly hired a marksman to shoot it out for her on cue. He didn't know about Iowa farm girls.)

These innocuous little publicity items, more or less true, were juxtaposed with totally invented ones, such as Donna Reed's having to have the color blue around her at all times because one of her father's hired hands back on the farm ("an Egyptian," read the releases) had impressed upon her that Egyptian nurses protected children from the evil eye by hanging a necklace of blue beads on the child and by always keeping small pieces of blue material on the nursery walls. According to the release, Capra was seeing to it that there was a bit of blue in every one of Miss Reed's scenes.

Stewart, a World War II bomber pilot with more than two thousand hours in the air, was said to be so afraid of driving a car that he insisted that the scene in which he and Reed proceed to the railroad station after their marriage be changed from a car to a taxi. "Stewart refuses to reveal the cause of his phobia or discuss it." This item was picked up by the St. Paul *Pioneer Press,* despite an earlier release in which Stewart, having been ordered not to fly as either a passenger or a pilot for the ninety days of production, had told the press, "A fine way to treat a grown-up man . . . but . . . anyway . . . I've been having a little too much motor trouble anyway." (Frank Capra had also written a memorandum to Stewart saying, "Cross streets cautiously, look in all directions, don't take any chances." With seventy consecutive working days scheduled for his star, he was obviously nervous about accidents.)

The publicity-mill climax was reached with a release that concerned the filming of the famous scene in which Reed and Stewart talk to Frank Albertson on the telephone and end up in a passionate embrace:

Jimmy Stewart's first postwar screen kiss had been postponed for weeks at his request. Finally, Frank Capra, producer-director of *It's a Wonderful Life,* a Liberty Film for RKO Radio Release and Jimmy's first picture since getting out of the service, told him zero hour had arrived.

"Let's skip it for a few more days," Jimmy pleaded. "A fellow's technique gets rusty. I'm not used to the idea yet."

"Nonsense," Capra replied. "It's all in a day's work. A kiss is a kiss, just two pairs of lips pressed together."

To make sure Jimmy would not bolt, Capra huddled his stars over a telephone, conducting a conversation with Frank Albertson, who wants to marry Donna in the picture. Jimmy was raining perspiration, but he began playing the scene with tense urgency. Donna immedi-

All in readiness for The Kiss...

And The Kiss itself. (Too much of a good thing: the handwriting scratched over reads "Killed, Johnston office.")

ately caught the mood. As the stars huddled over the telephone, her lush lips parted close to his. Stewart flung the telephone away and really gave it everything in high gear. He was "in romantic anguish," according to the press agent. He "smothered her with kisses." Donna, her face shining with love for Jimmy, responded accordingly. Capra, exultant, yelled, "Cut! That was simply wonderful!"

"Yeah!," said the script girl, "it was fine, all

right, except that they left out a whole page of dialogue."

Capra grinned. "With technique like that," he said, "who needs dialogue? Print it!"

On August 1, Hedda Hopper breathlessly reported that she now understood why movies cost so much to make. The scene in which Stewart runs his car into a tree during a snowstorm — all of thirty seconds on the screen — required two camera crews, thirty electricians, thirty special effects men, twenty-five props men, a makeup crew, a first-aid crew, four wardrobe people, a thousand tons of ice, and one hundred and fifty hot meals to feed everyone because it was shot at night.

While the publicity men did their work, Capra did his. When his meticulous research turned up the fact that the weather in the New York State area that Bedford Falls was allegedly situated in had rain during the bank run of 1933, Capra added rain to the scene. (He also put a joke boner into the same sequence. As Reed and Stewart leave on their honeymoon, a newspaper headline reads SENATE VOTES DOWN BONUS. That Senate action took place on June 18, 1932, but the historic bank holiday depicted on the screen took place in 1933.)

Capra worked long hours, growing more and more convinced that this film was the best he'd ever worked on. But to friends he said simply, "We'll see how it turns out — it's kind of a crazy story, with angels and things."

Early in production, Capra found that although he loved Lionel Barrymore's performance as the villain, Potter, he wasn't pleased with the way Barrymore *looked* in the role. Barrymore's face was not only familiar but greatly loved by moviegoers who had seen him in a series of likable-old-codger roles over the years. He had already appeared in Capra's own *You Can't Take It with You* — to name only one of his more sympathetic roles — as a man of humor, warmth, and faith. Capra feared this association and wanted Barrymore's appearance changed.

Sitting home one day, idly leafing through magazines, Capra came across a portrait by Grant Wood, the famous *American Gothic*. "This is how I want Potter to look," he told his makeup crew, taking them the portrait and a picture of Lionel Barrymore. "Match 'em up," were his instructions. The makeup staff devised a plastic cap which fitted over Barrymore's skull like a tight glove and changed the contour of his head considerably. At first the effect was too severe, but with modifications and appropriate makeup, Barrymore was transformed from a lovable curmudgeon into a man whose expression spoke of greed and malice.

There were a few other production problems. On May 21, Joseph Walker took over as camera-man from Victor Milner, who had become "ill," according to press releases. Walker, a former Capra collaborator, began production as a favor to his old friend. As soon as Joseph Biroc could be officially promoted from camera operator to chief cinematographer, he took over. [*]

As the film progressed, Capra maintained a grueling work schedule. According to his records, he lost ten pounds — and a whole lot of sleep. His daily work schedule on the film was strictly regimented:

6:00 a.m. Rise and eat breakfast. Go over day's schedule.

7:45 a.m. Arrive at studio.

7:50 a.m. Look at the rushes [scenes shot previous day].

8:30 a.m. Arrive on the set, ready to shoot. Except for a half hour for Lunch around Noon, shoot all day until 6:00 p.m.

When not actually directing a scene, approve future sets, look at sketches, costumes, and props. If necessary, rewrite or change script.

6:00 p.m. Cameras stop. Between 6:00 and 8:00 p.m., Conferences with assistant directors, prop men, crew and others. Crew frequently works all night to get ready for next day.

8:00 p.m. Leave studio and after arriving home, sit down to dinner. After finishing dinner, spend 2–3 hours working on script, laying out new material, making future plans.

11:00 p.m. To bed.

Interviewed about this pace, which allowed very little time alone and almost no time with family or friends, Capra commented, "There's no peace anytime you are shooting a picture. It's very rarely you can sit down and do nothing for a while, not even on Sunday. As long as you are working on a picture, there is always something to keep you busy. There are either sets to be seen or locations to be

[*] See pages 87–93 for a discussion of the cameramen and an interview with Biroc.

OVERLEAF, *the less-than-wonderful reality of movie-making, with all its stresses showing on the faces of the participants.*

inspected or conferences with writers. There is always something to keep you going."

Capra suspended production only once in his nearly three months of shooting. After several weeks of night shoots, the cast and crew were beginning to complain of insomnia. The record hot spell of the California summer of 1946 had taken its toll. Everyone needed a break, and Capra gave them one day off.

As the summer wore on, Capra frequently was interviewed about the film. Some of his remarks were kept in his files for future reference, and they reflect his thoughts as he worked day by day on *It's a Wonderful Life:*

On actors: "A poor script can be made into a good picture by using good actors. Poor actors will ruin a good script."

On his past successes: "The hell with the past. I'm only interested in the future."

On his current ideas about his famous "little man": "He doesn't want much. Just peace and freedom and a break. And he's fundamentally good, too. If he wasn't, we couldn't hire enough cops to keep him in order. I have a definite feeling that the people are right. People's instincts are good. Never bad. As right as the soil."

On directing Donna Reed: "A director who seeks to obtain the most in acting from his feminine players must be considerate, gentle and understanding. To have berated her would have sent her home in tears. To have demanded in a bellicose manner that she do thus and so would have failed, also. I treated her as I treat all women in my pictures — with consideration for their talent and ability, understanding of their desire to deliver on film a realistic delineation, and gentleness in helping them."

On how a director chooses a property: "Maybe a director has a kind of instinct. You get enthusiastic over an idea and you make up your mind it will make a good picture. It might not appeal to anyone else, but it appeals to you. So you start from there. The worst trouble is to keep up your original enthusiasm after you get working on the picture. When you are in the middle of it, or even after it is finished, the story never seems as good to you as when you made the original plans. That is because you use such big tools when you are making motion pictures."

On directing: "A director has to give a thousand decisions a day. You don't have time to think about them either. They have to be yes or no. You have your main people set before you begin a picture, but several hundred other players must be cast while the picture is in progress. Some of them may work for only a day, or in a single scene, but every one of them is important. Each one contributes their bit to the success of the whole production, so you must take the time to decide on every one. Of course, you have to do them on the fly. Every set-up must be carefully studied. Camera angles are important. They must be exactly right to get the scene. It may last only 30 seconds on the screen, but it takes a long time. The ultimate idea, of course, is to get everything right, the action, the photography, the sound, all of which go to make up the scene. Very seldom do they all click at the same time. So you generally have to compromise and take the best general average."

On the picture business: "To stay in business, and picture making is a big money business, you have to make pictures with universal appeal. Unless a picture has tremendous initial impact upon the public, it quickly passes from the first run to lesser run houses and exhausts its money potential. If it starts out slowly, its run is taken off at the end of the week, even if business shows signs of building on the fifth day. That's one of the big troubles. Pictures are not given a chance to find their audience."

On It's a Wonderful Life *and the character of George Bailey:* "It's a movie about a small town guy who thinks he is a failure and wishes he had never been born. He's surprised to learn that he was not a failure, that he fitted into the scheme of life and actually contributed much to the happiness of several people. I think that a lot of people everywhere will be able to associate themselves with the character and will perhaps feel a bit better for having known him. People are seeking spiritual and moral reassurance, and if the movies can't supply this, they will be serving no worthwhile purpose."

At last, on July 27, 1946, right on schedule, shooting was complete. It was a wrap. Capra had exposed 350,000 feet of film, 50,000 under his prewar average per feature. Months before, on the same day he began shooting, his Liberty partner William Wyler had begun his own first postwar production, *The Best Years of Our Lives,* a Samuel Goldwyn Production which would also be distributed by RKO. Wyler had wired Capra, "Last one in is a rotten egg." Capra was finished, but Wyler, a stickler for perfection, was still shooting. "I admit it," he said. "I'm a rotten egg." (*The Best Years of Our Lives,* however, would still be released *before It's a Wonderful Life,* in November 1946.)

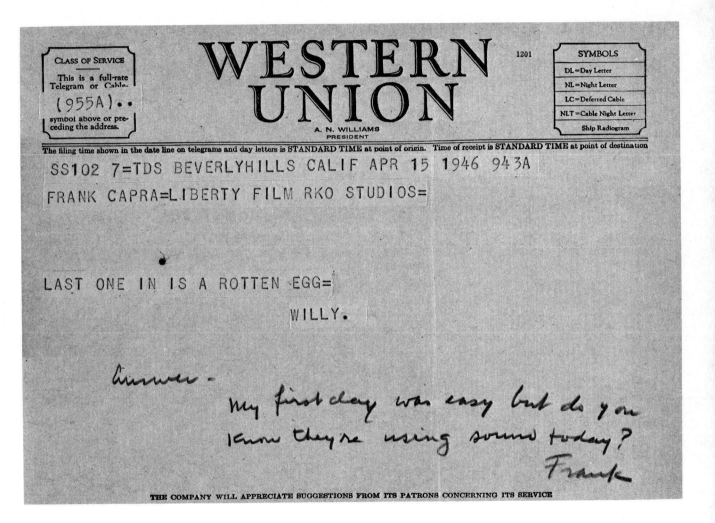

Celebrations and parties were planned in a spirit of optimism and confidence. On August 4, 1946, Capra and Stewart threw the *It's a Wonderful Life* picnic for everyone who worked on the film. They decided to hold it at a place called Arthur's Ranch, in the country outside Los Angeles, at a cost of $100 per day for usage, prudently negotiated down to $50 for the day by Capra's office. The celebration was attended by 372 people for a cost of $1,799.09, the total expense to be divided between Stewart and Capra. But when Frank Capra — the "round-it-off" film director — wrote Jimmy Stewart — the honest all-American boy — a check for what he considered his share, $899.55, he overpaid by a total of seven cents, at least by Stewart's all-American arithmetic. This led to a celebrated exchange:

"IT'S A WONDERFUL LIFE" PICNIC
AUGUST 4th, 1946

CASH DISBURSEMENTS:

Harold G. Hughes - Fire Warden. $10.00
Harry Killinger - Watchman.   36.00
Loggins Food Products - On account.   200.00

PRIZES:

Ladies' 3 Legged Race   5.00
Men's 3 Legged Race   7.00
Mixed Race   8.00
Children's Spoon Race   6.00
50 Yard Dash - Boys   6.00
Ladies' Sack Race   6.00
Men's Sack Race   6.00
Children's Watermelon Contest   13.00
                                                       $304.00

ACCOUNTS PAYABLE:

Liberty Films, Inc.   312.94
Weaver Photo Service   51.50
Weaver Photo Service   24.72
Personally Yours   200.00
Loggins Food Products (Balance due
   including $70.00 tip)   570.00
Lou Hafley (petty cash vouchers)   26.00
Arthur's Ranch   100.00
Schwab's Pharmacy   57.01
Mueller Dance Floor Company   55.00
Sanitary Portable Rest-Rooms Co.   97.92
                                                      $1799.09

cc Messrs. Stewart, Capra, Gadbois.

Note: All bills are on file at the office of Mr. Guy Gadbois,
        9494 Wilshire Blvd., Beverly Hills, Calif.
        Telephone No: CR 16291.

                              Maxine Graybill.

   mg:s

S STEWART

ire Boulevard

ls, California

                                        August 24, 1946

TO:

Frank Capra, Dr.

One-half expense-----

     "It's a Wonderful Life" picnic
     August 4, 1946

        To reimburse James Stewart $899.48

        Frank Capra check received
        8/26/46 $899.55

        James Stewart check herewith
        to balance   .07
                                       $899.55 $899.55

                              August 23, 1946

Mr. James Stewart
12731 Evanston Drive
West Los Angeles,
California

Dear Jimmy:

        Enclosed find Mr. Capra's
check in the amount of $899.55, his
share of the picnic, as per statement
submitted by Maxine Graybill.

        Best,

        Miriam Geiger

46

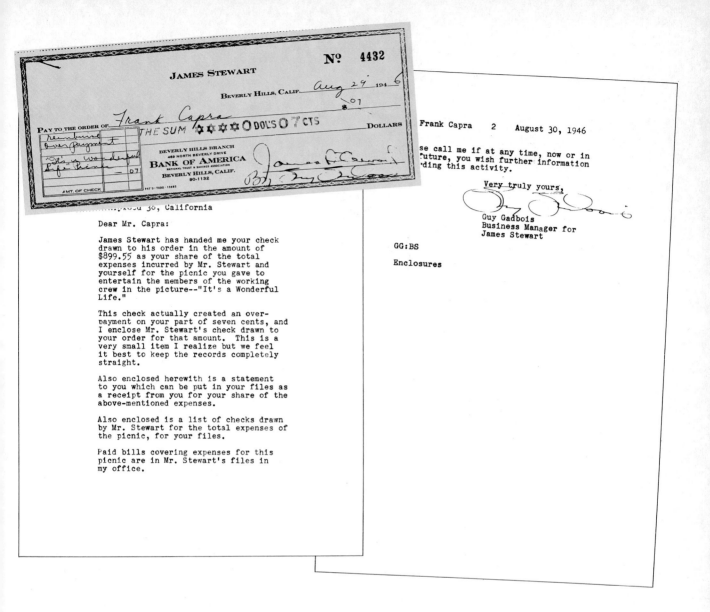

...wood 30, California

Dear Mr. Capra:

James Stewart has handed me your check drawn to his order in the amount of $899.55 as your share of the total expenses incurred by Mr. Stewart and yourself for the picnic you gave to entertain the members of the working crew in the picture--"It's a Wonderful Life."

This check actually created an over-payment on your part of seven cents, and I enclose Mr. Stewart's check drawn to your order for that amount. This is a very small item I realize but we feel it best to keep the records completely straight.

Also enclosed herewith is a statement to you which can be put in your files as a receipt from you for your share of the above-mentioned expenses.

Also enclosed is a list of checks drawn by Mr. Stewart for the total expenses of the picnic, for your files.

Paid bills covering expenses for this picnic are in Mr. Stewart's files in my office.

Frank Capra   2   August 30, 1946

...se call me if at any time, now or in ...uture, you wish further information ...ding this activity.

Very truly yours,

Guy Gadbois
Business Manager for
James Stewart

GG:BS

Enclosures

During the fall of 1946, the film was edited. Capra was pleased. Above all, he felt that Stewart's performance was Oscar-winning material. Dimitri Tiomkin began the scoring, using an eighty-piece orchestra. (This event was reported in the Holly-wood trade papers as beginning on December 2, 1946, but since a private screening was held for three hundred of Hollywood's elite only a week later, it seems unlikely that this date is correct.)

Liberty Films had finished its first movie, and Capra had won the "rotten egg" contest. He felt terrific, and since Liberty was a new company proud of its very first release, he decided that the first postwar film of two of Hollywood's most popular and solid citizens — Frank Capra and Jimmy Stewart — should be royally celebrated. This mood in-spired an occasion that typifies postwar Hollywood — a "Dinner-Dance and Private Showing" of *It's a Wonderful Life,* held at the Ambassador Hotel on December 9, 1946.

Virginia McPherson, writing a column called "Let's Gossip" for *Motion Picture* magazine, pro-vided a typically Hollywood write-up of the event:

Usually it's the movie queens who round up a couple hundred guests and toss the glittery parties. But this time a studio gets a deep curtsy from this corner for the fanciest whing-ding in many a movie moon. Yes — Liberty Films, Inc. And they took over half the sprawling Ambas-sador Hotel to do it. Frank Capra was the of-ficial host. Said he wanted to celebrate the

Dinner-Dance

and

Private Showing

"IT'S A WONDERFUL LIFE"

✳

Ambassador Hotel
Monday evening, December 9th

LIBERTY FILMS INC.

MENU

✳

Fresh Shrimp Supreme
1000 Island Dressing

Hearts of Celery   .   .   .   Mixed Olives

Tenderloin of Beef, Mushroom Sauce

Potatoes au Gratin   String Beans Julienne

Los Angeles Salad   .   .   .   French Dressing

Strawberry Romanoff Coupe   .   .   .   Demi Tasse

Sparkling Burgundy

completion of his film, *It's a Wonderful Life*. And every star in Hollywood showed up to help him. They drank toasts in champagne cocktails and packed away a scrumptious six-course dinner.

But we doubt if Yvonne DeCarlo knew what she was eating. She was too busy rhumba-ing with blond Robert Stack, her current escort about town. Ditto with Eleanor Powell and George Burns. They showed the amateurs what real "rug cuttin'" looks like, while Eleanor's husband, Glenn Ford, wolfed down two straw-berry-whipped-cream-concoction desserts.

Belle of the ball was white-haired Dame May Whitty, who snagged all the handsome leading men for partners. Her jitterbug routine with Richard Ney was the cutest thing we've seen yet. And while they were waiting for her to sit one out with 'em, Frank Morgan and Edward G. Robinson got up and waltzed a few rounds with each other. It practically brought down the house. We sat with gorgeous Merle Ober-on, who said she was so sleepy she could hardly

keep awake for the dessert course. "I've been digging in the garden all afternoon," she told us. "I can hardly pry my eyes open." She looked wide-awake and beautiful as ever, though.

After dinner all 300 stars had a special showing of *It's a Wonderful Life*. And it really was — as far as that evening was concerned anyway.

The *It's a Wonderful Life* dinner dance was covered live by radio, and the transcript exists in the Archives. In hushed tones, reverent with the importance of the people passing by, the announcer explains to the listening audience what the royal figures are wearing:

Lucille Ball in a short evening suit of silver and gold, brocaded in lamé and trimmed with mink . . . Colbert in black velvet with a mink coat . . . Roz Russell with a sequined scarf over her head and a black dinner dress, topped with a stone marten coat . . . Yvonne DeCarlo in ankle length dinner dress of black crepe with a top of black and peacock blue satin stripes . . .

Capra Unfurls "Life" At Elaborate Party

HOLLYWOOD—In an unusual approach to the prerelease screening of a picture, Liberty Films unfurled Frank Capra's "It's a Wonderful Life," which RKO will distribute, before a star-studded audience following an elaborate party hosted by Capra.

A dinner and special showing was scheduled at the Ambassador hotel to which were invited all the stars and players, some 100 strong, who have appeared in films produced and directed by Capra, William Wyler and George Stevens, the three producer-directors who with Samuel J. Briskin, executive producer, comprise Liberty. Following dinner, the showing was to be held in the Ambassador Theatre.

The guest list included:

Dana Andrews
Edward Arnold
Jean Arthur
Fred Astaire
Nils Asther
Mary Astor
Fay Bainter
Lionel Barrymore
Warner Baxter
William Bendix
Humphrey Bogart
Ward Bond
Beulah Bondi
Walter Brennan
George Brent
George Burns
Gracie Burns
Harry Carey
Jack Carson
Dave Chasen
Charles Coburn
Claudette Colbert
Constance Collier
William Collier jr.
Ronald Colman
Gary Cooper
Ricardo Cortez

Joan Crawford
Donald Crisp
Viola Dana
Bette Davis
Melvin Douglas
Irene Dunne
Dan Duryea
Douglas Fairbanks jr.
Henry Fonda
Joan Fontaine
Clark Gable
Reginald Gardiner
Greer Garson
James Gleason
Betty Grable
Cary Grant
Bonita Granville
Mildred Harris
Katharine Hepburn
Jean Hersholt
Samuel S. Hinds
Jack Holt
Miriam Hopkins
Edward Everett Horton
Walter Huston
Roscoe Karns
Priscilla Lane

* * *

All Hollywood comes to Capra's "Wonderful Life" party. Top, LEFT TO RIGHT: *Charles Coburn with Joel McCrea and Frances Dee; Greer Garson with William Wyler and Clark Gable; Jimmy Stewart with Margaret Sullavan.* CENTER: *William Wyler with Claudette Colbert.* BOTTOM, LEFT TO RIGHT: *Gary Cooper with Lionel Barrymore; Donna Reed with Frank Capra; Irene Dunne alone.*

Loretta Young in form-fitting black broadtail coat, and exquisite John Fredericks black lace hat . . . Ann Sothern in black velvet with an off-the-face hat . . . Greer [Garson] in short dinner dress which combined gold lamé with black velvet and a new short hair cut . . . Merle Oberon in a short dinner gown with ice blue satin and her famous gold and diamond jewelry.

Capra's files indicate that shortly before the dinner dance, he received word that the film's release would have to be moved up for a Christmas-day opening in fifty theaters across the country. RKO, the official distributor for the Liberty production, was not going to obtain Technicolor prints of *Sinbad the Sailor* in time for its previously scheduled holiday opening, because Technicolor was on strike. A tongue-in-cheek swashbuckler starring Douglas Fairbanks, Jr., Maureen O'Hara, and Anthony Quinn, *Sinbad* was perfect family entertainment. The only other film RKO had that might be suitable as a replacement was *It's a Wonderful Life,* with its holiday theme and setting. Prints were not ready, however, and a worried Capra ordered work to press forward.

On Friday, December 13, 1946 — an ominous date — the labs began rushing to make prints of *It's a Wonderful Life.* They would turn out four a day during each working day, and four at night during a rush overtime schedule, in order to complete fifty copies by Christmas day. The premiere was set for the Globe in New York City on December 20, a charity event, with official openings to follow around the USA during the next few days.

Although the general release date of *It's a Wonderful Life* would remain January 30, 1947, moving the film up accomplished three things: it filled RKO's release gap left by *Sinbad the Sailor,* gave Capra's film an appropriate Christmas audience, suitable for its theme, and made it eligible for the 1946 Oscar races. It all sounded perfect. Liberty Films was eager to help out RKO, and, after all, *It's a Wonderful Life was* a Christmas movie. Capra had not originally wanted to emphasize this aspect, because he felt that the film's message was universal and hoped its box office would last long past the holiday season. Also, it should be remembered that *It's a Wonderful Life* was an *independent* film — a

Liberty Production. As such, it would not normally have been given a priority release time or place. But under the circumstances, opening it at Christmas time seemed advantageous, since holiday movie-goers, if they liked it — and why shouldn't they like a Capra/Stewart film? — would give it solid word-of-mouth to carry it farther into 1947. As for the Oscar race, Capra felt confident. Who had given a better performance than Jimmy Stewart as George Bailey? Yes, there was Larry Parks in *The Jolson Story,* but musicals never won acting awards. There was Olivier in the British *Henry V,* but he *was* British and it *was* Shakespeare, and Capra figured Hollywood would stick with its own this time around. *The Best Years of Our Lives* had two strong leading men, Dana Andrews and Fredric March, which usually meant mutual cancellation in the acting

honors. It seemed like a good idea to get into the Oscar pool in 1946 and not to wait for everyone to remember *It's a Wonderful Life* nearly a year later for the 1947 awards.

In retrospect, however, it is possible to speculate that this hurried release might be what accounted for *It's a Wonderful Life* not achieving the hoped-for box-office success, and what probably doomed it to lose the Oscar race in all categories. First of all, as if to compete with Mr. Capra's fancy new film snow, nature showed what she could do by blasting the eastern United States with snow and ice and sub-zero temperatures during the last half of December, when *It's a Wonderful Life* opened. Ticket sales in theaters and movie houses hit rock bottom on cold nights, and with the need for last-minute Christmas shopping adding to the problem, the film opened "slow," causing Capra to have his first real worries about the picture's potential box-office success.

Secondly, although *It's a Wonderful Life* has found its lasting fame through holiday showings on television, it is possible that Americans, enjoying their Christmas season in that first full year of peace, felt depressed by the film's bleaker elements. Its conclusion is one of the most triumphant and joyous in all of film history, but along the way *It's a Wonderful Life* is a dark film — not without humor, of course, but with a depth and passion that make it something more than a lighthearted romp. Ironically, the film it replaced, *Sinbad the Sailor,* did very well (though not as well as expected) when it was ultimately released. *Sinbad* most likely would have made even more money had it been playing over the Christmas vacation, when everyone wanted a movie to take the kiddies to see.

Finally, *It's a Wonderful Life* found itself competing for Oscars with a film that matched the mood of postwar America as perfectly as any film could — *The Best Years of Our Lives*, which eventually was voted the Best Picture of 1946. If *It's a Wonderful Life* had been in contention for 1947 instead, it would have been up against weaker competition. The Best Picture nominations for 1947 were *Crossfire*, *Great Expectations*, *Gentleman's Agreement* (the winner), and, oddly enough, two other famous Christmas fantasies, *The Bishop's Wife* and *Miracle on 34th Street*.

The advertising materials prepared for *It's a Wonderful Life* sold the film in three main ways: as a Frank Capra film, since Capra was a proven box-office champ, an Oscar-winning favorite — one of the few directors whose name the public would recognize; as a happy family story, suitable to the postwar period, with smiling photos of the Bailey family grouped around the Christmas tree; and as a romance, with charming drawings of Stewart lifting Reed high above his head, and "It's a powerful love story" printed alongside their handsome profiles.

Looking at newspaper ads and lobby cards and posters outside theaters, the moviegoer got the impression that the movie was a happy-go-lucky, warm love story, reminiscent of the screwball comedies of the thirties — in particular, Capra's own *You Can't Take It with You*, which also starred Stewart and Lionel Barrymore. There was no suggestion of the darker aspects: the word "suicide" appeared nowhere. No copy spoke of a man confronting a crisis and triumphing over it. Although the Christmas theme was plugged briefly in December 1946, it was not made the major thrust of the campaigns for obvious reasons — the film would hit the majority of United States theaters well past the holidays. Also, the advertising campaign had originally been planned for a January release. The last-minute hurry-up left no time for major changes. Thus it was that *It's a Wonderful Life* went out to the American public as a happy-go-lucky Frank Capra movie, a 1930s model in a postwar world.

Legend has it that *It's a Wonderful Life* did not receive good reviews. This, however, is simply not true. What it did not receive was the Academy Award or outstanding box-office returns. However, sample reviews from around the country indicate that almost everyone liked *It's a Wonderful Life*, and many people loved it. The reviews were not entirely favorable, but the overall response was enthusiastic. Capra himself contributed to the legend of bad reviews in his autobiography, in which he says, "Some . . . Manhattan critics sprayed it with bladder juice." To support this, he quotes three negative reviews. *The New Republic*'s critic, Capra asserts, wrote: "Hollywood's Horatio Alger fights with more cinematic know-how and zeal than any other director to convince movie audiences that American life is exactly like the *Saturday Evening Post* covers of Norman Rockwell." He quotes Bosley Crowther in the *New York Times*: "For all its characteristic humors, Mr. Capra's *Wonderful Life* . . . is a figment of simple Pollyanna platitudes." And finally, *The New Yorker*: "So mincing as to border on baby talk. . . . Henry Travers, God help him, has the job of portraying Mr. Stewart's guardian angel. It must have taken a lot out of him."

Actually, no one could have expected the leftist *New Republic* or the sophisticated *New Yorker* to like anything by Capra. In general, it was the eastern critics who *were* critical. (Ironically, years later, *The New Yorker* would carry more than one tribute to the staying power of *It's a Wonderful Life*.) And as for Bosley Crowther, though his initial review of December 23, 1946, was certainly not a rave, it was more favorable than Capra indicates, and Capra's alleged quote does not appear in it. In its entirety, Crowther's review said:

> The late and beloved Dexter Fellows, who was a circus press agent for many years, had an interesting theory on the theatre which suited his stimulating trade. He held that the final curtain of every drama, no matter what, should benignly fall on the whole cast sitting down to a turkey dinner and feeling fine. Mr. Fellows should be among us to see Frank Capra's *It's a Wonderful Life* which opened on Saturday at the Globe Theatre. He would find it very much to his taste. For a turkey dinner, with Christmas trimmings, is precisely what's cooking at the end of this quaint and engaging modern parable in virtue being its own reward. And a whole slue of cozy small-town characters who have gone through a lot in the past two hours are waiting around to eat it — or, at least, to watch James Stewart gobble it up. For it is

Press clippings about the movie pinned to the bulletin board at RKO Publicity.

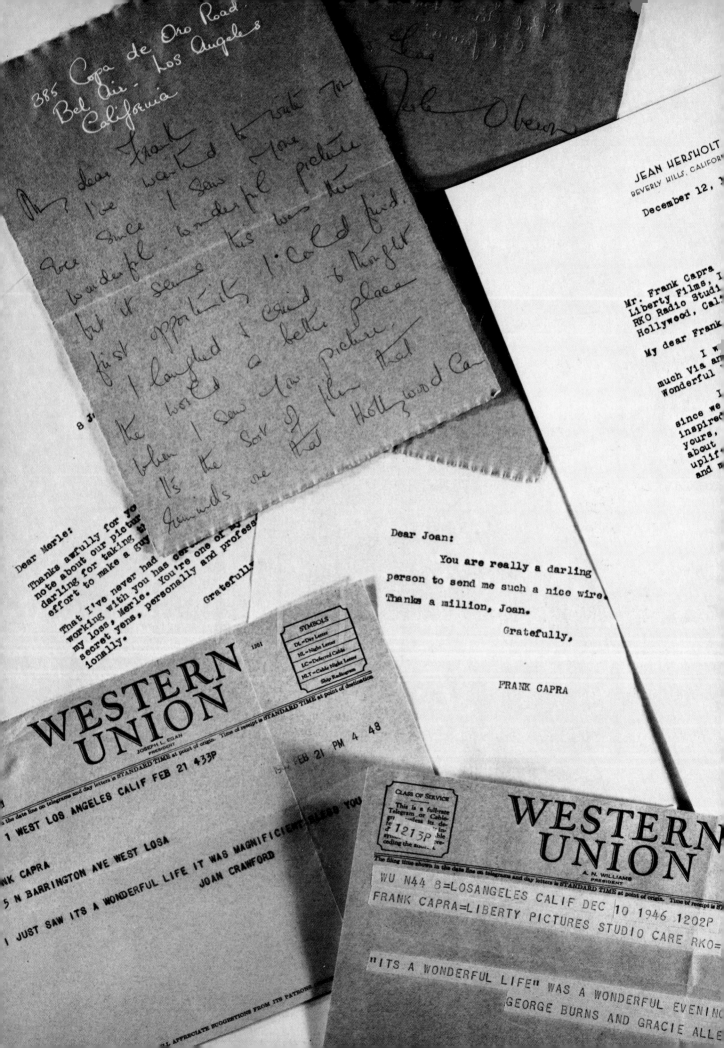

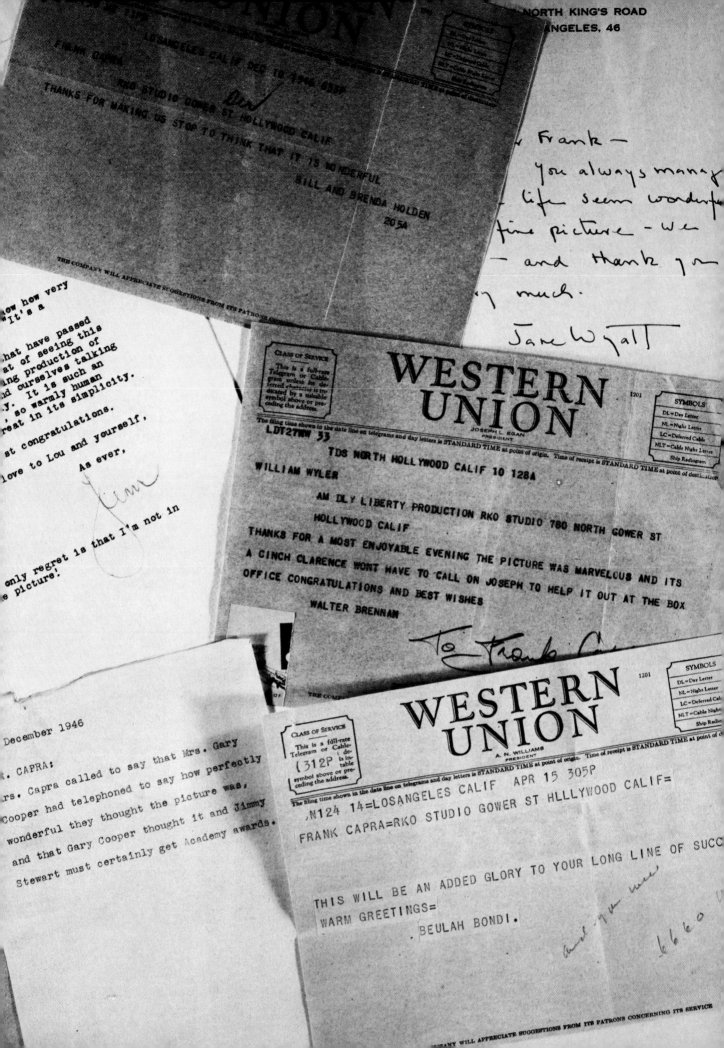

NORTH KING'S ROAD
ANGELES, 46

LOS ANGELES CALIF DEC 10 1946 635P

FRANK CAPRA

RKO STUDIO GOWER ST HOLLYWOOD CALIF

THANKS FOR MAKING US STOP TO THINK THAT IT IS WONDERFUL

BILL AND BRENDA HOLDEN
205A

r Frank —

You always manag

life seem wonderf

fine picture — we

— and thank yo

y much.

Jane Wyatt

THE COMPANY WILL APPRECIATE SUGGESTIONS FROM ITS PATRONS CON

now how very
"It's a

hat have passed
at of seeing this
ng production of
d ourselves talking
y. It is such an
so warmly human
reat in its simplicity.

st congratulations,

love to Lou and yourself,

As ever,

Jim

only regret is that I'm not in
e picture.

WESTERN UNION

JOSEPH L. EGAN
PRESIDENT

1201

This is a full-rate
Telegram or Cable-
gram unless its de-
ferred character is in-
dicated by a suitable
symbol above or pre-
ceding the address.

SYMBOLS

DL=Day Letter
NL=Night Letter
LC=Deferred Cable
NLT=Cable Night Letter
Ship Radiogram

The filing time shown in the date line on telegrams and day letters is STANDARD TIME at point of origin. Time of receipt is STANDARD TIME at point of destination

LDT27NW 33

TDS NORTH HOLLYWOOD CALIF 10 128A

WILLIAM WYLER

AM DLY LIBERTY PRODUCTION RKO STUDIO 780 NORTH GOWER ST

HOLLYWOOD CALIF

THANKS FOR A MOST ENJOYABLE EVENING THE PICTURE WAS MARVELOUS AND ITS
A CINCH CLARENCE WONT HAVE TO CALL ON JOSEPH TO HELP IT OUT AT THE BOX
OFFICE CONGRATULATIONS AND BEST WISHES

WALTER BRENNAN

To Frank Ca

WESTERN UNION

A. N. WILLIAMS
PRESIDENT

1201

SYMBOLS

DL=Day Letter
NL=Night Letter
LC=Deferred Cab
NLT=Cable Night
Ship Radio

CLASS OF SERVICE

This is a full-rate
Telegram or Cable-
(312P (de-
table
symbol above or pre-
ceding the address.

The filing time shown in the date line on telegrams and day letters is STANDARD TIME at point of origin. Time of receipt is STANDARD TIME at point of d

,N124 14=LOSANGELES CALIF APR 15 305P

FRANK CAPRA=RKO STUDIO GOWER ST HLLLYWOOD CALIF=

THIS WILL BE AN ADDED GLORY TO YOUR LONG LINE OF SUCC

WARM GREETINGS=

BEULAH BONDI.

December 1946

. CAPRA:

rs. Capra called to say that Mrs. Gary
Cooper had telephoned to say how perfectly
wonderful they thought the picture was,
and that Gary Cooper thought it and Jimmy
Stewart must certainly get Academy awards.

ANY WILL APPRECIATE SUGGESTIONS FROM ITS PATRONS CONCERNING ITS SERVICE

really Mr. Stewart who does most of the heavy suffering in this film, and it is he who, in the end, is most deserving of the white meat and the stuffing.

That is because Mr. Capra, back from the war, has resumed with a will his previously manifest penchant for portraying folks of simple, homely worth. And in this picture about a young fellow who wants to break away from his small-town life and responsibilities but is never able to do so because slowly they close in upon him, Mr. Capra has gone all out to show that it is really a family, friends and honest toil that makes the "wonderful life."

His hero is a personable fellow who wants to travel and do big things but ultimately finds himself running a building-and-loan association in a one-horse town, married and locked in constant struggle with the greedy old banker of the town. And when it finally looks as though the banker is about to drive him to ruin, he makes what appears a brash endeavor to take his own baffled life. Whereupon a heavenly messenger providentially intercedes and shows him, in fanciful fashion, what the town would have been like without him. The vision is so distressing that he returns to his lot with boundless joy — and is saved, also providentially, by the financial assistance of his friends.

In composing this moralistic fable, Mr. Capra and his writers have tossed in a great abundance of colloquial incidents and emotional tangles of a wistful, humorous sort. The boyhood of his hero, the frolic at a high school dance, the clumsy pursuit of a courtship — all are shown in an entertaining way, despite the too frequent inclinations of everyone to act juvenile and coy. And the heavier sections of the drama are managed in a tense, precipitate style. As the hero, Mr. Stewart does a warmly appealing job, indicating that he has grown in spiritual stature as well as in talent during the years he was in the war. And Donna Reed is remarkably poised and gracious as his adoring sweetheart and wife. Thomas Mitchell, Beulah Bondi, H. B. Warner and Samuel S. Hinds stand out among the group of assorted small-town characters who give the picture variety and verve. But Lionel Barrymore's banker is almost a caricature of Scrooge, and Henry Trav-

ers' "heavenly messenger" is a little too sticky for our taste. Indeed, the weakness of this picture, from this reviewer's point of view, is the sentimentality of it — its illusory concept of life. Mr. Capra's nice people are charming, his small town is a quite beguiling place and his pattern for solving problems is most optimistic and facile. But somehow they all resemble theatrical attitudes rather than average realities. And Mr. Capra's "turkey dinners" philosophy, while emotionally gratifying, doesn't fill the hungry paunch.

On the whole, however, reviews from around the United States were positive:

The Hollywood Reporter, December 11, 1946: "*It's a Wonderful Life* is just a wonderful picture; every foot of it pushes fresh air into lungs that have been clogged with pictures of many angles, of all types of subjects and for varied purposes. The Capra show is fine and clean, heart-wringing in spots, and in others, hilariously funny. It's a good American yarn, brilliantly written — dialogue that's so real it constantly sends shivers up your spine — and needless to say, expertly directed and acted by a superb cast. . . . It's the greatest of all Capra pictures, and in saying that, one must mean one of the greatest pictures of this or any other year."

United Press: "Never in all my years of covering Hollywood have I been so moved by a movie as by *It's a Wonderful Life.* The Capra film is the season's climax."

Box Office Digest, December 19, 1946: "Frank Capra is back with a bang. *It's a Wonderful Life* is an all-American picture — that goes for caliber and its appeal — a picture that is both an enjoyable and an enriching entertainment experience."

New York *Sun,* December 21, 1946: "Last night the Globe Theatre presented Broadway moviegoers with their finest Christmas present, a warm and merry comedy called *It's a Wonderful Life.* It has the laughter, the understanding, the poignancy of the best Capra pictures."

Los Angeles *Herald Express,* December 26, 1946: "Frank Capra's *It's a Wonderful Life* melted all the barnacles off my heart and left me feeling young and full of ideals again. I think it's the greatest holiday-week picture I ever saw."

New York *Daily News,* January 18, 1946:

"We've seldom seen such a moving and inspiring, entertaining and exciting picture as this one."

Chicago *Herald American*, December 27, 1946: "A glorious picture for the holiday season. . . . This one has the substance of which great movies are made."

Time, January 20, 1947: "Producer-Director Frank Capra and Actor James Stewart stage a triumphant Hollywood homecoming."

Life, December 30, 1946: "Movie of the Week . . . a masterful edifice of comedy and sentiment."

Newsweek, December 30, 1946: "A film in the old Capra manner."

Houston *Post*, March 7, 1947: "A movie of superlative value . . . bringing a human drama of essential truth."

Minneapolis *Sunday Tribune*, December 22, 1946: "*It's a Wonderful Life* is a wonderful motion picture. Bob Murphy, a motion picture projectionist, is a hard-boiled character as far as motion pictures are concerned. He sees many movies and may see each one often; and his verdict concerning a number which you happen to like may be strictly thumbs down. But when the operator walked out of the booth after showing *It's a Wonderful Life* and said that's what the motion picture art was invented for, he could find no dissenters among the onlookers, including this one. *It's a Wonderful Life* will be looked back on in years to come, in my mind, as one of the classics of filmdom."

Overall, reviewers of the film seem to break down into two groups: those who joyously loved it, were openly moved by it and are unafraid to say so; and those who express dismay at what they perceive as its sentimentality and who complain that Capra is old-fashioned. The former group sometimes apologize for loving the film, and the latter sometimes grudgingly admit it is well acted and has a kind of power. But both groups point to a quality that seemingly was its undoing — its passionate commitment to the common man and his way of life. The little man, Capra's famous character of the thirties, was back, and the film suggested that no matter how down he might feel and how tough his daily job might be or how small his accomplishments might seem, he counted for something. It was a message for the Depression era — when individuals wanted to be reassured, and when things were tough all over. In World War II, America had become group oriented. Not only that, the nation

had moved from a depressed economy to a booming one, from loser status to victorious winner. Although the final message of *It's a Wonderful Life* is that a man must have friends — that is, a group to support him — the film's primary focus is on a strained and desperate individual who questions his own worth.

The success or failure of *It's a Wonderful Life* at the box office has always been hard to determine. Although everyone agrees that it did not do as well as expected, it was listed among the top-grossing films of 1946–47 in the records of *Motion Picture Herald, Motion Picture Daily,* and *Film Daily.* Capra's scrapbooks on box-office figures are incomplete; the returns are kept at first but then abruptly stop.

The film opened at the Globe in New York City the day after the premiere, December 21, and at the Pantages in Los Angeles on December 24. For $1.25 plus tax, Frank Capra's magnum opus was ready for viewers. Stewart and Capra were brought to New York for interviews and personal appearances to help the publicity and potential box office. As the new year came in, the film was in nearly forty theaters around the country — the Grand in Chicago, the Orpheum in Kansas City, Minneapolis, and St. Paul, the Riverside in Milwaukee, the Golden Gate in San Francisco, and the Century in Buffalo. Despite the terrible winter of 1947, box office was good in the Middle West. *Variety* reported in its February 19, 1947 issue that *It's a Wonderful Life* was in the top ten in box-office grosses for the previous week, ranking number 9 in the following list:

1. *The Jolson Story*
2. *The Shocking Miss Pilgrim*
3. *Till the Clouds Roll By*
4. *Lady in the Lake*
5. *Sinbad the Sailor*
6. *Humoresque*
7. *The Yearling*
8. *The Best Years of Our Lives*
9. *It's a Wonderful Life*
10. *California*

But *Variety* also reported that business had dropped off sharply after the holidays, and various printed sources have said that RKO lost $525,000 on the film. (The RKO Picture Archives say the financial record of *It's a Wonderful Life*, disputed

INCOME ON TRAILER			
TOTAL	3,183,205.07	32,757.90	
Less: CHARGES AGAINST PRODUCERS ACCOUNT			81,291.38
Negative Cost or Advance	81,291.38		281,721.87
U. S. and Canada: Prints	281,624.32	97.55	59,900.66
Advertising	59,866.23	34.43	
Miscellaneous	225,706.04	16,840.01	242,546.05
FOREIGN OFFICES (as per schedule)	648,487.97	16,971.99	665,459.96
TOTAL			
Balance Due R K O			
Remittances			2,263,278.36
BANK OF AMERICA N.Y. & S.A.	2,263,278.36		145,603.05
LIBERTY FILMS INC.	145,603.05	12,741.56	138,577.25
RKO STUDIO RENTAL	12,583.69	3,044.35	3,044.35
PARAMOUNT PICT. CORP.			
	3,183,205.07	32,757.90	3,215,962.97

A detail from RKO's 1954 summary of the earnings of It's a Wonderful Life, *suggesting that the film made something over three million dollars—good, but not wonderful.*

for a long time between Liberty and RKO, is "very unclear.") On December 21, 1946, Samuel Briskin did a postmortem on the cost of the film for *Box Office* magazine. "Five years ago," wrote Briskin, "it might have been possible to make [*It's a Wonderful Life*] for $1,500,000. Three years ago it probably could have been made for $1,800,000. It actually cost $2,800,000. The increased costs go into every item from extras to stars, and the labor slowdowns stretch out the shooting time. To use an illustration, we used to be able to get the title cards made in 24 hours. On this film, it took us two weeks." Because production costs had gone up so much, Briskin pointed out later, "it is no longer possible to make cheap films, and there is no point in making expensive films without aiming for the highest attainable quality because they will not return a profit. . . ." On January 3, 1947, *Variety* reported that total production costs on *It's a Wonderful Life* were $3,000,000.

Capra's files provide no detailed, coherent financial picture of *IAWL* at all. One can only conclude that the film did not grow and gain strength at the box office as he had hoped. Whatever the

reasons — a rushed release, bad weather, mixed reviews, stiff competition from light entertainments such as *The Jolson Story* and *Till the Clouds Roll By,* not to mention its main nemesis, *The Best Years of Our Lives* — not long after its release it appeared to have been an ill-fated venture. One might even ask (and risk sounding like George Bailey for a moment) whether making *It's a Wonderful Life* had counted for anything at all.

Perhaps the most accurate thing to say about the box-office returns of *It's a Wonderful Life* is that they did not live up to expectations — either Frank Capra's expectations or those of the Hollywood rank and file who were used to blockbusters from Capra. Its domestic rentals after one year of release were listed by *Variety* as $3,300,000, and it was ranked twenty-seventh among the hundreds of films released in the 1946–47 box-office season. Since Capra had spent nearly $3,000,000 in making and promoting *It's a Wonderful Life,* its success was clearly tenuous, and its reception put Liberty Films in financial jeopardy. (About two years after *It's a Wonderful Life*'s release, Liberty Films was sold to Paramount.)

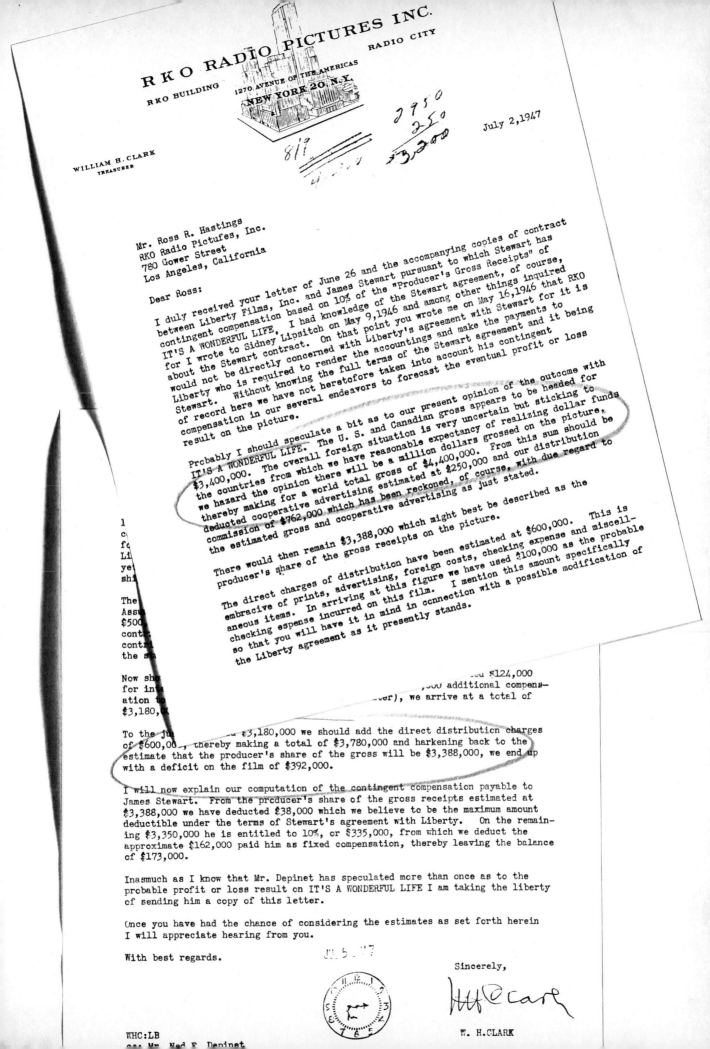

RKO RADIO PICTURES INC.

RKO BUILDING · 1270 AVENUE OF THE AMERICAS · NEW YORK 20, N.Y. · RADIO CITY

WILLIAM H. CLARK
TREASURER

2950
250
817
$3,200

July 2, 1947

Mr. Ross R. Hastings
RKO Radio Pictures, Inc.
780 Gower Street
Los Angeles, California

Dear Ross:

I duly received your letter of June 26 and the accompanying copies of contract between Liberty Films, Inc. and James Stewart pursuant to which Stewart has contingent compensation based on 10% of the "Producer's Gross Receipts" of IT'S A WONDERFUL LIFE. I had knowledge of the Stewart agreement, of course, for I wrote to Sidney Lipsitch on May 9,1946 and among other things inquired about the Stewart contract. On that point you wrote me on May 16,1946 that RKO would not be directly concerned with Liberty's agreement with Stewart for it is Liberty who is required to render the accountings and make the payments to Stewart. Without knowing the full terms of the Stewart agreement and it being of record here we have not heretofore taken into account his contingent compensation in our several endeavors to forecast the eventual profit or loss result on the picture.

Probably I should speculate a bit as to our present opinion of the outcome with IT'S A WONDERFUL LIFE. The U. S. and Canadian gross appears to be headed for $3,400,000. The overall foreign situation is very uncertain but sticking to the countries from which we have reasonable expectancy of realizing dollar funds we hazard the opinion there will be a million dollars grossed on the picture, thereby making for a world total gross of $4,400,000. From this sum should be deducted cooperative advertising estimated at $250,000 and our distribution commission of $762,000 which has been reckoned, of course, with due regard to the estimated gross and cooperative advertising as just stated.

There would then remain $3,388,000 which might best be described as the producer's share of the gross receipts on the picture.

The direct charges of distribution have been estimated at $600,000. This is embracive of prints, advertising, foreign costs, checking expense and miscellaneous items. In arriving at this figure we have used $100,000 as the probable checking expense incurred on this film. I mention this amount specifically so that you will have it in mind in connection with a possible modification of the Liberty agreement as it presently stands.

l
c
fo
Li
yet
shi

The
Assu
$500
cont
contr
the s

Now sh⋯⋯⋯⋯⋯⋯⋯⋯⋯⋯⋯ $124,000
for int⋯⋯⋯⋯⋯⋯⋯,000 additional compensation to⋯⋯⋯⋯⋯er), we arrive at a total of $3,180,0⋯

To the ju⋯⋯⋯ $3,180,000 we should add the direct distribution charges of $600,00_, thereby making a total of $3,780,000 and harkening back to the estimate that the producer's share of the gross will be $3,388,000, we end up with a deficit on the film of $392,000.

I will now explain our computation of the contingent compensation payable to James Stewart. From the producer's share of the gross receipts estimated at $3,388,000 we have deducted $38,000 which we believe to be the maximum amount deductible under the terms of Stewart's agreement with Liberty. On the remaining $3,350,000 he is entitled to 10%, or $335,000, from which we deduct the approximate $162,000 paid him as fixed compensation, thereby leaving the balance of $173,000.

Inasmuch as I know that Mr. Depinet has speculated more than once as to the probable profit or loss result on IT'S A WONDERFUL LIFE I am taking the liberty of sending him a copy of this letter.

Once you have had the chance of considering the estimates as set forth herein I will appreciate hearing from you.

With best regards.

Sincerely,

W. H. CLARK

WHC:LB
cc: Mr. Ned E. Depinet

Disappointed in the film's overall Christmas box office, Frank Capra turned his postholiday attention to promoting *It's a Wonderful Life* fully across America. To give it a much-needed boost, two publicity stunts were planned to appeal to the famous "little man" Capra's films were supposed to be about: the *It's a Wonderful Life* contest and the *It's a Wonderful Life* junket to Beaumont, Texas.

The first was simple enough. Four thousand dollars was invested in a writing contest in which entrants wrote a short essay about their personal experiences, telling why, for them, it had been "a wonderful life." Eight winners were to be chosen, and each would receive five hundred dollars plus a "personal greeting" from Frank Capra and Jimmy Stewart. According to the New York City *Radio Daily* of February 3, 1947, more than twelve hundred people entered the contest, and the eight winners were presented with their awards at the Warwick Hotel in Philadelphia. (No names are given, and no winning essays are reprinted.) According to the story, "the eight prize winners heard their own stories dramatized on WFIL; and each of them made a personal appearance on the stage of the Stanley Theatre, at the Philadelphia premiere of the picture. Likewise, each of them participated in a broadcast on WFIL marking the official end of the contest."

The other publicity stunt, a junket that sent Capra and Stewart to the small town of Beaumont, Texas, involved much more planning. This "big party" trip was quite unlike Capra's earlier party, the star-studded dinner dance. Very little lamé or mink was in evidence; but a great deal of enthusiasm, high spirits, and general American mayhem was. In fact, it might be said that in Beaumont, Texas, Frank Capra found himself caught up in a Preston Sturges movie. The trip was organized by Beaumont's Jefferson Amusement Company (Julius M. Gordon, president). Capra always laughs at any mention of the trip. In his autobiography, he wrote in detail of the horrible flight through bad weather he and Stewart endured to arrive in Beaumont, but he made a comedy out of their dilemma. His files contain a detailed notebook on the trip, marked in gilt on the cover: BEAUMONT, TEXAS WELCOMES JAMES STEWART AND FRANK CAPRA, MARCH 4, 1947.

The story of the Beaumont junket is a typical Hollywood publicity tale. Stewart and Capra were scheduled to arrive at 11:00 a.m. on Tuesday, March 4, by special chartered plane. But the bad weather Capra wrote about prevented their leaving Dallas on time, and they were more than four hours late. By the time they arrived, at 3:05 p.m., only one thousand out of the original five thousand people there at 11:00 a.m. were still at the airport.

The first man to greet Capra as he stepped off the plane was his first cousin, a Port Arthur liquor dealer whose mother was Capra's mother's sister. The two had never met before, and Capra felt himself being swept up by "a long lost relative" he'd never known he had. "Hordes of women — and some men," says a news article, "flocked downtown in the late morning to catch a glimpse of the famous Hollywood pair." Stewart and Capra made up for their lateness by charming everyone, as Stewart drawled, "Well, I guess we're a little late. Actually I guess I'd better say we're pretty late." The French High School band (70 pieces) and the Lamar College Band (105 pieces) had given up during the four-hour wait and returned to their classes. Consequently, Stewart and Capra arrived and paraded without musical accompaniment. Despite the late arrival, the streets were still lined, and nearly three thousand people were waiting at City Hall.

The official campaign book on the Beaumont visit contains many examples of the nearly incoherently reported event. Under a headline reading TRUMAN STRESSES GOOD NEIGHBOR POLICY, and a lesser head declaring STALIN QUITS AS RED ARMY COMMANDER, the Beaumont *Enterprise* featured the story PLANS TO WELCOME SCREEN STAR JAMES STEWART, MOVIE DIRECTOR FRANK CAPRA TODAY ARE COMPLETE. In the article, Stewart and Capra played second fiddle to what was really important to Beaumont — the local plans that had been made.

Mayor James F. Parker greeted the celebrities most cordially, welcoming them to the city and presented them with two, foot-long, Balsawood Keys.

Due to the lateness of the hour, it was impossible to carry out the Cocktail-Luncheon as planned, at the Mirror Room of Hotel Beaumont which had been specially decorated for the event. 4' × 8' blow-ups of Mr. Stewart and Mr. Capra were placed against a blue-drop

background with silver metalic [*sic*] letters in between the blow-ups reading: Welcome James Stewart and Frank Capra.

Place cards for the luncheon were die-cut folded cards using the "Welcome Academy Award Teams" angle. The die-cut was made around the illustration of the Oscar, and when the top part of the card was folded over, it made an easel allowing the Oscar to stand upright. The cards carried a ½" column screen cut of Stewart and Capra, and the title of the picture was printed in sepia with the individual name of each guest typed in red ink. Unfortunately, it was necessary to go ahead with the luncheon for the invited guests without Mr. Capra and Mr. Stewart at 2:30 p.m.

(It was also reported that at the luncheon a girl announced that she would like to ask Stewart if he knew Dick Tracy, but there is no report as to whether she ever asked or he ever answered.)

The Beaumont *Journal* summed up the day:

We received more than $500.00 in gratis radio time, and 460 inches of gratis news and art in the two Beaumont papers, the Port Arthur *News* and the Orange *Leader.* Beaumont will long remember the visit of James Stewart and Frank Capra, and it is hoped that they will long remember Beaumont, Texas.

Everybody was happy by nightfall. There had been much milling around in town all day. Stores had been crowded. Women and children had been stirred out of their winter lethargy. Except for Jefferson Amusement company officials who visibly aged under the strain of Mr. Stewart's delayed descent, a good time was had by all, and in the final analysis, that's why actors are born.

On February 9, 1947, as the Beaumont trip was being planned, the Oscar nominations were announced. As expected, *It's a Wonderful Life* figured prominently, with nominations for Best Picture (opposite *The Best Years of Our Lives, Henry V, The Razor's Edge,* and *The Yearling*), for Stewart as Best Actor (opposite Fredric March in *Best Years,* Laurence Olivier in *Henry V,* Larry Parks in *The Jolson Story,* and Gregory Peck in *The Yearling*); and for Capra as Best Director (opposite William Wyler for *Best Years,* David Lean for *Brief Encounter,* Robert Siodmak for *The Killers,* and

OVERLEAF: *Texas hospitality: the star and director arrive, and are fed, given the keys to the city, and awarded ribbons, like prize steers. It's a wonderful life.*

Welcome

❖

JIMMY
STEWART

FRANK
CAPRA

❖

JEFFERSON
AMUSEMENT CO.

Welcome
TO THE
ACADEMY
AWARD TEAM

JAMES ——AND—— FRANK
STEWART   CAPRA
STAR AND PRODUCER
OF THEIR NEW SCREEN SENSATION

"It's A Wonderful Life"

MR. FRANK CAPRA

MIRROR ROOM, Hotel Beaumont, MARCH 4, 1947

Clarence Brown for *The Yearling*). *IAWL* also received nominations for Best Sound Recording and Best Film Editing.

The powerful combination of Stewart and Capra had entered the Oscar race before, in 1939, when *Mr. Smith Goes to Washington* had also earned nominations for Best Picture, Best Actor, and Best Director, only to lose out to *Gone With the Wind*. They were in good company: *Ninotchka, Dark Victory, Love Affair, Stagecoach, The Wizard of Oz, Wuthering Heights, Goodbye Mr. Chips,* and *Of Mice and Men* were the other Best Picture nominees, and Stewart was contending with Robert Donat (the surprise winner for *Goodbye Mr. Chips* — the only major award to break *Gone With the Wind*'s Oscar stranglehold), Clark Gable (*GWTW*), Mickey Rooney (*Babes in Arms*), and Olivier (*Wuthering Heights*). Capra had been up against his close friend John Ford (*Stagecoach*), Wyler (*Wuthering Heights*), Sam Wood (*Goodbye Mr. Chips*), and Victor Fleming (the winner, for *Gone With the Wind*).

Both Capra and Stewart were already Oscar winners, Stewart for Best Actor in *The Philadelphia Story* (1940) and Capra for *It Happened One Night* (1934), *Mr. Deeds Goes to Town* (1936), *You Can't Take It with You* (1938), and also for *Prelude to War* in the "Why We Fight" series in 1942, with the award going to the U.S. Army Special Services.

In 1947, those earlier wins seemed long ago, in a distant time before World War II, which had deeply changed them both. Making *It's a Wonderful Life* had meant a great deal to Stewart and Capra; they wanted to win. They wanted it for their film, which they believed in, and for the reassurance it would bring to their return to the screen. Could they still do it? Of course. Would the public still *want* them to do it? Naturally. But would their peers still think they were the best at doing it? They wanted to know. Although they didn't talk about it, they both cared deeply about their nominations, and they loved the movie they had made. "The pace was that of a four-month non-stop orgasm," Capra had written. "All that I was and all that I knew went into the making of *It's a Wonderful Life*."

On the night of March 13, 1947, the distinguished Academy of Motion Picture Arts and Sciences presented its annual ceremonies, produced by Mervyn LeRoy and hosted by Jack Benny. Change was in the air. First of all, the Academy had revamped its voting rules. Instead of having the entire film community (nearly ten thousand people) select the nominees and then the final winners, as in the previous nine years, the rules were adjusted so that only Academy members would make the final selections. Also, after three years at Grauman's Chinese Theatre, the Oscar presentation was moved to the gigantic Shrine Auditorium, which seated sixty-seven hundred people. The general public was allowed to buy seats and mingle with the stars.

Things were different from the days when Stewart and Capra had been winners — so very different, in fact, that they came home losers. *It's a Wonderful Life,* a superbly written, directed, performed, and crafted film, did not win a single Oscar. The awards that Capra and Stewart specifically hoped for — Best Picture, Best Director, and Best Actor — all went to *The Best Years of Our Lives.* Wyler's film won four other Oscars as well, for a total of seven. Although Capra's diaries do not refer to the defeat, and his letters and conversations do not dwell on it, his Archives reveal how he must have felt. There is no coverage of the Oscar night — not a single clipping, not a single photograph or souvenir — and the scrapbooks on *It's a Wonderful Life* abruptly stop. Only the production and business files continue, later to be joined by bulging files of letters from devoted fans.

Whatever he felt privately, Capra congratulated his Liberty partner William Wyler, who had ironically brought *The Best Years of Our Lives*'s awards and money to Samuel Goldwyn, to fulfill a prior contractual obligation. Capra never criticized his colleague's film, although he did say that after the war, he was not himself interested in making films about ex-soldiers. He respected Wyler, who was not only a business partner but also a personal friend, and he liked *The Best Years of Our Lives.* When interviewed by Richard Glatzer in 1973 as to why "the postwar criticism of *It's a Wonderful Life* underrated it . . . (and) the realism of *The Best Years of Our Lives* seemed to be more what critics wanted in 1946," Capra replied:

I think that people understand films better now than they did then. They were labelled "corny" then because people didn't know what

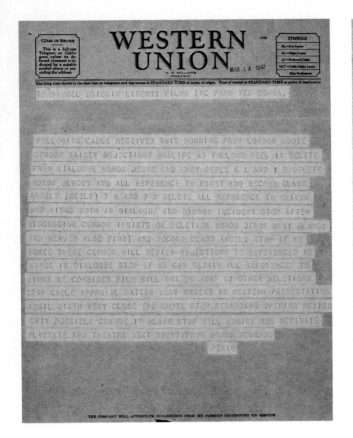

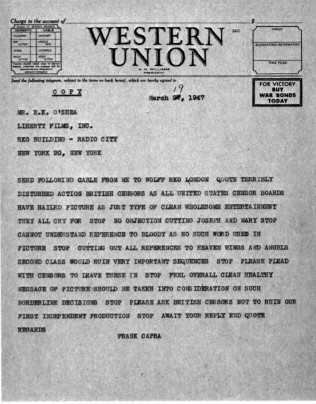

to call them. The critics particularly wanted the more obscure things, the more negative things. This positive attitude toward life, this optimism, this great reverence for the individual that is dramatized in all my films was a little bit too sticky for them at the time. Yet, are the people today any cornier than they were in those days? No, people today seem to be much more aware of something that is real, good, and true than even people of my day. So to me that's a big plus. There is no generation gap between my films and the present generation at all.

After the Oscar losses, Capra went ahead planning for the overseas release of *It's a Wonderful Life.* First of all, there was trouble with the London Censorship Board. Liberty received a cable (dated March 18, 1947, and shown above left) indicating the British censor's objections to certain scenes and lines of dialogue. On hearing that there were serious objections, Capra sent a cable (above right) to Wolff at RKO in London.

A compromise was finally reached. On March 25, the censors agreed it would not be necessary to delete all references to heaven and angels and first- and second-class angels. Most references would remain, and all objections to wings were waived. Clarence was still able to say "Thanks for the wings," and "Thanks for the flying appendages" failed to go down in Britain as one of those memorable lines from a Hollywood film.

With censorship settled, *It's a Wonderful Life* opened in London. Now came the really bad news. For the most part — there were a few exceptions — the British critics hated it. The *Daily Express,* April 7: "This isn't a film. It's a full gale of sentiment." The *Daily Mail,* April 3: "I found the experience more exhausting than uplifting." The *Daily Graphic,* April 3: "An orgy of sweetness . . . everybody is made good and happy. Positively everybody, except your critic." The *News Chronicle,* April 5: "At its best all this seems to me insipid, and at its worst an embarrassment to both flesh and spirit." The *Evening News,* April 3: "I believe this to be a very good film — for Americans." The *Sunday Pictorial,* April 6: "Just another movie." And the *Times* provided the most succinct crusher on April 5: "It is not a good film."

This was real rejection. But the *Daily Worker,*

the newspaper of the British Communist party, loved *It's a Wonderful Life*. On April 5 John Ross wrote: "One of those thought-stimulating films which Hollywood produces so rarely these days . . . a film of quality."

By spring 1947, it must have seemed to Capra that *It's a Wonderful Life* was over, finished. The British reception was the final letdown. The picnic had become a joke photo to keep as a memory, and the dinner dance a program that reminded people of what they'd eaten one night at the Ambassador Hotel. In Hollywood, you were only as good as your last picture. A good Hollywood yardstick was indicated by a Warner Bros. trailer which once advertised a movie by exclaiming, "A film so famous it will live for ten years!" That seemed extravagant enough for what was then perceived as a disposable medium.

For Capra, the reviews were in, the grosses tabulated, and, sadly, the Oscars lost. But *It's a Wonderful Life* could not really be counted as a failure. It had received many good reviews, and Capra had won the Hollywood Foreign Correspondents Association's "Golden Globe" award as the year's best director. It was on the National Board of Review's list of the ten best films of 1947 and was among the year's top-grossing films. Yet in Capra's mind it slowly seemed to fizzle out. He turned to other projects, assigning *It's a Wonderful Life* to his office shelves — perhaps even to his mental graveyard. To him it was dead, as his dreams for it had not been fully realized. It is possible that Capra's own disappointment accounts for the legend of the film's hostile reception that has grown in the ensuing years. Capra, the eternal storyteller, told a tale that reflected his own emotional reaction to what actually happened. Still, given Hollywood's tendency to discard its own past, *It's a Wonderful Life,* for all practical purposes, *was* dead by the end of 1947.

Slowly, however, a curious thing began to happen. *It's a Wonderful Life* began to stir and come alive again — or, to be fanciful, some mysterious Clarence seemed to pull it out of the water and give it a second chance.

At first, no one really noticed what was happening. People were always writing letters about movies they had seen, and there was always a period of "mop up" correspondence after any film was released. But this time, a *great many* people seemed to be writing those letters. It began with

lots of practical inquiries about specific details in the film. Capra answered them all.

"Where did you get that footage of George's brother's airplane?" "The scene was taken from Navy film, but the exact source was not identified. It is very probable, however, that it is the same sequence that was used in *The Fighting Lady*."

"Whatever happened to Potter and the eight thousand dollars?" "We photographed several solutions [Note: Production does not corroborate this], discussed many others, then threw them all away and decided to let heaven take care of him. Not very original, but there are some things heaven should do for us, especially when you can't think of them for yourself."

"Where can I find that house that the Martinis moved into? This is the type of home I expect to build — a one-story white bungalow. Just what I've been looking for a long time." "I have delayed in answering your letter about the house . . . hoping that I would be able to find out the information you requested. However, I regret to tell you that all I could ascertain is that the scene was shot in La Crescenta, a small town near Los Angeles, in the foothills."

One lengthy letter criticized the swimming pool scene as "slapstick, cheap slapstick at that, and there's no such thing as a pool like that," knocked the "papier-mâché rose-bush or whatever botanical contraption that bush Donna Reed hides in is supposed to represent," complained about the fact that Bailey offers Potter his life insurance policy as security ("That's silly"), and finished up on the way Henry Travers should be dressed to properly represent an angel ("about like a minister, broad-brimmed black hat or black derby, black frock-coat, and to intimate his celestial background — white vest and white necktie, and not to forget: an umbrella").

To all this Capra responded point by point. "First, the swimming pool sequence. That swimming pool actually exists at a local high school. The incident in the picture actually occurred. In fact, I got the idea from the actual occurrence.

"Second, the bush into which Donna Reed disappeared. That street scene was not 'ersatz.' The street, the houses, the fences actually are real and the shrubbery is growing. That is not a studio shot but an exterior street on the RKO ranch.

"Third, you say George Bailey should have offered some of the assets of his firm rather than his life insurance as security for a loan from Potter. This wouldn't do at all, because if the firm borrowed the money it would still be $8,000 short in its accounts. George had to get the money personally to make up the firm's shortage.

"Fourth, Henry Travers should have been dressed differently, more like a minister. Here you may have something, although . . . I doubt if any two people would agree on just how an angel visiting the earth should be dressed."

Capra thanked the man for his letter and later was rewarded by a second letter from him with these contradictory words: "Let's have more pictures like *It's a Wonderful Life!*"

Capra once told a group of Wesleyan University film majors: "I sat down to answer a letter about *It's a Wonderful Life* in about 1947, and when I next looked up, it was about 1957. What the heck happened? I wrote letters for years! It was television. TV. Films didn't die and disappear anymore. They never went out of circulation. Instead they went to TV and kept right on playing. They were as alive in '57 or '67 or '77 as they had been in 1947. I woke up one Christmas morning, and the whole world was watching *It's a Wonderful Life.* And they all wrote me about it!"

So more and more letters kept coming. People from all around the world wrote Capra about what the film meant to them — more letters than he had ever thought possible, longer letters, deeper letters, more meaningful letters. Letters from prisoners at San Quentin . . . letters from children and old people . . . letters from all countries . . . a heartbreaking letter from a would-be suicide. It was only the beginning. As Capra had said, letters would keep coming through the end of 1947, and into 1948. Letters would arrive in 1950 and still be coming in 1955, and throughout the 1960s. Finally, files were set up as "Sample Letters, *It's a Wonderful Life.*"

For Frank Capra, the film was kept alive long past 1946 by the people he had originally meant to reach with it — *his* audience, the movie fans. Kept in circulation by television showings at Christmas, it slowly gained prominence until by 1980, it was an American cultural phenomenon. *It's a Wonderful Life* did more than just become everyone's favorite holiday movie on the late show. It became, for many, *the* great American film.

A manifestation of this was duly reported in *The New Yorker* on January 15, 1979. "The Talk of the Town," under the headline "Wonderful," reported the story of Christopher Little and David White, who annually throw a small celebration with fifteen or twenty friends by screening *It's a Wonderful Life.* With mock solemnity, but proper respect, they gather to share and share again a movie that has meant something to them. "You still need Donna Reed and Jimmy Stewart to remind you that there may not yet be peace in the Middle East, the dollar may be unstable, inflation may be rampant, but it *is* a wonderful life," proclaimed the host, just before the lights went down.

Finally, *It's a Wonderful Life* moved into an exalted status in which academics began to analyze and comment on it:

Charles Maland in *Frank Capra,* 1980: "*It's a Wonderful Life* . . . is one of those rare works of narrative art in which an artist at last finds a form to express precisely the preoccupations he or she has been dealing with in a number of earlier works."

Ray Carney in his introduction to *American Modernism and the Movies,* 1986: "It is arguable that Frank Capra has more deeply touched and moved more people than any other artist of the twentieth century, perhaps more than any artist in history . . . all through one film, *It's a Wonderful Life.*"

Galen Guy Quick in a letter to the Capra Archives: "This film, staple Christmas fare . . . is not just a great piece of entertainment but a significant cultural document."

Robin Wood in *Film Comment:* "It is one of the greatest American films."

Andrew Sarris in the *Village Voice:* "[It] has become manifestly an all-time masterpiece."

William Pechter in *Partisan Review:* "*It's a Wonderful Life* is the kind of work which defies criticism. Almost, one would say, defies art. It is one of the funniest, bleakest, as well as being one of the most technically adroit films ever made; it is a masterpiece, yet rather of that kind peculiar to film: unconscious masterpieces. Like Mark Twain, Capra is a natural; a folk artist in the sense of drawing imaginatively for his substance on some of the most characteristic matter of America's national folk lore."

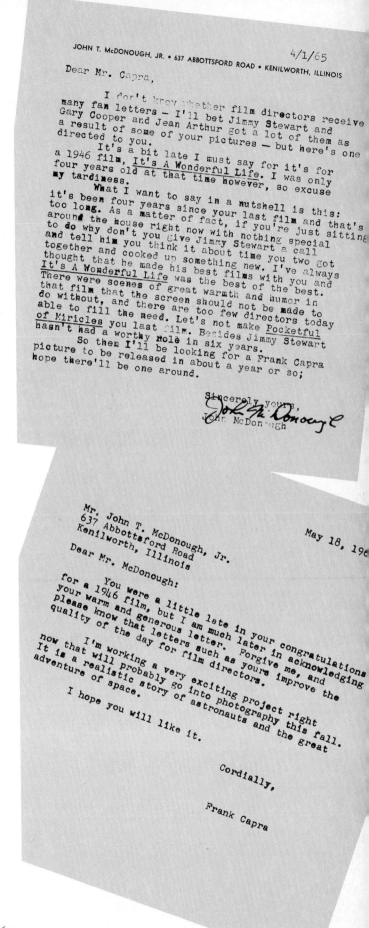

JOHN T. McDONOUGH, JR. • 637 ABBOTTSFORD ROAD • KENILWORTH, ILLINOIS

4/1/65

Dear Mr. Capra,

I don't know whether film directors receive many fan letters — I'll bet Jimmy Stewart and Gary Cooper and Jean Arthur got a lot of them as a result of some of your pictures — but here's one directed to you.

It's a bit late I must say for it's for a 1946 film, It's A Wonderful Life. I was only four years old at that time however, so excuse my tardiness.

What I want to say in a nutshell is this: it's been four years since your last film and that's too long. As a matter of fact, if you're just sitting around the house right now with nothing special to do why don't you give Jimmy Stewart a call and tell him you think it about time you two got together and cooked up something new. I've always thought that he made his best films with you and It's A Wonderful Life was the best of the best. There were scenes of great warmth and humor in that film that the screen should not be made to do without, and there are too few directors today able to fill the need. Let's not make Pocketful of Miricles you last film. Besides Jimmy Stewart hasn't had a worthy role in six years.

So then I'll be looking for a Frank Capra picture to be released in about a year or so; hope there'll be one around.

Sincerely yours,
John McDonough

Mr. John T. McDonough, Jr.
637 Abbottsford Road
Kenilworth, Illinois

May 18, 196

Dear Mr. McDonough:

You were a little late in your congratulations for a 1946 film, but I am much later in acknowledging your warm and generous letter. Forgive me, and please know that letters such as yours improve the quality of the day for film directors.

I'm working a very exciting project right now that will probably go into photography this fall. It is a realistic story of astronauts and the great adventure of space.

I hope you will like it.

Cordially,

Frank Capra

Wonderful

FOR reasons of their own, Christopher Little and David White firmly believe that this life, dammit, is a wonderful life. Annually, they throw a small party to celebrate that shared perception of reality. What they do at the party is this: they have a few drinks and eat a few ham sandwiches and then they watch an old movie on television. Specifically, they watch "It's a Wonderful Life" (1946, Frank Capra, three handkerchiefs, happy ending). Every year, it is the same movie, and every year, with slight variations, the same audience comes to watch—fifteen or twenty friends who agree that Jimmy Stewart is a great guy and Donna Reed is a swell and pretty girl and Lionel Barrymore makes a convincing villain. The eighth annual "It's a Wonderful Life" party took place one night shortly after Christmas in David White's apartment, on the East Side. When we arrived, a few minutes ahead of the rest of the guests, White, who used to be a reporter for the *Times* and now spends his days finishing a novel, was busy with last-minute preparations.

"This thing always gets shown on television around Christmastime, and we pore over every word of *TV Guide* trying to find out when," he said as he sliced ham. "Once, we got stuck with a late-afternoon showing, which meant that we had to invite people to start drinking at four o'clock. Believe it or not, there were some people who weren't willing to leave work early to come to the party. We had to strike them from the invitation list. Nothing strictly personal, of course, but they've been permanently banned. Well, it's not really a *permanent* ban. You can get back on the list if you've got a doctor's excuse or a note from your mother. This year, Channel 5 broadcast the move on Christmas Day at *twelve-thirty*—in the middle of the day. Indecent. Naturally, we couldn't get anyone to show up for that, so we decided to hold the party tonight, even though Christmas is over. Fortunately, with great foresight we taped the movie last year on a Betamax machine for just such a situation. I think it's a pretty good tape. We edited out all the commercials, so you won't be seeing any Kitchen Magician or Crazy Eddie ads. The Betamax is over there." He pointed to a compact machine on top of a desk. "At the appropriate moment, the ground-service crew will move the television set into the most advantageous viewing spot in the room."

People began to arrive now. Christopher Little, a photographer who lives in Chelsea, was among them. He shook White's hand, nodded gravely, and said, "Wonderful life, David."

"Wonderful life, Christopher," White said sternly.

Several people in the room had seen the movie more times than they could remember. Jane Bayard, an assistant curator at the Yale University Art Gallery, did remember. "This is the seventh time for me," she said. "I've seen it more than any other movie."

"It's a violation of the rules to watch this movie out of town or during the off-season," said Little. "Hawaii in July, for instance—strictly forbidden. Technically, it's possible not to like the movie but to love this party as an institution."

"No," said Jane Bayard. "I think it's necessary to love the movie."

"For sheer raw emotional power," said a friend of hers, an architect named Patrick Curley, "I don't think you can beat the scene where Jimmy Stewart leans over that bridge railing, having decided not to commit suicide after all, and says, 'I want to live! I want to live!' "

"Patrick was in Jerusalem during last year's party," Jane said.

"I looked all through the Jerusalem television listings," he said. "I guess the movie isn't that popular over there."

Our invitation had noted that a special guest was going to be present. As we were surveying the room looking for someone charismatic, Little said, "Trying to pick out the special guest, I see. I'm afraid that fell through. David's girlfriend, Margaret Stanback, works with a woman who used to be a friend of the next-door neighbor of the girlfriend of Jimmy Stewart's nephew. We thought the nephew would be here tonight, but he had to go to Florida. If we had held this party last week, he would have made it. We're thinking of waiting until the tenth annual celebration before we get Uncle Jimmy and Donna Reed involved. But I'm sure they'll accept."

It was almost time for the Betamax machine to be turned on. While Patrick Curley cleaned the television screen with Windex, David White made a brief speech. "You may wonder why you've all been invited here tonight," he said. "The story begins, in at least one important respect, the same way that the story of the birth of Jesus Christ begins, and that is that it begins on a dark and wintry night. It was 1970, and three desperate college students—Christopher Little, myself, and Christopher's sister Suzanne—home on vacation with nothing better to do, spent the evening watching a movie on television. That movie was 'The Miracle of the Bells.' And when it ended, at one-thirty in the morning, we flipped the channel selector and stumbled across another movie. Christopher watched a few frames and then uttered these immortal words: 'Wait, I've seen this movie before. It's a *great* movie.' Christopher spoke as if another miracle were at hand, and we could only have faith. And he was right. So now, even though Christmas is over and you've all unwrapped your neckties and blouses, you still need Donna Reed and Jimmy Stewart to remind you that there may not yet be peace in the Middle East, the dollar may be unstable, inflation may be rampant, but it *is* a wonderful life."

There was brief applause. Then the lights went out, the television screen brightened, the opening credits rolled, and the room filled with the sound of deeply contented sighing. About fifteen minutes into the movie, Christopher Little, who had been lying on the floor, stood up and went to mix himself a drink.

"I'll be right back," he said to no one in particular. "Tell me what happens, will you?"

Stephen Handzo in *Film Comment*: "*It's a Wonderful Life* is best described as *A Christmas Carol* from Bob Cratchit's point of view. . . . It is [Capra's] *Magnificent Ambersons*, his *How Green Was My Valley* — one man's life and the collective autobiography of a small town (the archetypal American microcosm) in the era spanning the two world wars. Abandoning his customarily linear narrative, Capra makes the entire film an extended flashback. Instead of the usual timespan of weeks and months culminating in a decisive act, the film chronicles decades through the character George Bailey — a Deeds who never got rich, a Smith who never got appointed to the Senate, a Doe who remained obscure — who just got old. Bailey is less a character than a container into which James Stewart pours every nuance of his own being, exposing his whole emotional range in a two-hour tour de force. Surpassing even *Mr. Smith Goes to Washington*, it remains Stewart's own favorite performance, as *Wonderful Life* is Capra's favorite of his films. It is also Capra's most Ford-like film, dealing with themes of community and continuity, and taking place in the generation just past. . . . *Wonderful Life* is one of the most personal visions ever realized in commercial cinema. Rich in performance, unflinching in its confrontation of the "permanent things" of human existence, it is probably the film for which Capra will ultimately be remembered. Capra has said that he tried for no less."

In private conversations, Capra often laughed in delight over comments such as "Capra's philosophic determinism" or "abandoning his customary linear narrative" and comparisons to Mark Twain. He took academics seriously, respected their ideas, and was grateful for their praise — but he liked to remind people of the London review which had said *It's a Wonderful Life* was "an embarrassment to both flesh and spirit."

It's a Wonderful Life is now part of America's annual Christmas ritual. It is shown on channel after channel. (In New York City, WNET once cut it and received more phone calls and letters than ever before in the station's history.) It can be rented or bought on videotape. The RKO Picture Archives report that hardly a week goes by without an inquiry about *It's a Wonderful Life*, and the Library of Congress reports the same regarding title searches on its copyright by those dreaming of

adapting it for some other use. The Capra Archives also receive mail, asking for everything from copies of the script to advice on remakes, and always asking for Mr. Capra's private address, "so that we can write him or say thanks." And *still*, every year, *It's a Wonderful Life* makes news and friends. Steven Spielberg: "Frank Capra led with his heart. His films made it shameful *not* to cry in the movies. He celebrated the noblest impulse of women and men, showed all of us our dark side, and then pointed a flashlight at the way out." Dustin Hoffman: "*It's a Wonderful Life* is a great, great, great film, and a great piece of work. When I saw Jimmy Stewart on the screen in that performance, he made me laugh, he made me cry, and he made me wish for a country which, perhaps, we haven't seen for a while."

This has been the story of the production of *It's a Wonderful Life* as taken from the Capra Archives. In his autobiography, *The Name Above the Title*, Frank Capra has told his version of the same story. In their interviews, James Stewart and Joseph Biroc tell theirs. Over the years, various articles and books have been written about the undocumented origins of the script . . . have indicated various starting dates for principal photography . . . and have explained the mysteries of the three cameramen who served on its production crew. Not one of these stories quite matches another, and not one of them, including Capra's, quite matches his own files and scrapbooks. As is the case with many things in history (and almost everything in Hollywood), legend, faulty memory, the desire for a colorful story, and the need to make things come out right interfere with a simple and orderly presentation. The Archives help to tell the truth, but they do not explain all discrepancies. Capra's personality is reflected in his tendency to save letters, reviews and tributes, photos and souvenirs, but not financial records, box-office returns, or budgets. He saved what he wanted to save, and his files are incomplete. Finally, fascinating though they are, the files give no explanation of what makes so many of us love *It's a Wonderful Life*, or want to watch it over and over again. For that, we have to look at the movie itself.

It's tempting to want to make a poor boy out of *It's a Wonderful Life*, the postwar kid who went home

OPPOSITE: *From* The New Yorker, *January 15, 1979.*

LEISURE & ARTS

A Christmas Movie's Wonderful Life

By JOHN MCDONOUGH

Once upon a time there was a man who found a Christmas story he thought would make a great movie. "The story of a lifetime," he said.

When the film came out in December 1946, it was an event. Life gave it a six-page photo spread. Newsweek put it on the cover. But, alas, this sentimental Christmas fantasy never got on a fast commercial track. Pretty soon it started losing money—over half a million dollars on a $2.7 million investment.

The company that produced it fell into financial ruin and ultimately liquidation. The picture itself became an orphan and passed from one corporate foster parent to another. They all ignored it. The film's fortunes finally hit bottom in 1974 when no one remembered to renew its copyright. At the age of 28 it went into the public domain, its exclusive commercial worth irretrievably lost.

Then something incredible happened. A guardian angel suddenly appeared in the form of television. Slowly stations learned they could show this picture any time they wanted and it wouldn't cost them a cent. And show it they did. Every Christmas millions of new viewers discovered it and came to adore it.

Critics began including it unashamedly on their "10 greatest ever made" lists. Recently, in a Chicago Tribune poll, this once forgotten little picture roared past such financial whoppers as "Star Wars" and "The Wizard of Oz" as readers' all-time favorite, placing just behind "Gone With the Wind," "Casablanca" and "Raiders of the Lost Ark." And so, after financial disaster and abandonment, the film became one of the most beloved pictures ever.

If this darkest-before-dawn scenario strikes a familiar note, then you've probably seen Frank Capra's classic Christmas chestnut, "It's a Wonderful Life." Because the film's own history bears some interesting parallels to its plot.

If you haven't seen the movie, just turn on your TV set practically at random next week and there's a good chance it will be on. For "It's a Wonderful Life" seems quietly to have replaced Charles Dickens's "A Christmas Carol" as the Great American Christmas Story.

To many, I suspect, this notion falls somewhere between poppycock and blasphemy. But check your TV schedule first. You will find "It's a Wonderful Life" everywhere, playing once, twice, often three times in virtually every television market in America. This Sunday it will actually go up against itself throughout the country via satellite superstations WTBS out of Atlanta (1:30 p.m. EST) and WGN in Chicago (1:30 p.m. CST).

Interregional Program Services has distributed the film to 152 subscribing public stations from coast to coast. National Telefilm Associates provides it to 175 additional commercial stations. And viewers who can't get their fill on TV can buy their own videotape for as little as $19.95.

For those who haven't seen it yet, "It's a Wonderful Life" concerns the trials of George Bailey, whose boyhood dreams of travel and adventure are steadily crushed by a life of petty obligations. As played by James Stewart, Bailey is no goody-goody; he's an imperfect adult exploding with latent rage. On Christmas Eve his final hopes come crashing down in financial ruin, leaving suicide his only out.

Enter Clarence Oddbody, guardian angel second class, who gives George a vivid look into the world as it might have been if he'd never been born. Mr. Capra draws us into a fantasy nightmare that bores into the deepest rings of earthly hell. The horrors build to a crescendo until George, teetering on the brink of the abyss, pleads to live again. For a few emotionally charged seconds the entire picture seems to stop. Then sprinkles of snow flutter down, and the nightmare is over. But not the movie. During the final 12 minutes Mr. Capra lays climax on top of climax, achieving a breathtaking emotional impact.

Not entirely by coincidence, one suspects, "It's a Wonderful Life" has a lot in common with Dickens's "A Christmas Carol." Lionel Barrymore, the classic Scrooge, humbugs about as Mr. Potter, a greedy Scroogelike banker. Both stories achieve their emotional uplift by subjecting their heroes to prophetic nightmares before permitting them redemption and a happy ending. And both use spirit characters to do the job. But there's a difference too, and it's fundamental. Dickens tells his story through Scrooge. Mr. Capra tells his

through George Bailey, one of us, a 20th-century Bob Cratchit on whom the Scrooges of the world are closing in.

"I think it's certainly overtaken Dickens as the most loved of all modern Christmas stories," says Time magazine critic Richard Schickel. "It has a charge that I don't think 'A Christmas Carol' comes close to, for all its early Victorian charm. And to think such a masterpiece lay neglected for so long!"

"It's the damnedest thing I've ever seen," concurs someone in a position to know—the 87-year-old Mr. Capra himself. "This film has a life of its own now, and I can look at it like I had nothing to do with it," he said in a recent interview. "I'm like a parent whose kid grows up to be president. I'm proud as hell, but it's the kid who did the work." He added: "I didn't even think of it as a Christmas story when I first ran across it. I just liked the idea."

Mr. Capra is grateful to the television exposure for helping his film find its audience. But not everyone shares his enthusiasm toward the movie's public-domain status. "It concerns me," says Paul Nobel, who himself programmed it this week on WNEW in New York. "It's a film that should be seen sparingly. I'm worried that too much exposure could wear it out."

A well-intentioned but minor-league TV remake, "It Happened One Christmas," came along in 1977 with Marlo Thomas striking a misbegotten blow for women's lib by taking on the Stewart role. Unimpressive as it was (Mr. Capra considered it plagiarism), some thought the new version would appeal to local stations obsessed with color and drive the black-and-white original off the air. But it didn't. Nor have other Christmas evergreens such as "White Christmas," "Miracle on 34th Street" or any of the four versions of "A Christmas Carol" eroded its appeal.

"They were all studio pictures," says Mr. Schickel of the other Christmas fare. "The quality of Capra's belief and passion informs 'It's a Wonderful Life' in a way that almost never happened in studio-made films. The irony is that as Capra's most successful '30s hits begin to fade ("It Happened One Night," "Mr. Deeds Goes to Town," etc.) this 'failure' ends up superseding them all and becoming the one for the ages."

empty-handed from the Oscar giveaway and who failed to make millions at the box office. In short, it's easy to do to it what George Bailey did to his own life — misunderstand its importance, right from the very beginning. It's not hard to imagine why the film did not do so awfully well in 1947. Given the way it was advertised, *It's a Wonderful Life* looked like either a light comedy or a romantic love story. Actually, it was something much darker, much deeper. Its ad campaigns told people to come for love, for laughs, for escape. If they did, they probably went home not only disappointed but a little disturbed. The war was over. It was Christmas. And people wanted to feel good.

What is the power of *It's a Wonderful Life*? Where does its magic come from? After forty years in release, and no matter how many times one sees it, *It's a Wonderful Life* still casts its spell. Why? What draws Americans to it?

At the most obvious level, it's that *It's a Wonderful Life* is a superbly crafted film, an example of the best that Hollywood had to offer — skilled direction, fine screenwriting, compelling acting by an impeccable cast, artful cinematography, and outstanding art direction, editing, costuming, and sound engineering. There is a kind of perfection in the craft. The cast seems to have been assembled at just the right moment for each of them. James Stewart is *the* American son: still young enough to appear idealistic, to look gangly, to have the future in his eyes, yet in real life a World War II veteran, weathered enough to depict the burdened man of responsibility whose integrity has become a chain that shackles him to Bedford Falls. Donna Reed, the Iowa farm girl with sparkling eyes, clear skin, and natural grace, probably embodies the concept of "all-American girl" better than anyone else in film history. (As someone once remarked, "They stopped making Donna Reeds in 1961. The rest of us have to go without.")

The remaining cast is equally perfect: Thomas Mitchell, the quintessential drunken uncle with fey impulses; Samuel S. Hinds, a better father figure than Lewis Stone, because we all knew Stone was too good to be true; Beulah Bondi, a great actress who could be believable as a sweet mother or a twisted "Ma Bailey"; Ward Bond and Frank Faylen — Bert and Ernie — who doubtless inspired their characters' namesakes on *Sesame Street;* Gloria Grahame, everybody's favorite bad girl — the girl you want to take home, but not to mother; and, of course, Lionel Barrymore, putting power and menace into the role of the unredeemed villain.

Bedford Falls itself is a compelling character, changing its costume from season to season. It has its bad days (rain and snow) and its good days (blossoming trees and singing birds). It gets dressed up for Christmas. Bedford Falls is so much a part of the movie, that one can ask: Is Bedford Falls angry, deep down inside, because, like George, it can't be Paris or New York or, at the very least, Albany? Its own Freudian rage is expressed in George's nightmare vision of Bedford Falls, the all-American worthwhile small town, as Pottersville, a Phenix City–like hellhole of bars, brawls, and bad times.

Consider the subtlety of the script of *It's a Wonderful Life*. It seems to spend very little time on the character of George's father, and it never shows us his death. And yet we've already seen him die, little by little, in his daily life, and it is his character that defines the older George. The father is first seen when George is a child going to ask him for help. ("Ask Dad. He'll know.") The elder Bailey is being confronted by Potter, and the child George stands up on behalf of his parent. ("Don't let him talk to you like that, Dad.") In a brief moment, the script establishes George's respect for his dad, his dad's difficulties with Potter, his sense of defeat at the villain's hands, his willingness to go on fighting, and a hint of the future, in which George himself will be a more formidable foe for Potter. Later, when George prepares to leave Bedford Falls, his last night in town shows a touchingly humorous family dinner-table scene. The old man, played by Hinds with just the correct mixture of resigned strength and downtrodden optimism, tells George that he had hoped his eldest son would take over the Building and Loan. George's tactless outburst — "I couldn't face being cooped up for the rest of my life in a shabby little office!" — causes the father pain, but George, the loving son, quickly catches himself and tells his dad, "I think you are a great guy." Their last words to each other are: "Pop, I think I'll get dressed and go over to Harry's party." "Have a good time, son." It's the last we see of the father, whose fatal stroke later that night interrupts George and Mary's first tentative love scene — and changes the direction of George's life.

An audience can see and understand the life, and death, of the father: his struggle with Potter, his humiliation in front of his small son, his tired but kind responses to the older boy's belief in a more glamorous future for himself, his willingness to accept the son's need to have fun on his last night in town instead of staying home. We've seen enough to know that the son is the stronger half of the father, a tougher adversary for old Potter (who will apparently live forever). We've seen that the son's inability to be truly cruel to his father's small-town life is the innate sense of responsibility that will ultimately link him forever to his father's role in Bedford Falls. All this is so superior to a death-bed scene in which the dying father reaches out a clutching hand to croak, "George . . . George . . . don't let the Building and Loan die with me. . . ." The script of *It's a Wonderful Life* both trusts and respects its audience.

Frank Capra's direction reflects that same trust and respect. As usual, Capra sets up an intimate relationship with the audience, in which specific characters react to events on our behalf. When George and Mary walk home after their dunking in the high-school swimming pool, a nameless man reading his evening paper on the front porch watches and responds to their shy interaction. When George sweeps the crying Mary into his angry, passionate embrace during their abortive telephone conversation with Sam, a cut to her eavesdropping mother on the stairs tells us every-thing — her fear of their passion, her total horror at what it means for Mary's future life. Seeing her response makes ours more specific — we are all for George and Mary's love. We choose to be on their side, where we will remain for the rest of the film, even when George behaves so shockingly toward his little family. The cut to Mary's mother solidifies our belief in George and Mary as a couple, and it also helps relieve our own overwhelming emotional response by allowing us to laugh. Whatever the scene, whatever the emotion, *It's a Wonderful Life* reflects these same qualities — trust and respect of its audience.

The story itself is a basic parable. It sets up a direct confrontation between Good (George Bailey) and Evil (Old Man Potter). There's only one hero, and there's only one villain. George's brother does not turn out to be a selfish sibling, using George heartlessly to reap the rewards of a better life, lived well away from Bedford Falls. On the contrary, he loves, even worships, his older brother.

He is grateful to George. He flies home through a blinding snowstorm just in time to deliver the ulti-mate tribute at the film's climax: "To my big brother, George, the richest man in town." In the same way, George's rival for Mary's hand, Sam Wainwright ("Hee haw!") remains George's friend and constant supporter. His jaunty wire — AD-VANCE UP TO $25,000 — is one of the finale's best moments. Coming from overseas, it shows that George's spirit, if not his body, has traveled widely, after all.

Perhaps *It's a Wonderful Life* continues to draw people close because, although Potter is the em-bodiment of the wrong way to live, the real villain of the piece is George himself. George vs. George: the way George is against the way he sees himself. What he thinks his life has been worth vs. what it's really worth. Self-doubt, personal pain. The story of a man who questions himself.

It's a Wonderful Life is the story of an "ordinary man." George is not brilliant or grand or heroic in the usual senses of those words. He does not invent things or get elected to office. He does not make money, win contests, or circumnavigate the globe. He does not compose music. He doesn't even invest in plastics! And yet, what makes George touch us is that he hates his ordinariness and rails against it. It is not, he feels, his true self. He feels something grand and brilliant and heroic inside, and what he longs for is a chance to express it, a place to let it flow loose. It is not George Bailey's "common man" status that makes us all identify with him and love him. It is his desire to transcend his commonness, because within, he *is* extraordinary.

It's a Wonderful Life is shrewdly deceptive in its own way. George is supposed to be leading a simple life in a typical American small town. Everyone who talks about *It's a Wonderful Life* thinks of it that way. But actually, George's life is directly touched by the great events of his history — the Depression, a bank run, World War II. His brother is the winner of the Congressional Medal of Honor! His mother has lunch with the Presi-dent's wife! George stays home, of course. He ap-peals both to our secure "at home" selves and to the fabulous selves we know we could be — if we could just get out of town.

It's a Wonderful Life is a paradox. It presents the perfect small-town life and shows its darker po-tential. It gives us a hero who lives the perfect life but hates it. Everything about it is ambivalent, contradictory, contains its own opposite. It is a warm romantic comedy that contains a film noir at its core. Actors like H. B. Warner (fixed in people's minds as Christ) and Lionel Barrymore (Hollywood's most lovable curmudgeon) are cast against type. *It's a Wonderful Life* contains truth, but it contains within itself the possibility of its own untruth. It is about dreams that turn into nightmares and nightmares that turn into dreams. It provides a victory, but not without a defeat. Its leading character wins but also loses — or loses but also wins. In the end, nothing changes for him. Nothing except everything. He does not leave Bedford Falls, but he accepts the meaning of his life there.

Despite all the contradictions, everything has its reason and its motivation. The younger brother, Harry, in his daredevil determination to prove to the older kids that he is not a coward, slides down the icy hill into near-death in freezing water. This same quality makes him a football hero in college, leads to his romance with a wealthy girl who takes him away from Bedford Falls, and ultimately makes a war hero out of him. In the same logical fashion, the brother who rescues him, George, becomes the man who rescues the Building and Loan, who rescues Bedford Falls from destruction by Potter, just as he rescued his brother, the drunken druggist, and the sick child the druggist would have poisoned.

George gets to learn how others would have lived if he had not performed these rescues — Uncle Billy in the insane asylum, his poverty-stricken mother in a boardinghouse, his wife, repressed and lonely, in the library, and Violet out on the streets as the town tramp. A world unrescued. The reason George gets to know all this is that he performs the ultimate rescue — instead of drowning himself, he saves Clarence when the canny angel throws himself into the river, preventing George's suicide. George is too busy saving others to kill himself. Suicide, the selfish act, is denied him. His instinct is that of the responsible rescuer.

It's a Wonderful Life doesn't suggest that George was lucky to have stayed all his life in Bedford Falls; it suggests that his having had to stay counts for something. It lasts because it is about dreams that don't come true, something that everyone, no matter how ordinary or how extraordinary, how rich or how poor, experiences at some level. It suggests that dreams that don't come true may hurt you, but they could come true as nightmares and hurt you even worse.

Frank Capra was disappointed with the world's initial response to *It's a Wonderful Life*. But, like the George Bailey he created, he came to realize that it had counted for something after all. It *was* a wonderful film. It earned no riches in its lifetime, but no movie is a failure that has friends.

JAMES STEWART

Interviewed by Leonard Maltin

LM: I want to really pry into your memory about *It's a Wonderful Life.* The first thing I want to ask you is — do you recall specifically when you first were approached by Frank Capra about it?

JS: I remember as if it were yesterday.

When I got home from the war, my seven-year contract had run out at MGM, so my agent, Leland Hayward, advised me not to sign up again with any studio. And I took his advice, but then I found myself . . . uhh . . . well, Hank Fonda and I sort of wandered around and flew kites and sat and talked. He didn't have anything either, but it sort of worried me. When you've been away for four and a half years, you know, maybe you forget how to act. Maybe the whole thing's gone, and all of that wonderful experience that you've had at MGM, that sort of training, that learning your craft by working at it, maybe after four and a half years without doing it at all, maybe it's gone.

LM: When were you discharged?

JS: Either September or October of '45. But I remember it very well. I got a telephone call, and a voice said, "This is Frank Capra." And I could have said "Hip-hip-hurray!" right there. He said, "I've got an idea for a story." And he said, "Come on over to the house and I'll tell you." So I went over and he gave me a sort of wandering idea of the story. It wasn't based on any book, it wasn't based on any actual happening, it was no play, it was just an idea that Frank had gotten from a couple of letters from friends. And the two main ideas were: one, no one is born to be a failure; and two, no one is poor who has friends. That was it. He told me all this, but then he said, "I don't know . . . I don't know," and I said, "*Frank!* PLEASE! I think it's wonderful!" and "When do we start?" And he gave the ideas to Hackett and Goodrich, two writers who had done wonderful work in the movies, and

in about three weeks they had a script. And in about a month and a half, he had a cast. I'd never had such a pleasant, wonderful experience, working with all these great people — some I'd worked with before the war, like Lionel Barrymore, and some new, like Donna Reed, who couldn't have been nicer. I don't think I ever worked on a picture where everything seemed to fit in or go so well.

LM: When Capra first explained the general idea to you, was he a good storyteller?

JS: No, not particularly. No. But I was determined to say, "Frank, let me do the picture." I was determined even if he had me playing a professional football player. [*Laughs.*] I was determined. It was just a wonderful piece of luck, Frank asking me to listen to a little story he had. I had no doubt in my mind at all, even though in telling the story Frank made sort of a mess. He said, "Well, in this story, you're in a small town and you have dreams of going out to all sorts of adventures and accomplishments. Your father has a Savings and Loan, and then the big shot in town builds these houses and charges the people terrible rent for them and takes all the business away from your father." That's about the way Frank told it. "You get into more trouble and things get worse and worse, and . . . uhh, you decide to kill yourself. So you get out in the middle of a bridge, and just climb up, and you're going to jump and . . . uhh . . . uhhhh, an angel comes down. His name is Clarence. An angel comes down, though he doesn't have his wings, and when you jump in the water, he jumps in the water, but he can't swim. So you save him. And . . . uhh . . . uhh, you get out, and you sort of — well, you sort of get your clothes dry and everything, and Clarence is there. And he seems sort of strange to you, but you say, in the course of conversation, 'I wish I had never been born.' And, like that, it happens." All of a sudden Frank interrupted himself and said,

"This really sounds kind of . . . kind of . . . What do you think of it so far?" And I said, "Frank, if you want to do a movie about me committing suicide and an angel that hasn't won its wings named Clarence, I'm your boy. Anything, Frank. Anything."

LM: Were you nervous when you started on it?

JS: Yeah. Yeah. But, as I say, it was so wonderful to be with all those people. They all sort of helped. Frank did, of course, but all those others. Frank Faylen. Beulah Bondi. Ward Bond. Lionel Barrymore. Every once in a while, Barrymore would get me in a corner, and he'd say, "You know, you're doing fine." He'd say, "Don't worry about it. Everything's going to be fine. You've got the idea, you got the character, so just take it easy." It was just a terrific thing for me. I'll never forget it. We had a great time. And when we finished the picture, Frank sort of topped things off. We all got invitations to a picnic, down in the Malibu Hills someplace. He had everything. He had throwing horseshoes. He had burlap-sack races. He had everything you could ever think of from all the picnics you'd ever been on — every game, everything. It was a picnic lunch, and there had to be eighty-five, ninety people there.* Every member of the cast, every member of the crew, and all the cutters. Everybody. And it was a beautiful day. Capra just carried this out, and everybody was so grateful to him. The whole thing worked.

In those days, they had a way of taking pictures of large groups, like of classes in school, where they put everyone on bleachers. Everyone stood still, and the camera moved, going from place to place, right side to left side, to get everyone of the group in the picture. Well, we all got up. Capra got up. Lionel Barrymore in the middle of it. And Capra told me to come to the left end of the thing. The cameraman said, "Okay, everybody, all right now, everybody." And as soon as it started off and he had taken us on the left side, Frank said, "We're going to be in this picture twice," and we ran back of the stand to the other side of the thing. That picture was just great. I still have it somewhere.

LM: I love looking at that picture. It's almost like looking at the movie.

JS: Yeah, and that's the way the picnic was. The *It's a Wonderful Life* picnic had a wonderful life, too. Frank understood those things.

LM: Do you remember the first time you ever met him?

JS: I think probably when I did *You Can't Take It With You* — I don't remember meeting him before then. It was a terribly fortunate thing for me. I'd been loaned out quite a few times by Metro, and Frank was at Columbia. Everybody said that Frank and Harry Cohn were fighting, but that wasn't true — they got along fine together; they had tremendous respect for one another. About a year later, he asked me for *Mr. Smith Goes to Washington.* I think that Capra is actually responsible for getting me into the big stuff. Metro, of course, had an enormous population of stars and directors and everything, so I was just one of the bunch there, being loaned out to Warners, Fox. I think that *Mr. Smith* gave me a real accomplishment. Capra gave me something of a milestone there. I wouldn't have gotten the part in *The Philadelphia Story* if it weren't for *Mr. Smith,* and then I got the Academy Award for that. But I sort of think — I really believe — that I have to give credit and thanks for that Academy Award to Frank Capra.

LM: How does Capra direct? Does he talk to you a lot? Or does he kind of leave you to yourself to work things out?

JS: Well, he's *so* prepared. He has the story, and he has all these values. He has these things that he knows he wants to get up there on the screen. He doesn't talk to you much, but he talks a lot to the cameraman. They talk about . . . well, would it be better to move the camera, do we need more than one camera for this, should we do it differently from another angle. There was a lot of that. In *Mr. Smith,* he had six cameras in the Senate scene. It was on that movie that I stopped going to rushes. I never went to very many, ever, but it got so I really hated them at Metro. With Frank — Frank said, I live right on your way to Brentwood, you just turn right, and I have a projection room, so you can stop by and see the rushes with me. Well, the first time I did that, the rushes lasted an hour and forty minutes — you know, there was take after take after take, from every angle, and then another camera take after take. He really covered himself — every

_____
* The actual number was 372.

78

scene from every angle. Well, I didn't stay. The next night it was clearly going to be even longer! After an hour I turned to Frank. He was fast asleep! Well, I didn't wake him up or anything. I waited through the whole thing. But at last I said, "Frank, I got sort of against rushes when I was at Metro. If it's all right, I don't want to see any more."

Frank planned. He had it all on film any way he might need it. That came from his conversations with the cameraman. He'd say, "Let's try this. . . ." He worked that way with actors, too. He didn't say, "I want you to do this," he'd say, "Let's try it this way." By the time of *It's a Wonderful Life,* I pretty much had the thing licked. Frank could just say to me, "Now go in and do the scene." We all felt "Now it's up to us. This is what we're being paid for. Go in and act." I never remember him saying . . . sitting down at the table and saying, "Now what is your feeling about the motivation in this scene?" No, no, he didn't.

LM: Any rehearsal before shooting?

JS: Mostly for the cameraman. To see if the camera could get everything, if the camera should be moving. If there was more than one camera working on the thing, he wanted to coordinate the two. Then he would give us one if we were having a little bit of trouble with timing or something. He'd give us a couple and then always say, "Is everybody ready? Shall we try it?" Sometimes he got what he wanted after a lot of takes, sometimes the first time. But he always knew what he wanted.

LM: Did he routinely do a lot of takes?

JS: No. In *Mr. Smith,* in the long filibuster thing, it took over a week. And he had it covered everywhere. As I said, he had six, *six* cameras. When the thing started to build, and I started to yell in front of everybody, he came up and said, "You are going to start losing your voice because you've been

talking for days." Well, I was sort of prepared for that. I sort of practiced by myself, and thought I had a kind of believable rasp in my voice. But after I'd put in a long day talking, talking, talking, Frank came up to me and said, "You know, Jim, you don't convince me that you have a sore throat and that it's hard for you to talk. You sound exactly like you're doing what you're doing — and that is *doing it like this, all raspy*. I mean," he said, "anybody can do it like that." This worried me. On the way home I stopped at an eye, ear, nose, and throat doctor. I said, "Is there any way you can give me a sore throat?" He looked at me, and he said, "Well, I've heard you Hollywood folks are crazy, but you take the cake. You want me to give you a sore throat. It's taken me twenty-five years of study and practice to keep people from getting a sore throat, to cure the sore throat, and you come in here and want me to give you a sore throat." And he shook his head. He said, "I'll give you the sorest throat you've ever had." He dropped bichloride of mercury in, not near my vocal cords, but just in around there. It wasn't dangerous. And he said, "How's that?" and I said *"Rasp-rasp-rasp."* He said, "This is going to wear off, so I think I'd better come to the set." Now I hadn't thought of that. Then I knew if he came, Frank would know all about what I'd done, and he'd say, "Here is a mechanical actor if I ever saw one." But sure enough, the next morning, the doctor was on the set. What happened to his practice during the day I don't know, but he was fascinated and he stayed in my dressing room. I said, "Do you mind if I don't introduce you to Mr. Capra?" Every once in a while I would come in during the day and say, "It's getting better, Doctor," and he would give me a little more and then he would go back to reading or something. He stayed most of the day. At the end, Frank said that it was fine. I couldn't keep it from him — I told him what I had done. He said, "Fine, all right, you gave me what I wanted." But it worried me for a while.

LM: Did he shoot *It's a Wonderful Life* in sequence?

JS: He did. He was very adamant about that. He would go out of his way, and spend more money than you should, by doing it in sequence. We had an awful lot of night stuff. We ran this little quiet scene outside the house in the middle of the night, and the birds started to sing. Capra said *"Cut!"* He

said, "Is somebody doing that? Or are they real birds? We can't have birds singing in the middle of the night." No one knew what to do but the animal man. He came the next night bringing two crows. They were on strings. He sat up in the tree and strung out his crows. The birds were scared of them, so it solved the problem. We had no more birds singing at night.

LM: Were you at all intimidated by having to play the young scenes in the film? Do you remember if they did anything special to age you during the process of the film?

JS: I asked Frank about it. He said, "Well, leave it to me. If I think something ought to be done about your aging or getting younger, I'll let you know." He didn't feel there was any problem. As a matter of fact, I was having so much fun on the film that it didn't bother me at all. It never occurred to me.

LM: Did he change much after you got to the set? Did he get ideas for changing things in a scene — dialogue, anything?

JS: He wasn't one to stick strictly to the dialogue. You could go off and get a little dialogue-wise, get him to change things. He didn't mind that. But he didn't do very much scene changing, because he was just so well prepared. He had this *complete* idea, right up here. He was just so well prepared that not many changes were necessary.

LM: What kind of set did he like? What kind of atmosphere on the set?

JS: Plain. Plain. Everybody doing their job. Everybody knowing when to be quiet. Knowing there's no need for big whistle blowing or anything to keep people quiet. Everybody did their work. There was very little commotion and very little tension. There just wasn't any. Frank could always handle any trouble. In *Mr. Smith* there we were shooting outside the Lincoln Memorial. A policeman came up to Frank and said, "Ah, pardon me, is that fellow [the cameraman] taking a picture of that fellow out there with the statue?" And Frank said yes. "Well," the policeman said, "that is not allowed. There is a law against that." And Frank said, "Well, they gave me permission to come down here and shoot." The policeman said, "You can't shoot the man and the statue at the same time." Frank said, "What kind of a law is that?" The guy said, "It's the

kind we enforce. Otherwise people will put their kids in Lincoln's lap and take a picture of them." And, well, Frank, he just said, "Well, I swear to you he's not going to get on Lincoln's lap. He is going to stand in front of him." And the cop said, "I don't care. You can't do that. It's against the law." Frank said, "Okay." It was the middle of the afternoon, but Frank said, "That's a wrap." The policeman walked away, and Frank quietly went to see the Memorial guards. He talked to them, and very quietly, very quickly, they put the camera and the lighting equipment and everything back in a corner, and the guards watched it for us that night. As I got in the car to go to the hotel, Frank said, "Oh, Jim, I've got an early call for you tomorrow. Five o'clock a.m." So there I was, crack of dawn next morning, standing out in front of Abraham Lincoln. Frank had all the equipment out, and we got the shot. You can bet that policeman wasn't up yet!

LM: Do you remember how and where you shot the scene in *It's a Wonderful Life* with the gymnasium floor opening up?

JS: Down at Beverly Hills High School. It's actually there. It's a basketball floor — a gymnasium — and the floor opens up and there is a swimming pool under it. How Frank found it, I don't know. But it's right down at Beverly High.

LM: What about the rest of the cast you worked with? Was Lionel Barrymore's wheelchair a problem?

JS: It was just an inspiration to see how he worked, every line right on the button and everything. As I said, I will always be grateful to him for the encouragement he gave to me. It was just wonderful. In fact, I can still see Frank enjoying every minute of our scenes together and wondering when Barrymore was going to steal the moment. There were so many good ones in that film. Tommy Mitchell. Frank would just let him move around and do it his own way. I remember the scene in which all the banks closed and everybody who'd invested in the Building and Loan came to get their money. This is when Donna Reed and I were on our way to our honeymoon. I came up and decided that we could give just so much to each person, and we should ask the people how much they needed. And I had a speech when all the people were there. I said, "Please don't take all of your money, and then we

can keep going." So I got the money, and one by one they would come past and I would say, "How much do you want? How much do you want?" "I'll have seventy-five dollars." "How much do you want?" "I'll have sixty dollars, that's enough." And then comes Ellen Corby. Frank told her what to say, but he didn't tell me that she was going to say it. You know, she's about this tall, and she could barely see over the counter, and she said, "Twelve dollars and eighty cents." And this threw me completely! I reached over the counter and kissed her on the cheek. That's how Frank Capra worked. That's how he created things, by letting us all help him.

LM: What about Beulah Bondi?

JS: She was my mother seven times! I always had a sort of special respect and love for her. I started treating her just the way I did my own mother. I did a television thing, and I needed a mother. I said, "Get Beulah Bondi. She's really my mother." Well, they came back and said they couldn't find her. She lived in Florida, but she'd left there. Well, it turned out she was fishing. You know, this wasn't too long ago. She'd got to be in her nineties, and she was fishing up near Yellowstone. And they got her in to do one day's work. She said, "Sure, it's me, I'm his mother, nobody can play his mother but me," so down she came, and she did the day's work all right. "Bye," she says. "I've got ten more days of fishing and then I'm going back to Florida."

LM: Henry Travers.

JS: Henry! Of course, he was just exactly right, just exactly right for Clarence. And this was another quality Frank had. He just hits the right note as far as casting is concerned. There couldn't have been anybody better than Henry Travers for Clarence, there just couldn't. His timing and his looks and the way he played it straight. You could see him absolutely guarding himself against anything that would be a comic-strip type of thing. Because he was an angel. He didn't have any wings, but he was an angel. It was fascinating. It was just a joy to see him work and to work with him. In that scene where we're drying off after being in the water, I kept hearing these things that he was saying. Frank had said, "Let's not rehearse it. Let's keep it natural. Just go ahead with it and we'll see how it plays, but do the whole darn thing no matter what." We

did, and I was just fascinated with that man. His timing, and always putting the humor where it belonged. Looking up every once in a while when I talked, and then, when I said that I wished I'd never been born . . . the way he did it. The take wasn't fake, but it — you know, it was just sort of amazed. He fascinated me. Frank once told me that when he said to himself, "Who will I get for the angel?," Henry Travers came right into his mind.

LM: Samuel S. Hinds, your father?

JS: Oh, I have been in lots of pictures with him. I think he's a good character actor. A very fine actor. And so was the girl . . . the pretty little girl, Gloria Grahame. It was one of her first really good roles. Frank picked her. She was just exactly right for the thing — exactly right for the relationship between us. And then again, in the sequence when I hadn't been born she was a streetwalker, and she was perfect for that, too. Frank has this absolute genius for getting people into the right part.

LM: What about the casting of Donna Reed? She has said that she felt very nervous to be working with you and with Capra, and that she knew you two felt a little uneasy because you hadn't worked in a while because of the war, but that everything went just beautifully. What were your first impressions of her?

JS: I fell in love with her right off the bat. She just seemed to be everything . . . everything just seemed to come to her. I can't put my finger on a single time when we ever rehearsed. I always said, "Do you want to go over it?" and she always said, "No, let's do it." And then we'd ask Frank, "Is it all right? Can we just do it?" I mean, that telephone scene, you know. I worked on it off and on, and Frank said, "Do you want to go over it?" and I said, "Not unless she does." And she said, "Oh, no, I don't." And we did that scene with one take. Can you believe it? We did it in one great, unrehearsed take.

LM: Do you prepare a lot? Did you work at home a lot?

JS: Always, I always have. By myself. No tape recorder. There's all different ways of acting, or of preparing yourself for the next day's work. Some like to sit around and discuss the scene with me. Frank doesn't care for this, and I don't either. I say, do your own presentation and present it. If it doesn't work, then you can start messing around with it.

LM: What happened when *It's a Wonderful Life* was finished?

JS: Well, Frank got the picture together. We went to the preview. And the picture went out. Did no business. And it not only did no business — the fact that it did no business hindered the continuation of Frank's company, Liberty Films, that he had founded with George Stevens, Willy Wyler, and Sam Briskin. Uhh . . . uhh . . . you know, that's a pretty good crowd . . . but they were depending upon this picture to get the money to keep them going. They weren't able to do so, and the company was absorbed by Paramount. Frank made a few more pictures, but I think it discouraged him a little. Later, he got the idea of going out and lecturing to universities. Personally, I think Frank Capra has done more for the picture business than anybody I know. Because he's introduced it to people, not as glamour but in terms of what you could get up there on the screen. How you should tell a story. I think that his book is the best that's ever been written about Hollywood. I don't see how you could top Frank Capra as a director.

LM: How did the critics like *It's a Wonderful Life*?

JS: Actually, I don't remember what they said. I've been looking around to see if I had any of the reviews, but I can't find anything. The reviews weren't very good. They weren't bad. They were just sort of so-so.

LM: Do you remember the night of the preview? Do you remember what that was like, the night that you first saw the film?

JS: Yeah, I remember. A lot of people were there. Gable was there. The preview was very successful — they liked it very much. But I think they were just glad to see Frank Capra back and making pictures again. That was the main thing.

LM: What do you think about the general response to the film at the time of its release?

JS: It has always been amazing to me that after the war people didn't want this story. They had been through too much. They wanted wild slapstick comedy, they wanted westerns — stuff like that. It just took a while for the country to sort of quiet down. Then we could start to think about family and community and responsibility to family and work and so on.

LM: Did the failure of this film, the relative failure, hurt you?

JS: I imagine that it did. Someone suggested I needed a little more maturity in my characterization. The picture that did that for me was, I think, *Call Northside 777*.

LM: For years, I have heard you say that *It's a Wonderful Life* was your favorite film. That was also before its resurgence in popularity, a popularity that I guess TV is responsible for. Have you sensed, over the years, a steady buildup of interest in the movie?

JS: I still get quite a bit of fan mail, and I would say that around 95 percent favor *It's a Wonderful Life*. They say they've seen it, you know, fifteen or twenty times. Every once in a while they mention *Winchester '73* or *The Man Who Shot Liberty Valance* or *Shenandoah*. And that's all. The great majority think that my best film is *It's a Wonderful Life*. They've seen it every Christmas. They make it sort of like putting up the Christmas tree. They put up the tree, they get people in, and they all watch *It's a Wonderful Life*. It's part of the annual ritual now. That means a great deal to me. And I know it means an awful lot to Capra, because in his book, he says it's his favorite, too.

LM: Did you have any sense of that while you were making it? How are your antennae when you're making a film? Have you had good ideas of which ones were going to work and which ones weren't?

JS: No. No. I don't think that's possible. That's one of the wonderful things about the picture business. Nowadays they obviously think they can, but all they're really doing is — if they've made one and it has gone big, six months later they make a sequel. I don't think that's really "knowing." I think the only people who knew what would work were the so-called moguls. The Louis B. Mayers and the Harry Cohns and the Warners. They had this sixth sense, they weren't afraid to take chances, and their judgment as to what type of thing the audience would like hasn't been replaced in today's business, and probably never will be.

LM: You know, if you'd made *Harvey* today, you'd probably have to make *Harvey II* next.

JS [*laughs*]: Well, certainly no one ever suggested a sequel to *It's a Wonderful Life*. But what an experience it was! We all just went by what we thought was right, what felt good, and did the best job we could do. All of us. Every single person. And we were helped by Frank Capra. The best thing that ever happened to my career was that he gave me a chance to watch him get that magic up on the screen the way he does.

LM: How does he do it?

JS: It's very hard to describe. I think that you've got to go back to the value that Frank puts on life, on work, on responsibility, and on genuine family togetherness. Those are the values he has, and he has them very strong. Love of country, love of God — he's tremendously strong on those. And he's able to get them up on the screen without preaching. Now *how* he does this is Frank Capra. It's his secret. His genius. His magic. That's Frank Capra.

JOSEPH BIROC

Interviewed by Leonard Maltin

It's a Wonderful Life is unique in having had the services of no less than three of Hollywood's top cameramen of the day. The original cinematographer, Victor Milner, had been borrowed from Paramount to photograph the movie. Shortly after shooting began, however, he left "because of illness." Capra himself supports this explanation, but everyone else today says quite candidly that although the two men did not quarrel openly, their relationship did not work out well. Research indicates that Milner photographed the gymnasium dance sequence and the apothecary shop sequence before he was "let go."

At that point, Joseph Walker, Capra's trusted friend and favorite cameraman, came to take over the cinematography. Walker and Capra had worked together successfully many times before, and Walker, as a favor, shot the greater part of the movie. Unfortunately, he had to leave before filming was completed, due to a prior commitment to film a Rosalind Russell picture for Columbia.

The camera operator for *It's a Wonderful Life,* under both Milner and Walker, was Joseph Biroc. Biroc was promoted to full director of cinematography and finished filming. He and Walker share credit for cinematography, and this interview represents his memories of the film.

LM: What do you think about *It's a Wonderful Life* becoming more and more popular over each passing year?

JB [*laughs*]: They will have to give it an Emmy or an Oscar for longevity. It was a good picture when it came out, but it did not seem *that* great because there were so many pictures that were made. They were just grinding them off, entertainment for the public. No one expected the kind of longevity *It's a Wonderful Life* has had.

LM: Do you remember having any kind of special feeling for it as you were working on it? Did it seem like an especially good picture?

JB: No. Nothing. Just another picture.

LM: Let's go through the history of the film as you recall it, and particularly from your point of view. When did you get hired on?

JB: Well, I had just got out of the service. I was an operator in the Signal Corps, doing camera work. Just took off my civilian clothes and put on the Army clothes; took off the Army clothes and was a civilian. Did exactly the same thing. I was three years in Europe, assigned to Supreme Headquarters, so I was active nearly all the time. They knew we were from Hollywood. They knew our qualifications, and knew what we could do, and if anything really important came up they always came back to us. So I was pretty active. I went all over Europe. Many special assignments. Once I got into the service, I was a full-fledged cameraman, shooting 35 sound. When I came back I had presumably a year of work that the studio was supposed to give us after the service, but I went onto another picture as a picture's operator. When the picture finished they put me on *It's a Wonderful Life.* As an operator. The head of the camera department told me I was going to go on a picture, with a cameraman I didn't particularly care to work with from Paramount. That was Vic Milner. One of the top cameramen in the business.

LM: You had a contract?

JB: No, no, I had no contract. If you were efficient and knew your business, they just kept you going and hoped eventually to push you up a little bit higher. So I began *It's a Wonderful Life.* We made a lot of tests with Vic Milner and Capra. We made a lot of film tests, a lot of lens tests, a lot of other stuff. Milner was a little nitpicky. I was never that type. He didn't know what he wanted to do with the meters — the meters weren't too well known then — but I was very fortunate. I had one from an old western that I had done several years ago. He was doing it the wrong way, and I said, "Victor, you aren't doing it right. Too much light coming in. There is no way that light can come in from here into that meter and hit it. There is no way, because the thickness of that meter doesn't allow the light to get in there." You couldn't convince him. You just couldn't convince him. So I said, "Well, hell, it's not worth it." I had just got out of the service, and I wasn't ready for that type of nitpicking, you know. And the same way when we started the picture. I was the operator. Victor Milner was the cameraman, and the first day on the film was the thing where the pool opens. That was the first or the second day on the film, shot on location at Beverly Hills High School. And he was nitpicking there for hours and hours. We didn't get our first take until almost lunchtime. Of course it was a big scene, and it was difficult to light. It's a big open space, and no way to get light down to the middle. We couldn't get lights up high, or get them down. We didn't have parallels, like we had in the studio. So pretty soon Milner started getting in trouble. His idea of working with Capra was to get an Academy Award. That's all he thought about. That's all he ever thought about. Getting an Academy Award. And you don't *get* an Academy Award — I mean, you don't work for one. As hard as you work, you may never get it. It's just an accident that happens, and it falls into your lap. Just because the picture is great, the photography doesn't have to be good. So anyhow, at the end of about five weeks of shooting, Milner started coming in a little bit later every morning. By then, we're working out at the RKO ranch in the valley, and he calls me several times from the lab and he says, "There is something wrong at the lab with the film here, can you take over?" I said, "Vic, I can't take over." We're twenty-five minutes from the studio, and the union rule is I have to call for them to get another cameraman out here. The studio is only twenty, twenty-five minutes away. I was still an operator, you see, not a full-fledged cameraman. So that happened a couple of mornings, and Capra noticed it. He knew something was wrong. Finally, when we were doing the sequence with the druggist Gower, Milner was having trouble, and he never got over it.

He told me to take over. And I said I can't take over.

LM: The union wouldn't have allowed you to take over?

JB: Absolutely. Absolutely. I had no authority to do that. The union wouldn't have allowed me to do that. The studio wouldn't have allowed me to do it — we had at that time ten, eleven, or twelve men on salary at RKO. And he was an outside cameraman from Paramount that came in to do the picture.

LM: What do you think that it was that was making him feel that way? Did he feel just frustrated that he wasn't getting the results that he wanted?

JB: He felt that he wasn't getting an Academy Award picture. That was the only thing that he wanted to do this picture with Capra for. The only thing.

LM: What was it that got him frustrated? Did he feel that the results weren't good enough, the picture wasn't good enough?

JB: The picture itself was good. It was a good script. There was nothing wrong with the rushes. The rushes were fine. I saw them every night, and I was well pleased at what I saw.

LM: Was Capra pleased?

JB: Capra, he never said anything. If there was something wrong, he is the first guy that would have told ya. So I think that it was Milner's own frustration. He left the picture. He got paid for twenty weeks, and he only worked five. As soon as he left, Joe Walker came in. Joe Walker came in, I think, on a Monday. We finished all the stuff at the ranch, and we started in the studio on a Monday. I had never worked with Joe. He was a wonderful man. A great guy. Toward the end of filming, Walker had to go back. He had a commitment to do a Rosalind Russell picture back at Columbia. So he worked the five weeks he had free, and at the end of the five weeks he left. In the last two weeks they had been talking about what cameraman they were going to bring in to take the picture over. Hot or cold, Joe would be leaving. They had to have a top man because they had a top cast. Jimmy Stewart, the star — Barrymore, Donna Reed, though she was only a kid. She was only eighteen, I think, at the time. Tom Mitchell. People like that had to go work with a good cameraman. And finally I said to Joe, "Who is going to take the show over if you go back to Columbia?" He said he'd suggest someone who'd been on the show ever since it started. Capra said, "Who is that?" he says, "Biroc." So with that Capra got up and came over to me. I'm sitting on the crane — it's laying on the ground, you know. And he said, "How would you like to take the picture over?" I said, "Who, me?" I looked around. There was nobody around. He said, "Yeah." He grinned ear to ear. He says, "Yeah." I said, "Gee, that would be wonderful." He said, "Okay, it's yours. That's it." So from that minute on I was the cameraman. Joe was there three more days. We worked six days a week then. So Joe was there to help me get started. If I needed advice, I'd ask him. I'd say, "Joe, do you think that would look pretty good in the background there, are the paths broken up enough there?" He'd look out of his glasses and he'd say, "Well, we'll see tomorrow afternoon, or tomorrow night." [*Laughs.*] Meaning, when we'd see the rushes. But if there was anything seriously wrong, he would go to the gaffer and tell the gaffer to do something. I didn't know that until way later, when the gaffer told me what Joe had been doing. He was a wonderful man. He protected me on my first big job. So that's how it happened. I was twenty years as an operator before promotion. Now when a guy is an operator for a year, he thinks he's being held down. A tremendous amount of the people that are working now are not competent. They don't have the experience. So you have nothing to draw back on. If something goes wrong you have to find a way to do it, and if you can't find a way, someone has to tell you, or the director has to tell you, or you don't do it.

LM: From your point of view as an operator, did you see different photographic styles? I mean, was there a different look to what Victor Milner shot from what Joe Walker shot?

JB: Basically, no. They both worked basically alike. Victor was too meticulous. Joe would do everything that he wanted to do in the back of his head. And very few people, or anything else, could change it. He knew what he wanted to do, but he wasn't adamant about having it done the way he wanted it. If something else came up to make it a little bit dif-

ferent, like some of my suggestions for doing things, he'd say, "Not bad, not bad," and he'd incorporate that into what he had in mind to do. But Victor wouldn't do that. He would say, "No, no, no, it won't work, it won't work, no." So you get hit on the head a couple of times, your head gets soft, you start quitting. But with Joe you at least had a chance to say no. The quality of their work was basically the same. Joe worked a little bit softer. He got along wonderfully with the top stars, the women stars, because he knew what they needed to make them look good. But he didn't bend over backwards. He didn't have to do that. He was that good.

LM: And what about the working relationship with Capra? Did Capra have a definite look he wanted in mind for every scene?

JB: He definitely would have a certain thing — an effect that he wanted, a certain thing he wanted to do, a certain type of work he wanted. He would talk to Joe about it and Joe would say, "Oh, there's no problem, it's easy." Joe was that way. He would say, "That's fine." Or if he didn't like it, he'd say, "It won't work" — that particular look was going to take away from either the acting or the entire scene or the sequence. From the whole style of the picture that you're trying to get. So Capra would say, "Fine." But nine out of ten times Joe did everything on his own.

LM: Did Capra always start off with his own idea, too? What he wanted?

JB: They always started off that way.

LM: I mean, did Capra always have an instruction to start off setting up a scene?

JB: For the picture overall, yes. He knew the overall quality he wanted.

LM: From what I understand, the picture was shot pretty close to in sequence, because Capra wanted it that way.

JB: I don't remember now whether the whole picture was shot that way or not. No, I don't think so. For the rain sequences and the snow sequences, we had people come back. They were tied up so they could come back. No, I wouldn't say that. I don't remember it that close.

LM: It looked to me as if all the night shooting really must have been done at night.

JB: Oh, yes. Oh, yes. Definitely. Definitely. That's how I started, on the night stuff. [*Laughs.*] In a cemetery. With snow on the ground. Worst thing in the world to work with. The snow was just so brilliant you couldn't light it. Matter of fact [*laughs*], the first night that I worked we had a hundred and twenty electricians. One hundred and twenty. And the gaffer said, "We're short of men. We don't have the men that we need." He said, "All we have is a hundred or a hundred and ten or a hundred and five," something like that!

LM: So the first scene you shot was Stewart going to the graveyard?

JB: Yes, I did all of that. Also the bridge. Jumping into the water.

LM: It must have been a real baptism of fire for you.

JB: Oh, you're not kidding. Worst thing in the world. But like I say, very fortunately they started me off on the right foot. Capra started me thinking differently entirely from being an operator. I was an eager beaver all my life, and I was always trying to find out things and always trying to help. And naturally I wanted to get ahead, and Capra was great. He was great. He was great. He could see [*laughs*] that I knew what the hell I was doing. Even in those days he worked entirely different from most directors. He would shoot a sequence with the widest lens available then. They would get a good take there, then he would do it with the next widest, and then the next. Each time we would take people out. Each take you shot, you got the main action all the time, but the outside people were slowly dropped out. He did very few individual close-ups; his stuff was mainly with groups. He liked the groups to get together, to keep the feeling of the picture together. That was the way we worked. He thought I was great, so I could do no wrong. And when someone treats me that way, I always have the courage to get more. To do more.

LM: You are saying that instead of shooting a master shot, and then an over-the-shoulder shot and that kind of coverage, he would just keep shooting the same thing but just get —

JB: Closer. Closer, closer, closer, and closer. Then if he felt there was someplace in there he really needed coverage, he would do over the shoulders and big heads. But everything was covered by gradually getting closer and closer with the lenses.

LM: So your camera position would change hardly at all.

JB: Very little. Very little. The light seldom changed. Until you started getting into something new. If you started getting too close to the stars, you would have to try to improve the lighting a little bit. This is something about Capra that's pretty unique. It shows how much he emphasized his groups of people — everybody counts — in his films. It carries out the ideas of his stories.

LM: Did Capra like a lot of camera movement?

JB: There was quite a bit. Yes. We were on the crane all the time. All the time. He planned it. However, he never was set in his mind how he wanted to do a scene, until they started doing it and started rehearsing it. Then he started moving people. He would move people around to see groups. By the time they rehearsed it five or six times, ten times — why, he'd know exactly what he wanted. He'd see his group as an alive, moving unit for the camera.

LM: Do you think he had in mind early on that he would want to do a certain length of take that would involve camera movement?

JB: It was always in the back of his mind to keep the camera moving. His editing a picture was unique, too. Now most editors are going to get behind. They get behind. Pretty soon the film starts piling up. Nowadays, directors wait till the end of shooting and then start editing. They can't stand to cut, so they end up with a nine-hour picture. Then they have to cut it down little by little, or cut sequences out. Capra was different. Capra would run the picture as he went along, and seldom cut a sequence. But he ran everything complete — say, like in the fifth, sixth, eighth, or tenth week into the picture. There may have been a couple of sequences that he edited down to the way he wanted it, but the rest of it was long shots. He'd run the whole picture as long shots and maybe medium shots. Then run it maybe as long shots, maybe no medium shots. And the next maybe all medium shots and no long shots, and he would say, "Well, cut this out . . . cut that out . . . cut this out . . . cut that out.

Cut this one up. This one looks interesting. Edit that down. Just cut it down the way you want. Make the best out of it." And that would be it. So by the time he finished a picture, he was down to almost what he needed. Now he didn't have to worry about seven, eight, nine, ten hours of show. He wasn't faced with a mess at the end, that he would have to edit and then bring down. He'd done it all before.

LM: So was he picking his takes as he went along?

JB: Yes. A lot of times he would have two. He would say, "Leave the two in there, leave them in there." Later on, he might cut one or two close-ups and medium shots into that sequence. Then he would forget it. And then when he got enough film to run about an hour, two hours, or three hours, then he would run it through and get rid of what he didn't need. "Get rid of that, we don't need that." That way he took twenty minutes or a half an hour out of the picture.

LM: So he would edit as he went along?

JB: Oh, yes. Each weekend. I mean that he would work on Sundays, work with the editor on Sundays. Capra didn't want to lose the performance of certain people, so you couldn't cut that out. You had to hold that sequence in. So he sometimes had the camera crew go back and do one or two close shots of somebody in there to build the sequence up.

LM: So he did do pickups then?

JB: Yes.

LM: But do you think that was the advantage of the way he worked?

JB: Absolutely. Absolutely.

LM: As he's going along, if he wanted to go back to redo something he could.

JB: Absolutely. It didn't mean that much to go back to it. Because most of the time in those days they kept the sets up. But he had, like I say, he had a different style of working. And he knew what he was doing every minute of the day. Anybody could go up to him and ask him a question, and he'd say, "No, I don't think that would work" because such-and-such a thing happened. He was a man who knew what he wanted and could picture it all in his head. He could keep it in his head. And he was willing to cut and throw away. He didn't bore people.

LM: How would you describe the atmosphere on his set?

JB: Excellent! Everybody was jovial. Everybody had a good time. Everybody was happy. I don't think there was a dull moment on the whole picture.

LM: He wanted it that way, didn't he?

JB: *He* was that way.

LM: Was Capra very open to suggestions in general? Was he an accessible director that way?

JB: Well, I would say yes. Because anytime that I suggested something to him, he would say fine, okay, go ahead. I would say as far as I'm concerned, he was generous with people.

LM: Did you go to see the rushes every day?

JB: When I first took over, he would run the stuff at his home or at the studio. And I would come in and ask him how the stuff was, and he would say fine. And I would say how about such-and-such a scene, and he would say, "It will work out fine." That was it. That was the end of it. I couldn't find out a thing! While he was looking at them at home, we were working nights. So I would ask him. We would come in at four thirty in the afternoon, and it was in the summer that we did most of that stuff. So you'd have to wait until eight at night before it got dark. He'd say the stuff is very nice.

That's it. That's the end of it. He wasn't going to elaborate on it.

LM: When was the first time you saw the picture? Did you see a rough assembly, or didn't you see it until it was finished?

JB: Well, the first preview. Every picture that I was ever on, I saw every preview, all of them. Then after the show they would get together and say such-and-such a thing — we should do this, or we should do that, or such-and-such a sequence should be brought up a little bit more, or the whole thing was too dark. Well, probably by that time the lab had taken care of most of that. *It's a Wonderful Life* was a good picture. That's all I thought or felt. It wasn't sensational. At least it wasn't sensational to me.

LM: What did you think of your own work when you saw *It's a Wonderful Life*? What did you think of the first stuff you had shot as first cameraman?

JB: I never liked anything that I shot. Even today, I don't like it. I always say, Well, why didn't I do *this*? I could have done *that*. I never liked my work. Always picked it apart.

LM: When you saw the finished picture, could you see a marked difference in the stuff that you shot from the stuff that Joe Walker shot from the stuff that Vic Milner shot?

JB: No. But in those days a good cameraman always worked as a good cameraman. There was a basic style that the good cameramen even today use. Also, all three of us were working for Capra, remember. Giving him the look he wanted. The only difference between the shadow side with the three of us was that Joe worked on the softer side, so it wasn't too black. The contrast was there, but very soft. Vic worked a little bit stronger — the dots were a little bit stronger. I very seldom use full light. Very, very seldom, so my shadows are black. My shadow is a shadow. And another thing, having started off with Capra in such a high key, I never got down to shooting with the lens wide open. Never, in all my life. Never got down to shoot wide open. Unless you were doing that stuff at night. But I always liked that contrast. So when I started on my own, doing independent pictures, I'd light exactly the same way that I would for the daytime, only I would stop the lens down, a full whole stop. And that automatically made it that much darker.

LM: Was *It's a Wonderful Life* a good film to get started with?

JB: Oh, sensational. Sensational. I'm on top. First picture, I'm on top. And I got screen credit with two other top cameramen.* And with Capra it was always the top. And you know, like we said at the beginning, it turns out my first movie as a full-fledged cameraman is probably the longest-lived one I ever made. It's the one people love. It's the one film everyone remembers.

---

* Actually, he shared credit only with Walker.

Frank Capra's *It's a Wonderful Life* started life as a little story that no one wanted to publish. But it finally got a chance to earn its wings — mostly because its author, Philip Van Doren Stern, never lost faith in it. Mr. Van Doren Stern wrote about his story on the occasion of the release of *It's a Wonderful Life*.

New York *Herald Tribune,*
December 15, 1946

It's a Wonderful Life Started as the
By Product of a Shave

By Philip Van Doren Stern

It began nearly eight years ago — on Feb. 12, 1938, to be exact. That morning while I was shaving, I got an idea for a story. The idea came to me complete from start to finish — a most unusual occurrence, as any writer will tell you, for ordinarily a story has to be struggled with, changed around and fixed up. After I had finished shaving, I sat down and typed out a two-page outline, which I dated. However I did nothing about writing the story for more than a year. Then I dug up the outline and made an attempt at putting the story down on paper. I was just learning how to write fiction, so that first version was pretty terrible. Fortunately, I knew it was, so I had the sense to put it away. A few years later I tried again. The results were still no good.

I waited until the spring of 1943 before trying again. Meanwhile I had been telling the story to various people, and I was encouraged by their response to it. I got out the old manuscript and rewrote my earlier versions, this time adding a Christmas background and the title "The Greatest Gift." I then showed it to my magazine agent who said that she liked it, but that it would be difficult to sell a fantasy to the magazines.

It was. After she had tried everything from *The Saturday Evening Post* to the local farm journals it was evident that no magazine would touch it. But by this time I had become fond of the story that nobody wanted. I revised it again and had 200 twenty-four-page pamphlets printed at my own expense. I sent these out to my friends as Christmas cards, and one of them went to my Hollywood agent. She wrote back, asking permission to offer the story to the movies. I thought she was crazy, but naturally I told her to go ahead. Three months passed. Then, one evening, just as I arrived home, I heard the telephone ringing. It was Western Union calling to read me a telegram from Hollywood, announcing that the story had been sold for $10,000.

The Greatest Gift

THE LITTLE TOWN straggling up the hill was bright with colored Christmas lights. But George Pratt did not see them. He was leaning over the railing of the iron bridge, staring down moodily at the black water. The current eddied and swirled like liquid glass, and occasionally a bit of ice, detached from the shore, would go gliding downstream to be swallowed up in the shadows.

The water looked paralyzingly cold. George wondered how long a man could stay alive in it. The glassy blackness had a strange, hypnotic effect on him. He leaned still farther over the railing . . .

"I wouldn't do that if I were you," a quiet voice beside him said.

George turned resentfully to a man he had never seen before. He was stout, well past middle age, and his round cheeks were pink in the winter air, as though they had just been shaved.

"Wouldn't do what?" George asked sullenly.

"What you were thinking of doing."

"How do you know what I was thinking?"

"Oh, we make it our business to know a lot of things," the stranger said easily.

George wondered what the man's business was. He was a most unremarkable person, the sort you would pass in a crowd and never notice. Unless you saw his bright blue eyes, that is. You couldn't forget them, for they were the kindest, sharpest eyes you ever saw. Nothing else about him was noteworthy. He wore a moth-eaten fur cap and a shabby overcoat. He was carrying a small black satchel. A salesman's sample kit, George decided.

"Looks like snow, doesn't it?" the stranger said, glancing up appraisingly at the overcast sky. "It'll be nice to have a white Christmas. They're getting scarce these days — but so are a lot of things." He turned to face George squarely. "You all right now?"

"Of course I'm all right. What made you think I wasn't?"

George fell silent before the stranger's quiet gaze.

The man shook his head. "You know you shouldn't think of such things — and on Christmas Eve of all times! You've got to consider Mary — and your mother, too."

George opened his mouth to ask how this stranger could know his wife's name, but the fellow anticipated him. "Don't ask me how I know such things. It's my business. That's why I came along this way tonight. Lucky I did, too." He glanced down at the dark water and shuddered.

"Well, if you know so much about me," George said, "give me just one good reason why I should be alive."

"Come, come, it can't be that bad. You've got your job at the bank. And Mary and the kids. You're healthy, young and — "

"And sick of everything!" George cried. "I'm stuck here in this mudhole for life, doing the same dull work day after day. Other men are leading exciting lives, but I — well, I'm just a small-town bank clerk. I never did anything really useful or interesting, and it looks as if I never will. I might just as well be dead. Sometimes I wish I were. In fact, I wish I had never been born!"

The man stood looking at him in the growing darkness. "What was that you said?" he asked softly.

"I said I wish I'd never been born," George repeated firmly.

The stranger's pink cheeks glowed with excitement. "Why, that's wonderful! You've solved everything. I was afraid you were going to give me some trouble. But now you've got the solution yourself. You wish you'd never been born. All right! Okay! You haven't!"

"What do you mean?"

"You haven't been born. Just that. No one here knows you. You have no responsibilities — no job — no wife — no children. Why, you haven't even a mother. You couldn't have, of course. All your troubles are over. Your wish, I am happy to say, has been granted — officially."

"Nuts!" George snorted and turned away.

The stranger caught him by the arm.

"You'd better take this with you," he said, holding out his satchel. "It'll open a lot of doors that might otherwise be slammed in your face."

"What doors in whose face? I know everybody in this town."

"Yes, I know," the man said patiently. "But take this anyway. It can't do any harm, and it may help." He opened the satchel and displayed a number of brushes. "You'd be surprised how useful these brushes can be as introduction — especially the free ones." He hauled out a plain little hand brush. "I'll show you how to use it." He thrust the satchel into George's reluctant hands and began: "When the lady of the house comes to the door, you give her this and then talk fast. You say, 'Good evening, madam, I'm from the World Cleaning Company, and I want to present you with this handsome and useful brush absolutely free — no obligation to purchase anything at all.' After that, of course, it's a cinch. Now you try it." He forced the brush into George's hand.

George promptly dropped the brush into the satchel and closed it with an angry snap. "Here," he said, and then stopped abruptly, for there was no one in sight.

The stranger must have slipped away into the bushes growing along the riverbank, George thought. He certainly wasn't going to play hide-and-seek with him. It was nearly dark and getting colder. He shivered and turned up his coat collar.

The street lights had been turned on, and Christmas candles in the windows glowed softly. The little town looked remarkably cheerful. After all, the place you grew up in was the one spot on earth where you could really feel at home. George felt a sudden burst of affection even for crotchety old Hank Biddle, whose house he was passing. He remembered the quarrel he had had when his car had scraped a piece of bark out of Hank's big maple tree. George looked up at the vast spread of leafless branches towering over him in the darkness. He felt a sudden twinge of guilt for the damage he had done. He had never stopped to inspect the wound — he was afraid to have Hank catch him even looking at the tree. Now he stepped out boldly into the roadway to examine the huge trunk.

Hank must have repaired the scar or painted it over, for there was no sign of it. George struck a match and bent down to look more closely. He straightened up with an odd, sinking feeling in his stomach. There wasn't any scar. The bark was smooth and undamaged.

He remembered what the man at the bridge had said. It was all nonsense, of course, but the nonexistent scar bothered him.

When he reached the bank, he saw that something was wrong. The building was dark, and he knew he had turned the vault light on. He noticed, too, that someone had left the window shades up. He ran around to the front. There was a battered old sign fastened on the door. George could just make out the words:

FOR RENT OR SALE
Apply JAMES SILVA, Real Estate

Perhaps it was some boys' trick, he thought wildly. Then he saw a pile of ancient leaves and tattered newspapers in the bank's ordinarily immaculate doorway. A light was still burning across the street in Jim Silva's office. George dashed over and tore the door open.

Jim looked up in surprise. "What can I do for you?" he said in the polite voice he reserved for potential customers.

"The bank," George said breathlessly. "What's the matter with it?"

"The old bank building?" Jim Silva turned around and looked out of the window. "Nothing that I can see. Wouldn't like to rent or buy it, would you?"

"You mean — it's out of business?"

"For a good ten years. Went bust. Stranger 'round these parts, ain't you?"

George sagged against the wall. "I was here some time ago," he said weakly. "The bank was all right then. I even knew some of the people who worked there."

"Didn't know a feller named Marty Jenkins, did you?"

"Marty Jenkins! Why, he — " George was about to say that Marty had never worked at the bank — couldn't have, in fact, for when they had both left school they had applied for a job there and George had gotten it. But now, of course, things were different. He would have to be careful. "No, I didn't know him," he said slowly. "Not really, that is. I'd heard of him."

"Then maybe you heard how he skipped out with fifty thousand dollars. That's why the bank went broke. Pretty near ruined everybody around here." Silva was looking at him sharply. "I was hoping for a minute maybe you'd know where he is. We'd like to get our hands on Marty Jenkins."

"Didn't he have a brother named Arthur?"

"Art? Oh, sure. But he don't know where his brother went. It's had a terrible effect on him, too. Took to drink, he did. It's too bad — and hard on his wife. He married a nice girl."

George felt the sinking feeling in his stomach again. "Who did he marry?" he demanded hoarsely. Both he and Art had courted Mary.

"Girl named Mary Thatcher," Silva said. "She lives up on the hill just this side of the church — Hey! Where are you going?"

But George had bolted out of the office. He ran past the empty bank building and turned up the hill. For a moment he thought of going straight to Mary. The house next to the church had been given to them by her father as a wedding present. Naturally Art Jenkins would have gotten it if he had married Mary. George wondered whether they had any children. Then he knew he couldn't face Mary — not yet, anyway. He decided to visit his parents and find out more about her.

There were candles burning in the windows of the little weather-beaten house on the side street, and a Christmas wreath was hanging on the glass panel of the front door. George raised the gate latch with a loud click. A dark shape on the porch hurled itself down the steps, barking ferociously.

"Brownie!" George shouted. "Brownie, stop that! Don't you know me?" But the dog advanced menacingly. The porch light snapped on, and George's father stepped outside to call the dog off. He held the dog by the collar while George cautiously walked past. He could see that his father did not know him. "Is the lady of the house in?" he asked.

His father waved toward the door. "Go on in," he said cordially. "I'll chain the dog up. She can be mean with strangers."

His mother, who was waiting in the hallway, obviously did not recognize him. George opened his sample kit and grabbed the first brush that came to hand. "Good evening, ma'am," he said politely. "I'm from the World Cleaning Company. We're giving out a free sample brush. No obligation. No obligation at all . . ." His voice faltered.

His mother smiled at his awkwardness. "I suppose you'll want to sell me something. I'm not really sure I need any brushes."

"I'm not selling anything," he assured her. "This is just — well, it's just a Christmas present from the company."

His father entered the hall and closed the door.

"Won't you come in for a while and sit down?" his mother said. "You must be tired, walking so much."

"Thank you, ma'am. I don't mind if I do." He entered the parlor and put his bag down on the floor. The room looked different somehow, although he could not figure out why.

"I used to know this town pretty well," he said. "I remember a girl named Mary Thatcher. She married Art Jenkins, I heard. You must know them."

"Of course," his mother said. "We know Mary well."

"Any children?" he asked casually.

"Two — a boy and a girl."

George sighed. He looked around the little parlor, trying to find out why it looked different. Over the mantel piece hung a framed photograph which had been taken on his kid brother Harry's sixteenth birthday. He remembered how they had gone to Potter's studio to be photographed together. There was something queer about the picture. It showed only one figure — Harry's.

"That your son?" he asked.

His mother's face clouded. She nodded but said nothing.

"I think I met him, too," George said hesitantly. "His name's Harry, isn't it?"

His mother turned away, making a strange choking noise. Her husband put his arm clumsily around her shoulder. His voice, which was always mild and gentle, suddenly became harsh. "You couldn't have met him," he said. "He's been dead a long while. He was drowned the day that picture was taken."

George's mind flew back to the long-ago August afternoon when he and Harry had visited Potter's studio. On their way home they had gone swimming. Harry had been seized with a cramp, he remembered. He had pulled him out of the water and had thought nothing of it. But suppose he hadn't been there!

"I'm sorry," he said miserably. "I guess I'd better go. I hope you like the brush. And I wish you both a very Merry Christmas." There, he had put his foot in it again, wishing them a Merry Christmas when they were thinking about their dead son.

Brownie tugged fiercely at her chain as George went down the porch steps and accompanied his departure with a rolling growl.

He wanted desperately now to see Mary. He wasn't sure he could stand not being recognized by her, but he had to see her.

The lights were on in the church, and the choir was making last-minute preparations for Christmas vespers. The organist had been practicing "O Holy Night" evening after evening until George had become thoroughly sick of it. But now the music almost tore his heart out. He stumbled blindly up the path to his own house.

When he knocked at the door, there was a long silence, followed by the shout of a child. Then Mary came to the door.

At the sight of her, George's voice almost failed him. "Merry Christmas, ma'am," he managed to say at last. His hand shook as he tried to open the satchel.

When George entered the living room, unhappy as he was, he could not help noticing with a secret grin that the too-high-priced blue sofa they often had quarreled over was there. Evidently Mary had gone through the same thing with Art Jenkins and had won the argument with him, too.

George got his satchel open. One of the brushes had a bright-blue handle and varicolored bristles. It was obviously a brush not intended to be given away, but George handed it to Mary. "This would be fine for your sofa," he said.

"My, that's a pretty brush," she exclaimed. "You're giving it away?"

He nodded solemnly. "Special introductory offer."

She stroked the sofa gently with the brush, smoothing out the velvety nap. "It is a *nice* brush. Thank you. I — " There was a sudden scream from the kitchen, and two small children rushed in. A little, homely-faced girl flung herself into her mother's arms, sobbing loudly, as a boy of seven came running after her, snapping a toy pistol at her head. "Mommy, she won't die," he yelled. "I shot her a hunnert times, but she won't die."

He looks just like Art Jenkins, George thought. Acts like him, too.

The boy suddenly turned his attention to George. "Who're you?" he demanded belligerently. He pointed his pistol at him and pulled the trigger. "You're dead!" he cried. "You're dead. Why don't you fall down and die?"

There was a heavy step on the porch. The boy looked frightened and backed away. George saw Mary glance apprehensively at the door.

Art Jenkins came in. He stood for a moment in the doorway, clinging to the knob for support. His eyes were glazed. "Who's this?" he demanded thickly.

"He's a brush salesman," Mary tried to explain. "He gave me this brush."

"Brush salesman!" Art sneered. "Well, tell him we don't want no brushes." Art lurched across the room to the sofa, where he sat down suddenly.

George looked despairingly at Mary. Her eyes were begging him to go. He went to the door, followed by Art's son, who kept snapping his pistol at him and saying, "You're dead — dead — dead!"

Perhaps the boy was right, George thought when he reached the porch. Maybe he was dead, or maybe this was all a bad dream from which he might eventually awake. He wanted to find the man on the bridge again and try to persuade him to cancel the whole deal.

He hurried down the hill and broke into a run when he neared the river. George was relieved to see the stranger standing on the bridge. "I've had enough," he gasped. "Get me out of this — you got me into it."

The stranger raised his eyebrows. "I got you into it! You were granted your wish. You got everything you asked for. You're the freest man on earth now. You have no ties. You can go anywhere — do anything. What more can you possibly want?"

"Change me back," George pleaded. "Change me back — please. Not just for my sake but for others, too. You don't understand. I've got to get back. They need me here."

"I understand," the stranger said slowly. "I just wanted to make sure *you* did. You had the greatest gift of all conferred upon you — the gift of life, of being a part of this world and taking a part in it. Yet you denied that gift." As the stranger spoke, the church bell high up on the hill sounded, calling the townspeople to Christmas vespers. Then the downtown church bell started ringing.

"I've got to get back," George said desperately. "You can't cut me off like this. Why, it's murder!"

"Suicide rather, wouldn't you say?" the stranger murmured. "You brought it on yourself. However, since it's Christmas Eve — well, anyway, close your eyes and keep listening to the bells." His voice sank lower. "Keep listening to the bells . . ."

George did as he was told. He felt a snowdrop touch his cheek — and then another and another. When he opened his eyes, the snow was falling fast, so fast that it obscured everything around him. The stranger could not be seen, but then neither could anything else. The snow was so thick that George had to grope for the bridge railing.

As he started toward the village, he thought he heard someone saying "Merry Christmas," but the bells were drowning out all rival sounds, so he could not be sure.

When he reached Hank Biddle's house he stopped and walked out into the roadway, peering down anxiously at the base of the big maple tree. The scar was there, thank heaven! He touched the tree affectionately. He'd have to do something about the wound — get a tree surgeon or something. Anyway, he'd evidently been changed back. He was himself again. Maybe it was all a dream, or perhaps he had been hypnotized by the smooth-flowing black water.

At the corner of Main and Bridge Streets he almost collided with a hurrying figure. It was Jim Silva. "Hello, George," Jim said cheerfully. "Late tonight, ain't you? I should think you'd want to be home early on Christmas Eve."

George drew a long breath. "I just wanted to see if the bank is all right. I've got to make sure the vault light is on."

"Sure it's on. I saw it as I went past."

"Let's look, huh?" George said, pulling at Silva's sleeve. He wanted the assurance of a witness. He dragged the surprised real-estate dealer around to the front of the bank, where the light was gleaming through the falling snow. "I told you it was on," Silva said with some irritation.

"I had to make sure," George mumbled. "Thanks — and Merry Christmas!" Then he was off, running up the hill.

He was in a hurry to get home, but not in such a hurry that he couldn't stop for a moment at his parents' house, where he wrestled with Brownie until the friendly old bulldog waggled all over with delight. He grasped his startled brother's hand and wrung it frantically, wishing him an almost hysterical Merry Christmas. Then he dashed across the parlor to examine a certain photograph. He kissed his mother, joked with his father and was out of the house a few seconds later, slipping on the newly fallen snow as he ran on up the hill.

The church was bright with light, and the choir and the organ were going

full tilt. George flung the door to his house open and called out at the top of his voice: "Mary! Where are you? Mary! Kids!"

His wife came toward him, dressed for church and making gestures to silence him. "I've just put the children to bed," she protested. "Now they'll — " But not another word could she get out of her mouth, for he smothered it with kisses, and then he dragged her up to the children's room, where he violated every tenet of parental behavior by madly embracing his son and his daughter and waking them up thoroughly.

It was not until Mary got him downstairs that he began to be coherent. "I thought I'd lost you. Oh, Mary, I thought I'd lost you!"

"What's the matter, darling?" she asked in bewilderment.

He pulled her down on the sofa and kissed her again. And then, just as he was about to tell her about his queer dream, his finger came in contact with something lying on the seat of the sofa. His voice froze.

He did not even have to pick the thing up, for he knew what it was. And he knew that it would have a blue handle and varicolored bristles.

THE EARLY SCRIPTS

More than a year before Frank Capra purchased "The Greatest Gift" from RKO, three complete versions of the script had already been written. These three scripts — all unsatisfactory — have for many years been presumed lost or destroyed. Capra had bought them as part of his original deal but had discarded them for a complete rewrite by Frances Goodrich and Albert Hackett. He frequently referred to the three scripts in interviews, crediting them to Marc Connelly, Dalton Trumbo, and Clifford Odets, but indicating he did not recollect saving them.

Copies of all three are in the Capra Archives. The project was worked on for nearly two years before Frank Capra came along, and reading the original story outlines and scripts indicates that without Capra, RKO would have been wise to leave the film unmade.

The slow evolution of *It's a Wonderful Life* begins at RKO in 1944 with the basic story. A man stands on a bridge in despair, wishing he had never been born. Suddenly, a mysterious stranger appears and grants his wish. The grim experience of seeing his world without him makes the man willing to keep on living. The original screenwriter, Marc Connelly (author of *The Green Pastures*), added a visual Heaven — a specific place with characters sitting around discussing the man's fate. He also added a literal interpretation of the hero's inner conflict. The Connelly first rough draft creates *two* Georges — the original man on the bridge who wants to end it all, and the "other George," the wealthy, philandering man he might have become. (This man is originally designated as "George-plus.") When George embarks on his heavenly journey, he does not find a world with no George. He finds a world with a bad George.

The first rough draft by Connelly (incomplete; August 18, 1944) begins with the introduction of the physical Heaven:

FADE IN

1 FULL SHOT — *a summer sky full of billowy clouds, with a suggestion of a rural landscape at the bottom of the frame. (Accompanying this is orchestral music seemingly inconsistent with the lyric quality of the scene. It should be a hodgepodge of popular contemporary tunes, with an occasional discordant clashing of distant military bugle calls.)*

After a moment, the CAMERA MOVES UP *and* AWAY FROM *the clouds, into a region of planets, meteors, and comets. The eye can identify the moon, the earth, Saturn and its rings, etc. (The vulgar character of the music described above is supplanted by a lyrical, more celestial melody.) The* CAMERA SLOWS DOWN *as it reaches an astral empyrean. Distant stars suddenly become brighter. (The music takes on the nobility of the* Eroica.*) The* CAMERA MOVES SLOWLY, LATERALLY, *suggesting that the firmament is now revolving about the camera. (The music diminishes as two human voices are heard over it. The first voice, the Voice of Authority, in its mellow baritone suggests divine dignity and compassion. The second voice reflects the quick, nervous, engagingly humorous inflections one associates with Barry Fitzgerald.)*

VOICE OF AUTHORITY
(summoning an angel)
L, one, six, eight, three, R, five, one, four — B-two-nine.

There is a rapid arpeggio on the strings of an orchestra, indicating the arrival of B-29.

B-29'S VOICE
B-29 reporting.

VOICE OF AUTHORITY
You are the guardian angel of the mortal George Roscoe Platt?

B-29'S VOICE
Yes, Authority.

VOICE OF AUTHORITY
You have neglected your duty —

B-29'S VOICE
To George Roscoe Platt? I beg your pardon. I happen to know he's the salt of the earth. He's one of the most decent fellahs —

VOICE OF AUTHORITY
I am not referring to the state of his soul. But you have neglected his daily existence.

B-29'S VOICE
(with asperity)
There's been a standing order since Creation that mortals be trusted a bit to work out their own destiny —

VOICE OF AUTHORITY
(with deep, quiet anger)
— But that at crucial moments their guardians must be in attendance!

B-29'S VOICE
(weakly)
Oh. I didn't know there was a crisis. (Briskly) Well, if Your Authority will excuse me, I'll fly right down and —

VOICE OF AUTHORITY
(interrupting)
Wait. The crisis will not be reached until twenty-two minutes after six, Earth Time. At that moment, you will find George Roscoe Platt at the Water Street Bridge, in Bedford Falls.

B-29'S VOICE
(casually)
Six twenty-two. Then I've got lots of time.

VOICE OF AUTHORITY
You will spend it in examining his life history.

B-29'S VOICE
Righto. I'll get the book.

VOICE OF AUTHORITY
(gently)
I've already sent for it.

From an infinite distance, as the Voice of Authority continues, a small object approaches swiftly until, at the conclusion of the Voice of Authority's speech, it fills most of the frame.

VOICE OF AUTHORITY
You need not read it all. Merely those moments in his life which have brought about the approaching crisis. When you are certain all is well, you will return to Headquarters for further instructions.

INSERT OBJECT.   *It is a book. On its cover are stamped the words:*
GEORGE ROSCOE PLATT

The Connelly scripts evolve toward a concentration on George's guilt over his failure to make a great deal of money. In Connelly's revised first draft (October 12, 1944), George knows Mary could have married a plastics magnate, and this triggers his thoughts of suicide. "Angel B-29" shows George that Mary's life would have been miserable if she had married a George that prospered. The plot develops more than one love triangle, stresses middle-class neuroticism, and presents a series of sour characterizations. In denouncing his bad self to the town, the good George intones:

> Bedford Falls — the city which has gone from twenty-sixth to twelfth in manufacturing — the city that has made George Platt [bad version] and others rich — is itself so poor that it cannot repair its own streets! There are not enough school facilities to educate your children! The Public Health Bureau consists of only one man, while the Bedford River carries filth and disease up and down the Valley! There is no recreation grounds where your children can play! Slums have spread over the town like a cancer! Your town is advertised in national magazines as the spawning ground of cheap labor! And why?

Potterville is described, if not envisioned.

In this first-draft revised Connelly script, George is a politician who never gets around to marrying poor Mary, and who contemplates suicide because he has lost the race for governor. This version has *three* Georges! The first is the film's true hero, the popular, most-likely-to-succeed George. The second is an unscrupulous politician, the man he might have been. The third is the totally imaginary George — the former "George-plus" — an arrogant, philandering, wildly wealthy business tycoon (George as both George and Potter). This version attempts to move the film away from the fantasy of a visible heaven and an earth-visiting angel. It presents the recurring motif of "the calliope player," a symbolic commentator rather than an angel. He pumps away triumphantly to celebrate George's good moments, mocks his political fall, and eggs him on to suicide like a demon figure.

In the incredible finale, George meets George on the bridge for fisticuffs. As good George swings his right, his bad self steps back just in time to be knocked off the bridge by the passing calliope, which has been lurking around waiting to help in a plot resolution. No doubt using the calliope was intended to satisfy someone's fears about the censorship board's possible response to George's killing "himself," real or unreal. At script's end, Mary, hearing the far-off sound of a bell tinkling, says her grandmother told her that meant an angel was getting its wings.

In this humorless and unrewarding script, Bedford Falls is a Potterville with or without George. The script stresses realism, and thus begins with a description of Bedford Falls instead of a celestial world:

FADE IN

1   FULL SHOT — TOWN OF BEDFORD FALLS — DAY
This scene is taken from a hilly bluff which leads down to a placid little river, on the other side of which nestles the town of Bedford Falls. The bluff is covered with trees in their natural state. In the river immediately below it we see a half a dozen boys, naked as fish, diving and shouting and playing in the water. The town in the background is an idealization of the small town in which every boy or girl should have been born. The streets are lined with shady elms; the homes are small, neat and brightly painted; each has its garden. One of the central features of the town is the oblong white church with its tall spire which stands out in our SHOT. *This* SHOT *is an important one, because it will contrast with a later* SHOT, *and will greatly assist in establishing the point of our story.* OVER THE SCENE *begins the ringing of a church bell.*

The version of the script that is next chronologically (which has no writer's name on it) alters the ending to present more threatening dialogue and more dynamic physical action. "Now I'm going to beat the daylights out of you!" George tells George. "Don't back away or you won't get the good of this one. . . ." As he swings his right this time, there is a flash of lightning and bad George topples backward. Appalled, George looks first in the water, then upward to the control house on the bridge. The bridge is swinging back, blocking off any attempt at rescue. B-29 (this version's angel) is releasing the controls, grinning hugely as he does so.

In an agony of guilt, George dashes to the embankment rail and jumps into the river, swimming frantically in the darkness. B-29 is waiting for him when he finally drags himself, empty-handed, out of the black and mysterious water. "Of course you killed him," B-29 says calmly in answer to George's anguished cry. "You should have killed him years ago. . . . You should have got rid of him before he ever got hold of your imagination. He's represented all the nonsense you've allowed to get in the way of a happy life. You see, George, that's all that was ever the matter with you. Always ashamed of being yourself — wanting to be somebody else. . . . Now go back and enjoy your real life, George. Maybe you'll find it's not so bad after all."

B-29's boss, the Voice of Authority, however, has his own opinion on the situation. The final words of the film are his skeptical comment: "Knowing mortals as I do, you had better be ready to fly down again in a year or two."

In his final version, Capra would more or less combine the introductions worked on by Connelly and the unidentified writer. He would begin with scenes of Bedford Falls in the snow, with the sound of voices praying for George, and move upward toward the sky filled with stars and the sound of "heavenly voices" discussing George's problem. The endings were totally scrapped; George's problems were resolved at home, with him reunited with family and friends.

The Clifford Odets scripts begin to bring into focus the elements found in the final movie: the accident on the ice in which Harry nearly drowns; the Gower Drug Store sequence; a moonlit dance where George and Mary court, interrupted by news of the death of George's father; George's marriage to Mary, in which he beats out his chief rival, Sam Wainwright. The first half of the script is quite similar to the movie in structure, but not in tone. The second half, however, goes off the track. George's mother remarries with George's blessing but Harry's opposition, causing conflicts. Uncle Billy loses the money, but there is no Potter waiting to capitalize on the error. Violet asks George for money to leave town, but her kiss on his cheek as thanks begins the rumor that they are having an affair. An unwieldy plot unfolds, in which George, looking for the lost money, asks his mother and stepfather to help him "in his trouble." They think he means Violet and refuse. As it turns out, Uncle Billy's crackpot wife has pasted the eight thousand dollars in her stamp collection!

The Odets version presents yet another beginning. Little Zuzu Bailey (the surname is Odets's contribution) wanders into a "music conservatory" which turns out to be in heaven. Her grandfather, George's dead father, is interrupted from harp practice by her appearance. (He is "Angel 1163.") Back on earth, Zuzu is actually lying near death, and her appearance in heaven alerts Grandpa that there is "great peril" in George's life. A heavenly official conducts Grandpa to a projection room and directs the projectionist to run off whatever film he has on the life of George Bailey, Jr. George describes his despair:

> It's all a mask. How it happens is more than I can say. Boys don't wear masks, but men do. We put them on to hide our fears and inadequacies. But some fine day something cracks the mask . . . and you're looking at your own, dear naked self. And you say, like me, "I wish to God I'd never been born! Oh, how I wish I'd never been born!"

A low organ rumble shivers the air; the bridge seems to tremble. The wind drops down to a faint breeze. George doesn't notice.

Odets also uses the idea of two Georges, the villainous one "a Babbitt, a cold-eyed, business-wise fish." However, he makes more of a stab at humor, or at least at acknowledging the fantasy level of the film. When the police are chasing George (originally to have been played by Cary Grant), "Angel 1163" tells George: "According to the police, a stranger, looking like Cary Grant, the movie actor, stole a car last night."

Odets brings his version to a dramatic moment in which the two Georges grapple wildly on the bridge:

> GEORGE
> Take your coat off, Bailey! You've nagged me for the last time in your life!
>
> BAILEY
> *(backing down)*
> I don't understand . . . did I ever hurt you?
>
> GEORGE
> *(roaring)*
> Did you ever hurt me? Why, you've given me a thousand sleepless nights! You were what I wanted to be — you were poison in my brain, you amalgamated runt! You mocked me and taunted me, called me failure —
>
> *George hits him several times. Bailey steps back, stumbles and falls off the bridge. A howl goes up from the shore. . . . The organ tone rumbles heavily.*
>
> GEORGE
> Smith [his name for "Angel 1163"] . . . I killed that man . . .
>
> 1163
> *(quietly)*
> Why didn't you do it years ago?
>
> GEORGE
> They'll find the body, won't they?
>
> 1163
> No, he won't be missed — he's unimportant.

Although each of these scripts contains something we can recognize, none comes close to being *It's a Wonderful Life*. None knows *who* George Bailey is, what his conflict is, or why he's really driven to suicide. Motives are invented, and violence is inserted for credibility. (In the second full script, Uncle Billy blows his own head off). Most importantly, all fail to create a real sense of Bedford Falls as a community.

These earlier versions all lack depth, humor, and friendship. When George returns to his past to see what the world would have been without him, his good deeds seem to be merely that — a few good deeds. The reverse point is made: Bedford Falls didn't really need George Bailey — it just needed the absence of his awful self.

Frank Capra changes that. He eliminates the two Georges, creates a town full of believable characters, makes Mary into a warm human being, and manages to make it all funny as well as sad and frightening. When Odets brings in the problem of lost money, both losing it and finding it are external to George. (His little boy finds it pasted in the crazy aunt's stamp collection.) In the final film, the loss of the money is the loss of George's freedom, his honor, his credibility in the community, and his life's work. It is both personal enough and terrible enough to make us believe in his suicidal response.

THE FINAL SCRIPT AS SHOT

The Capra Archives contain two complete scripts for *It's a Wonderful Life:* the estimating script (March 20, 1946), which was used to estimate the final budget of the film, and which contains all of Capra's personal notes, rewrites, production plans, and general character observations; and the final script as shot (March 4, 1947), which is published in full here.

The estimating script is the document that best reveals Frank Capra's talent and style. It shows how he worked and thought and planned and questioned as he prepared to shoot the final movie. It contains not only his handwritten notes about character, blocking, camera angles, etc., but also his thoughts about the characters, their lives and motivations. Samples of these handwritten notes have been reproduced —- with appropriate "translations" for those who have trouble with his penmanship! — on pages 333–338. However, the estimating script does not correspond to the final film as shot; in fact, it is substantially different. The difference between these two scripts is a testament to Capra's genius, to his writing and directing ability, and to his feisty contention that any motion picture he made was *his* creation: "One man, one movie." Without downplaying the considerable, marvelous contributions of his entire filmmaking team — his cast and crew and, above all, his scriptwriters — it is clear that Capra transformed *It's a Wonderful Life* into his own personal vision of George Bailey's story. Using everything given him by his talented collaborators, Capra shaped the characters and the story

into the movie represented by the final script reprinted here.

Capra's participation in the scripting process is not fully documented, although his estimating script illustrates how he worked. Capra's general philosophy regarding scripts was expressed in an interview with the *New York Times* on December 21, 1947, in which he used *It's a Wonderful Life* to illustrate his ideas:

> No script can be taken as gospel. It must be adapted to actors, to the set. Scripts may be written, but pictures aren't written. A picture isn't like a book to be read by one person in the privacy of a home, to be put down and taken up again. It is constructed for an average audience of 500 people, sitting in a theatre, and expected to absorb it all at one sitting. Any good scene can be expanded almost indefinitely. And frequently it isn't until you start shooting that you appreciate the possibilities.

Capra tells the interviewer that the famous hitchhiking scene of *It Happened One Night was* in the script, but that no one expected it to be given so much footage. The judge's doodling in *Mr. Deeds Goes to Town* was a Capra touch, and the detachable newel post in *It's a Wonderful Life* was an on-the-set inspiration. Capra also points out that had he not learned about the swimming pool underneath the gym floor at Beverly Hills High School, that scene would never have been in the film. "The writer couldn't have found a gym with a contraption like that."

It's a Wonderful Life

FINAL SCRIPT AS SHOT

MARCH 4, 1947

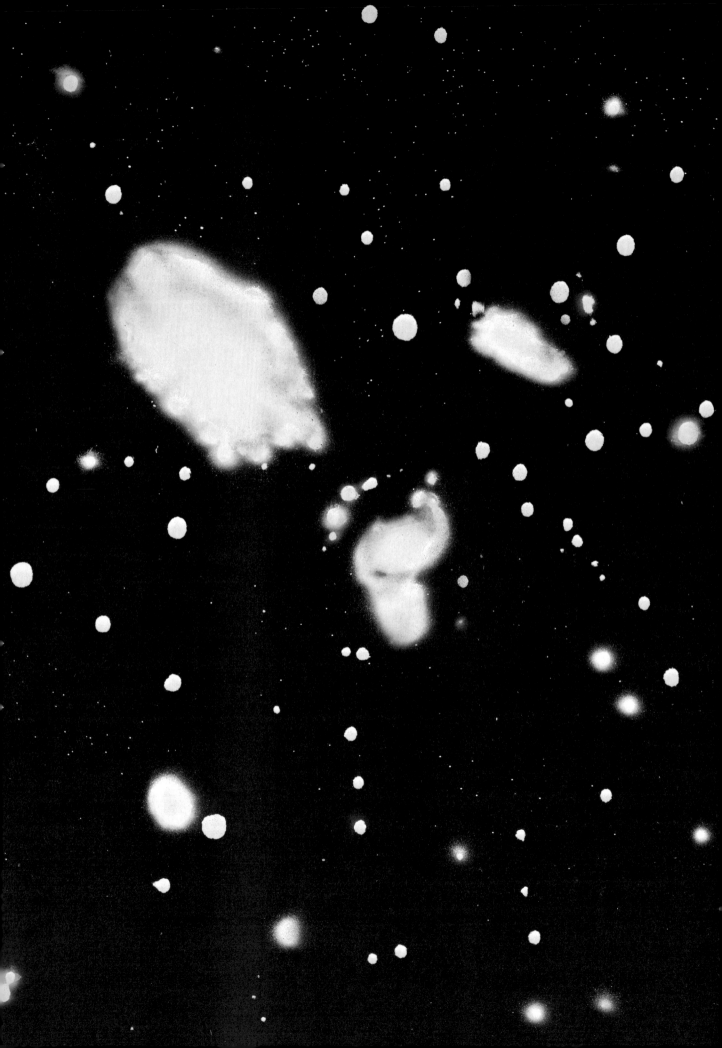

FADE IN — NIGHT SEQUENCE

SERIES OF SHOTS *of various streets and buildings in the town of Bedford Falls, somewhere in New York State. The streets are deserted, and snow is falling. It is Christmas Eve. Over the above scenes we hear voices praying:*

> GOWER'S VOICE
> I owe everything to George Bailey. Help him, dear Father.

> MARTINI'S VOICE
> Joseph, Jesus and Mary. Help my friend Mr. Bailey.

> MRS. BAILEY'S VOICE
> Help my son George tonight.

> BERT'S VOICE
> He never thinks about himself, God, that's why he's in trouble.

> ERNIE'S VOICE
> George is a good guy. Give him a break, God.

> MARY'S VOICE
> I love him, dear Lord. Watch over him tonight.

> JANIE'S VOICE
> Please, God. Something's the matter with Daddy.

> ZUZU'S VOICE
> Please bring daddy back.

CAMERA PULLS UP *from the Bailey home and travels up through the sky until it is above the falling snow, and moving slowly toward a firmament full of stars. As the camera stops we hear the following heavenly voices talking, and as each voice is heard, one of the stars twinkles brightly:*

> FRANKLIN'S VOICE
> Hello, Joseph, trouble?

> JOSEPH'S VOICE
> Looks like we'll have to send someone down — a lot of people are asking for help for a man named George Bailey.

> FRANKLIN'S VOICE
> George Bailey. Yes, tonight's his crucial night. You're right, we'll have to send someone down immediately. Whose turn is it?

> JOSEPH'S VOICE
> That's why I came to see you, sir. It's that clock-maker's turn again.

> FRANKLIN'S VOICE
> Oh — Clarence. Hasn't got his wings yet, has he? We've passed him up right along.

> JOSEPH'S VOICE
> Because, you know, sir, he's got the I.Q. of a rabbit.

FRANKLIN'S VOICE

Yes, but he's got the faith of a child — simple. Joseph, send for Clarence.

A small star flies in from left of screen and stops. It twinkles as Clarence speaks:

CLARENCE'S VOICE

You sent for me, sir?

FRANKLIN'S VOICE

Yes, Clarence. A man down on earth needs our help.

CLARENCE'S VOICE

Splendid! Is he sick?

FRANKLIN'S VOICE

No, worse. He's discouraged. At exactly ten-forty-five P.M. tonight, Earth time, that man will be thinking seriously of throwing away God's greatest gift.

CLARENCE'S VOICE

Oh, dear, dear! His life! Then I've only an hour to dress. What are they wearing now?

FRANKLIN'S VOICE

You will spend that hour getting acquainted with George Bailey.

CLARENCE'S VOICE

Sir . . . If I should accomplish this mission — I mean — might I perhaps win my wings? I've been waiting for over two hundred years now, sir — and people are beginning to talk.

FRANKLIN'S VOICE

What's that book you've got there?

CLARENCE'S VOICE

"The Adventures of Tom Sawyer."

FRANKLIN'S VOICE

Clarence, you do a good job with George Bailey, and you'll get your wings.

CLARENCE'S VOICE

Oh, thank you, sir. Thank you.

JOSEPH'S VOICE

Poor George . . . Sit down.

CLARENCE'S VOICE

Sit down? What are . . .

JOSEPH'S VOICE

If you're going to help a man, you want to know something about him, don't you?

CLARENCE'S VOICE
Well, naturally. Of course.

JOSEPH'S VOICE
Well, keep your eyes open. See the town?

The stars fade out from the screen, and a light, indistinguishable blur is seen.

CLARENCE'S VOICE
Where? I don't see a thing.

JOSEPH'S VOICE
Oh, I forgot. You haven't got your wings yet. Now look, I'll help you out. Concentrate. Begin to see something?

The blur on the screen slowly begins to take form. We see a group of young boys on top of a snow-covered hill.

CLARENCE'S VOICE
Why, yes. This is amazing.

JOSEPH'S VOICE
If you ever get your wings you'll see all by yourself.

CLARENCE'S VOICE
Oh, wonderful!

EXT. FROZEN RIVER AND HILL — DAY — 1919

CLOSE SHOT — *group of boys. They are preparing to slide down the hill on large shovels. One of them makes the slide, and shoots out onto the ice of a frozen river at the bottom of the hill.*

BOY
(as he slides)
Yippee!!

CLARENCE'S VOICE
Hey, who's that?

JOSEPH'S VOICE
That's your problem, George Bailey.

CLARENCE'S VOICE
A boy?

JOSEPH'S VOICE
That's him when he was twelve, back in 1919. Something happens here you'll have to remember later on.

SERIES OF SHOTS *as four or five boys make the slide down the hill and out onto the ice. As each boy comes down the others applaud.*

CLOSE SHOT — *George Bailey at bottom of slide.*

GEORGE
(through megaphone)
And here comes the scare-baby, my kid brother, Harry Bailey.

CLOSE SHOT — *Harry, on top of hill, preparing to make his slide.*

HARRY
I'm not scared.

BOYS
(ad lib)
Come on, Harry! Attaboy, Harry!

MED. SHOT — *Harry makes his slide very fast. He passes the marks made by the other boys, and his shovel takes him onto the thin ice at the bend of the river. The ice breaks, and Harry disappears into the water.*

CLOSE SHOT — *George.*

GEORGE

I'm coming, Harry.

MED. SHOT — *George jumps into the water and grabs Harry. As he starts to pull him out he yells:*

GEORGE

Make a chain, gang! A chain!

WIDER ANGLE — *the other boys lie flat on the ice, forming a human chain. When George reaches the edge with Harry in his arms, they pull them both to safety.*

JOSEPH'S VOICE

George saved his brother's life that day. But he caught a bad cold which infected his left ear. Cost him his hearing in that ear. It was weeks before he could return to his after-school job at old man Gower's drugstore.

DISSOLVE

EXT. MAIN STREET — BEDFORD FALLS — SPRING AFTERNOON

MED. SHOT — *Five or six boys are coming towards camera, arm in arm, whistling. Their attention is drawn to an elaborate horsedrawn carriage proceeding down the other side of the street.*

MED. PAN SHOT — *The carriage driving by. We catch a glimpse of an elderly man riding in it.*

CLOSE SHOT — *the boys watching the carriage.*

> GEORGE
> Mr. Potter!

> CLARENCE'S VOICE
> Who's that — a king?

> JOSEPH'S VOICE
> That's Henry F. Potter, the richest and meanest man in the county.

The boys continue until they reach Gower's drugstore. The drugstore is old-fashioned and dignified with jars of colored water in the windows and little else. As the kids stop:

> GEORGE
> So long!

> BOYS
> *(ad lib)*
> Got to work, slave. Hee-haw. Hee-haw.

INT. DRUGSTORE — DAY

MED. SHOT — *George comes in and crosses to an old-fashioned cigar lighter on the counter. He shuts his eyes and makes a wish:*

> GEORGE
> Wish I had a million dollars.

He clicks the lighter and the flame springs up.

> GEORGE *(cont'd)*
> Hot dog!

WIDER ANGLE — *George crosses over to the soda fountain, at which Mary Hatch, a small girl, is seated, watching him. George goes on to get his apron from behind the fountain.*

> GEORGE
> *(calling toward back room)*
> It's me, Mr. Gower. George Bailey.

CLOSE SHOT — *Mr. Gower, the druggist, peering from window in back room. We see him take a drink from a bottle.*

GOWER

You're late.

MED. SHOT — *George behind soda fountain. He is putting on his apron.*

GEORGE

Yes, sir.

WIDER ANGLE — *Violet Bick enters the drugstore and sits on one of the stools at the fountain. She is the same height as Mary and the same age, but she is infinitely older in her approach to people.*

VIOLET
(with warm friendliness)
Hello, George.
(then, flatly, as she sees Mary)
'Lo, Mary.

MARY
(primly)
Hello, Violet.

George regards the two of them with manly disgust. They are two kids to him, and a nuisance. He starts over for the candy counter.

GEORGE
(to Violet)
Two cents worth of shoelaces?

VIOLET
She was here first.

MARY
I'm still thinking.

GEORGE
(to Violet)
Shoelaces?

VIOLET
Please, Georgie.

George goes over to the candy counter.

VIOLET *(cont'd)*
(to Mary)
I like him.

MARY
You like every boy.

VIOLET
(happily)
What's wrong with that?

117

GEORGE
Here you are.

George gives Violet a paper sack containing licorice shoelaces. Violet gives him the money.

VIOLET
(the vamp)
Help me down?

GEORGE
(disgusted)
Help you down!

Violet jumps down off her stool and exits. Mary, watching, sticks out her tongue as she passes.

CLOSE SHOT — *George and Mary at fountain.*

GEORGE
Made up your mind yet?

MARY
I'll take chocolate.

George puts some chocolate ice cream in a dish.

GEORGE
With coconuts?

MARY
I don't like coconuts.

GEORGE
You don't like coconuts! Say, brainless, don't you know where coconuts come from? Lookit here — from Tahiti — Fiji Islands, the Coral Sea!

He pulls a magazine from his pocket and shows it to her.

MARY
A new magazine! I never saw it before.

GEORGE
Of course you never. Only us explorers can get it. I've been nominated for membership in the National Geographic Society.

He leans down to finish scooping out the ice cream, his deaf ear toward her. She leans over, speaking softly.

CLOSE SHOT — *Mary, whispering.*

MARY
Is this the ear you can't hear on? George Bailey, I'll love you till the day I die.

She draws back quickly and looks down, terrified at what she has said.

CLOSE SHOT — *George and Mary.*

GEORGE
I'm going out exploring some day, you watch. And I'm going to have a couple of harems, and maybe three or four wives. Wait and see.

He turns back to the cash register, whistling.

ANOTHER ANGLE — *taking in entrance to prescription room at end of fountain. Gower comes to the entrance. He is bleary-eyed, unshaven, chewing an old unlit cigar. His manner is gruff and mean. It is evident he has been drinking.*

GOWER

George! George!

GEORGE

Yes, sir.

GOWER

You're not paid to be a canary.

GEORGE

No, sir.

He turns back to the cash register when he notices an open telegram on the shelf.
He is about to toss it aside when he starts to read it.

INSERT: THE TELEGRAM. *It reads:*

"We regret to inform you that your son, Robert, died very suddenly this morning of influenza stop. Everything possible was done for his comfort stop. We await instructions from you.

EDWARD MELLINGTON
Pres. HAMMERTON COLLEGE."

BACK TO SHOT. *George puts the telegram down. A goodness of heart expresses itself in a desire to do something for Gower. He gives the ice cream to Mary without comment and sidles back toward Gower.*

INT. PRESCRIPTION ROOM OF DRUGSTORE — DAY

CLOSE SHOT — *Gower, drunk, is intent on putting some capsules into a box.*

GEORGE
Mr. Gower, do you want something . . . Anything?

                    GOWER
No.

                    GEORGE
Anything I can do back here?

                    GOWER
No.

George looks curiously at Gower, realizing that he is quite drunk. Gower fumbles and drops some of the capsules to the floor.

CLOSE SHOT — *capsules spilling on floor at their feet.*

BACK TO SHOT — *George and Gower.*

                    GEORGE
I'll get them, sir.

*He picks up the capsules and puts them in the box. Gower waves George aside, takes his old wet cigar, shoves it in his mouth and sits in an old Morris chair in the b.g. George turns a bottle around from which Gower has taken the powder for the capsules. Its label reads "*POISON*." George stands still, horrified.*

                    GOWER
Take those capsules over to Mrs. Blaine's. She's waiting for them.

George picks up the capsule box, not knowing what to do or say. His eyes go, harassed, to the bottle labelled poison. George's fingers fumble.

                    GEORGE
Yes, sir. They have the diphtheria there, haven't they, sir?

                    GOWER
Ummmm . . .

Gower stares moodily ahead, sucking his cigar. George turns to him, the box in his hand.

                    GEORGE
Is it a charge, sir?

                    GOWER
Yes — charge.

                    GEORGE
Mr. Gower, I think . . .

                    GOWER
Aw, get going!

                    GEORGE
Yes, sir.

INT. DRUGSTORE — DAY

MED. SHOT — *George comes out into main room. As he puts on his cap he sees a Sweet Caporals ad which says:*

INSERT: "ASK DAD HE KNOWS" — SWEET CAPORAL

BACK TO SHOT: *With an inspiration, George dashes out the door and down the street. Mary follows him with her eyes.*

EXT. STREET — DAY

MED. SHOT — *George runs down the street until he comes opposite a two-story building with a sign on it reading: "Bailey Building and Loan Association." He stops. Potter's carriage is waiting at the entrance. Suddenly he runs up the stairs.*

INT. OUTER OFFICE BLDG. AND LOAN — DAY

FULL SHOT. *The offices are ancient and a bit on the rickety side. There is a counter with a grill, something like a bank. Before a door marked:* PETER BAILEY, PRIVATE, *George's Uncle Billy stands, obviously trying to hear what is going on inside. He is a very good-humored man of about fifty, in shirt-sleeves. With him at the door, also listening, are Cousin Tilly Bailey, a waspish-looking woman, who is the telephone operator, and Cousin Eustace Bailey, the clerk. The office vibrates with an aura of crisis as George enters and proceeds directly toward his father's office.*

CLOSE SHOT — *Uncle Billy listening at the door. As George is about to enter his father's office, Uncle Billy grabs him by the arm.*

> UNCLE BILLY
> Avast, there, Captain Cook! Where you headin'?

> GEORGE
> Got to see Pop, Uncle Billy.

> UNCLE BILLY
> Some other time, George.

> GEORGE
> It's important.

> UNCLE BILLY
> There's a squall in there that's shapin' up into a storm.

During the foregoing, Cousin Tilly has answered the telephone, and now she calls out:

> COUSIN TILLY
> Uncle Billy . . . telephone.

> UNCLE BILLY
> Who is it?

> COUSIN TILLY
> Bank examiner.

INSERT: CLOSEUP *Uncle Billy's left hand. There are pieces of string tied around two of the fingers, obviously to remind him of things he has to do.*

BACK TO SHOT. *Uncle Billy looking at his hand.*

> UNCLE BILLY
> Bank examiner! I should have called him yesterday. Switch it inside.

He enters a door marked: WILLIAM BAILEY, PRIVATE. *George stands irresolute a moment, aware of crisis in the affairs of the Bailey Building and Loan Association, but aware more keenly of his personal crisis. He opens the door of his father's office and enters.*

INT. BAILEY'S PRIVATE OFFICE — DAY

MED. SHOT — *George's father is seated behind his desk, nervously drawing swirls on a pad. He looks tired and worried. He is a gentle man in his forties, an idealist, stubborn only for other people's rights. Nearby, in a throne-like wheelchair, behind which stands the goon who furnishes the motive power, sits Henry F. Potter, his squarish derby hat on his head. The following dialogue is fast and heated, as though the argument had been in process for some time.*

> BAILEY
> I'm not crying, Mr. Potter.

> POTTER
> Well, you're begging, and that's a whole lot worse.

> BAILEY
> All I'm asking is thirty days more . . .

> GEORGE
> *(interrupting)*
> Pop!

> BAILEY
> Just a minute, son.
> *(to Potter)*
> Just thirty short days. I'll dig up that five thousand somehow.

> POTTER
> *(to his goon)*
> Shove me up . . .

Goon pushes his wheelchair closer to the desk.

> GEORGE
> Pop!

> POTTER
> Have you put any real pressure on those people of yours to pay those mortgages?

> BAILEY
> Times are bad, Mr. Potter. A lot of these people are out of work.

> POTTER
> Then foreclose!

> BAILEY
> I can't do that. These families have children.

MED. CLOSE SHOT. *Potter and Bailey.*

> GEORGE
> Pop!

POTTER
They're not my children.

BAILEY
But they're somebody's children, Mr. Potter.

POTTER
Are you running a business or a charity ward?

BAILEY
Well, all right . . .

POTTER
(interrupting)
Not with my money!

CLOSE SHOT. *Potter and Bailey.*

BAILEY
Mr. Potter, what makes you such a hard-skulled character? You have no family — no children. You can't begin to spend all the money you've got.

POTTER
So I suppose I should give it to miserable failures like you and that idiot brother of yours to spend for me.

George cannot listen any longer to such libel about his father. He comes around in front of the desk.

GEORGE
He's not a failure! You can't say that about my father!

BAILEY
George, George . . .

GEORGE
You're not! You're the biggest man in town!

BAILEY
Run along.

He pushes George toward the door.

GEORGE
Bigger'n him!

As George passes Potter's wheelchair he pushes the old man's shoulder. The goon puts out a restraining hand.

BAILEY
Run along.

GEORGE
Bigger'n everybody.

George proceeds towards the door, with his father's hand on his shoulder. As they go:

POTTER
Gives you an idea of the Baileys.

INT. OUTER OFFICE BLDG. AND LOAN — DAY

CLOSE SHOT — *George and his father at the door.*

GEORGE
Don't let him say that about you, Pop.

BAILEY

All right, son, thanks. I'll talk to you tonight.

Bailey closes the door on George and turns back to Potter. George stands outside the door with the capsules in his hand.

WIPE TO:

INT. BACK ROOM — GOWER'S DRUGSTORE — DAY

CLOSE SHOT — *Gower talking on the telephone. George stands in the doorway.*

GOWER
(*drunkenly*)
Why, that medicine should have been there an hour ago. It'll be over in five minutes, Mrs. Blaine.

He hangs up the phone and turns to George.

GOWER *(cont'd)*
Where's Mrs. Blaine's box of capsules?

He grabs George by the shirt and drags him into the back room.

GEORGE

Capsules . . .

GOWER
(*shaking him*)
Did you hear what I said?

GEORGE
(*frightened*)
Yes, sir, I . . .

Gower starts hitting George about the head with his open hands. George tries to protect himself as best he can.

GOWER
What kind of tricks are you playing, anyway? Why didn't you deliver them right away? Don't you know that boy's very sick?

GEORGE
(*in tears*)
You're hurting my sore ear.

INT. FRONT ROOM DRUGSTORE — DAY

CLOSE SHOT — *Mary is still seated at the soda fountain. Each time she hears George being slapped, she winces.*

INT. BACK ROOM DRUGSTORE — DAY

CLOSE SHOT — *George and Gower.*

> GOWER
>
> You lazy loafer!

> GEORGE
> *(sobbing)*
> Mr. Gower, you don't know what you're doing. You put something wrong in those capsules. I know you're unhappy. You got that telegram, and you're upset. You put something bad in those capsules. It wasn't your fault, Mr. Gower . . .

George pulls the little box out of his pocket. Gower savagely rips it away from him, breathing heavily, staring at the boy venomously.

> GEORGE *(cont'd)*
> Just look and see what you did. Look at the bottle you took the powder from. It's poison! I tell you it's poison! I know you feel bad . . . and . . .

George falters off, cupping his aching ear with a hand. Gower looks at the large brown bottle which has not been replaced on the shelf. He tears open the package, shakes the powder out of one of the capsules, cautiously tastes it, then abruptly throws the whole mess to the table and turns to look at George again. The boy is whimpering, hurt, frightened. Gower steps toward him.

> GEORGE *(cont'd)*
> Don't hurt my sore ear again.

But this time Gower sweeps the boy to him in a hug, and sobbing hoarsely crushes the boy in his embrace. George is crying too.

> GOWER
> No . . . No . . . No . . .

> GEORGE
> Don't hurt my ear again!

> GOWER
> *(sobbing)*
> Oh, George, George . . .

> GEORGE
> Mr. Gower, I won't ever tell anyone. I know what you're feeling. I won't ever tell a soul. Hope to die, I won't.

> GOWER
> Oh, George.

INT. LUGGAGE SHOP — DAY — (1928)

MED. SHOT. *It is late afternoon. A young man is looking over an assortment of luggage. Across the counter stands Joe Hepner, the proprietor of the store — he is showing a suitcase.*

> JOE
>
> An overnight bag — genuine English cowhide, combination lock, fitted up with brushes, combs . . .

> CUSTOMER
>
> Nope.

As CAMERA MOVES UP CLOSER *to him, he turns and we get our first glimpse of George as a young man.* CAMERA HAS MOVED UP *to a* CLOSEUP *by now.*

> GEORGE
>
> Nope. Nope. Nope. Nope. Now, look, Joe. Now look, I . . . I want a big one.

Suddenly, in action, as George stands with his arms outstretched in illustration, the picture freezes and becomes a still. Over this hold-frame shot we hear the voices from Heaven:

> CLARENCE'S VOICE
>
> What did you stop it for?

> JOSEPH'S VOICE
>
> I want you to take a good look at that face.

> CLARENCE'S VOICE
>
> Who is it?

> JOSEPH'S VOICE
>
> George Bailey.

> CLARENCE'S VOICE
>
> Oh, you mean the kid that had his ears slapped back by the druggist?

> JOSEPH'S VOICE
>
> That's the kid.

> CLARENCE'S VOICE
>
> It's a good face. I like it. I like George Bailey. Tell me, did he ever tell anyone about the pills?

> JOSEPH'S VOICE
>
> Not a soul.

> CLARENCE'S VOICE
>
> Did he ever marry the girl? Did he ever go exploring?

JOSEPH'S VOICE
Well, wait and see.

CLOSE SHOT — *the screen. The arrested* CLOSEUP *of George springs to life again.*

GEORGE
Big — see! I don't want one for one night. I want something for a thousand and one nights, with plenty of room for labels from Italy and Baghdad, Samarkand . . . a great big one.

JOE
I see, a flying carpet, huh? I don't suppose you'd like this old second-hand job, would you?

He brings a large suitcase up from under the counter.

GEORGE
Now you're talking. Gee whiz, I could use this as a raft in case the boat sunk. How much does this cost?

JOE

No charge.

GEORGE

That's my trick ear, Joe. It sounded as if you said no charge.

JOE
(indicating name on suitcase)

That's right.

GEORGE
(as he sees his name)

What's my name doing on it?

JOE

A little present from old man Gower. Came down and picked it out himself.

GEORGE
(admiring the bag)

He did? Whatta you know about that — my old boss . . .

JOE

What boat you sailing on?

GEORGE

I'm working across on a cattle boat.

JOE

A cattle boat?

GEORGE
(as he exits)

Okay, I like cows.

WIPE TO:

INT. GOWER'S DRUGSTORE — DAY

MED. SHOT — *The place is practically the same except that it is now full of school kids having sodas, etc. A juke box and many little tables have been added. It has become the hangout of the local small fry. There are now three kids jerking sodas.*

Gower is a different man now — sober, shaven and good humored. He is behind the counter when George comes in. Gower's face lights up when he sees George.

GEORGE

Mr. Gower . . . Mr. Gower . . . thanks ever so much for the bag. It's just exactly what I wanted.

GOWER

Aw, forget it.

GEORGE

Oh, it's wonderful.

GOWER
Hope you enjoy it.

George suddenly sees the old cigar lighter on the counter. He closes his eyes and makes a wish.

GEORGE

Oh . . . Oh. Wish I had a million dollars.

As he snaps the lighter the flame springs up.

GEORGE *(cont'd)*

Hot dog!

George shakes Gower's hand vigorously, and exits.

EXT. MAIN STREET BEDFORD FALLS — DAY

PAN SHOT — *as George crosses the street. Uncle Billy, Cousin Tilly and Cousin Eustace are leaning out of the second-floor window of the Building and Loan offices.*

> UNCLE BILLY
> Avast there, Captain Cook. You got your sea legs yet?

> COUSIN EUSTACE
> Parlez-vous Français? Hey, send us some of them picture postcards, will you, George?

> UNCLE BILLY
> Hey, George, don't take any plugged nickels.

> COUSIN TILLY
> Hey, George, your suitcase is leaking.

George waves up at them and continues on across the street.

EXT. MAIN STREET — DAY

MED. SHOT — *as George crosses the street. He spots Ernie and his cab, and Bert the motor cop, parked alongside.*

> GEORGE
> Hey, Ernie!

> ERNIE
> Hiya, George!

> GEORGE
> Hi, Bert.

> BERT
> George . . .

> GEORGE
> Ernie, I'm a rich tourist today. How about driving me home in style.

Bert opens the door of the cab and puts George's suitcase inside.

> ERNIE
> Sure, your highness, hop in. And, for the carriage trade, I puts on my hat.

As George is about to enter the cab, he stops suddenly as he sees Violet (now obviously a little sex machine) come toward him. Her walk and figure would stop anybody. She gives him a sultry look.

REVERSE ANGLE — *The three men by the cab, but including Violet.*

> VIOLET
> Good afternoon, Mr. Bailey.

GEORGE
Hello, Violet. Hey, you look good. That's some dress you got on there.

CLOSE SHOT — *Violet. She reacts to this.*

VIOLET
Oh, this old thing? Why, I only wear it when I don't care how I look.

CAMERA PANS WITH *her as Violet swings on down the sidewalk.*

REVERSE SHOT — *cab. As Violet goes by George and Bert raise their heads above the top of the cab.*

MED. SHOT — *on Violet's back as she goes. As she crosses the street an elderly man turns to look at her, and is almost hit by a car that pulls up with screeching brakes.*

CLOSE SHOT — *George and Bert at cab. Ernie sticks his head out from the driver's seat.*

> ERNIE
> How would you like . . .

> GEORGE
> *(as he enters cab)*
> Yes . . .

> ERNIE
> Want to come along, Bert? We'll show you the town?

Bert looks at his watch, then takes another look at Violet's retreating figure.

> BERT
> No thanks. Think I'll go home and see what the wife's doing.

> ERNIE
> Family man.

DISSOLVE TO:

INT. BAILEY DINING ROOM — NIGHT

MED. SHOT — *Pop Bailey is seated at the dinner table. Mrs. Bailey and Annie, the cook, look up toward the vibrating ceiling. There are* SOUNDS *of terrific banging and scuffling upstairs. Annie pounds on the ceiling with a broom.*

> MOTHER
> *(calling out)*
> George! Harry! You're shaking the house down! Stop it!

> POP
> Oh, let 'em alone. I wish I was up there with them.

> MOTHER
> Harry'll tear his dinner suit. George!

ANOTHER ANGLE — *Mrs. Bailey is calling up the stairs.*

> ANNIE
> That's why all children should be girls.

> MOTHER
> But if they were all girls, there wouldn't be any . . . Oh, never mind.
> *(calling up stairs)*
> George! Harry! Come down to dinner this minute. Everything's getting cold and you know we've been waiting for you.

GEORGE'S VOICE

Okay, mom.

She goes up the stairs.

Pop is smiling and poking his plate. A commotion is heard on the stairs, the boys imitating fan-fare MUSIC. *Down they come holding their Mother high between them on their hands. They bring her into the dining room and deposit her grace-fully into Pop's lap.*

BOYS

Here's a present for you, Pop.

Pop kisses her. Mother gives Pop a quick hug then turns with all the wrath she can muster on the two boys.

MOTHER

Oh, you two idiots! George, sit down and have dinner.

HARRY

I've eaten.

MOTHER

Well, aren't you going to finish dressing for your graduation party? Look at you.

HARRY

I don't care. It's George's tux.

Annie crosses the room, holding her broom. Harry reaches out for her.

ANNIE

If you lay a hand on me, I'll hit you with this broom.

HARRY

Annie, I'm in love with you. There's a moon out tonight.

As he pushes her through the kitchen door, he slaps her fanny. She screams. The noise is cut off by the swinging door. George and his mother sit down at the table.

GEORGE

Boy, oh, boy, oh, boy — my last meal at the old Bailey boarding house.

MOTHER

Oh, my lands, my blood pressure!

CLOSE SHOT — *Harry, as he sticks his head through the kitchen door.*

HARRY

Pop, can I have the car? I'm going to take over a lot of plates and things.

MOTHER

What plates?

HARRY

Oh, Mom — I'm chairman of the eats committee and we only need a couple of dozen.

MOTHER

Oh, no you don't. Harry, now, not my best Haviland.

She follows Harry into the kitchen, leaving Pop and George. As she goes:

GEORGE

Oh, let him have the plates, Mother.

CLOSE SHOT — *George and his father, eating at the table. There is a great similarity and a great understanding between them.*

POP

Hope you have a good trip, George. Uncle Billy and I are going to miss you.

GEORGE

I'm going to miss you, too, Pop. What's the matter? You look tired.

POP

Oh, I had another tussle with Potter today.

GEORGE

Oh . . .

POP

I thought when we put him on the Board of Directors, he'd ease up on us a little bit.

GEORGE

I wonder what's eating that old money-grubbing buzzard anyway?

POP

Oh, he's a sick man. Frustrated and sick. Sick in his mind, sick in his soul, if he has one. Hates everybody that has anything that he can't have. Hates us mostly, I guess.

MED. SHOT — *the dining room. Harry and his Mother come out of the kitchen, Harry carrying a pie in each hand, and balancing one on his head.* CAMERA PANS WITH *them as they cross.*

HARRY

Gangway! Gangway! So long, Pop.

POP

So long, son.

GEORGE

Got a match?

HARRY

Very funny. Very funny.

MOTHER

Put those things in the car and I'll get your tie and studs together.

HARRY

Okay, Mom. You coming later? You coming later, George?

GEORGE

What do you mean, and be bored to death?

HARRY

Couldn't want a better death. Lots of pretty girls, and we're going to use that new floor of yours tonight, too.

GEORGE

I hope it works.

POP

No gin tonight, son.

HARRY

Aw, Pop, just a little.

POP

No, son, not one drop.

CLOSE SHOT — *George and Pop at the table. Annie comes in with some dishes.*

ANNIE

Boys and girls and music. Why do they need gin?

She exits.

GEORGE

Father, did I act like that when I graduated from high school?

POP

Pretty much. You know, George, wish we could send Harry to college with you. Your mother and I talked it over half the night.

GEORGE

We have that all figured out. You see, Harry'll take my job at the Building and Loan, work there four years, then he'll go.

POP

He's pretty young for that job.

GEORGE

Well, no younger than I was.

POP

Maybe you were born older, George.

GEORGE

How's that?

POP

I say, maybe you were born older. I suppose you've decided what you're going to do when you get out of college.

GEORGE

Oh, well, you know what I've always talked about — build things . . . design new buildings — plan modern cities — all that stuff I was talking about.

POP

Still after that first million before you're thirty.

GEORGE

No, I'll settle for half that in cash.

Annie comes in again from the kitchen.

POP

Of course, it's just a hope, but you wouldn't consider coming back to the Building and Loan, would you?

Annie stops serving to hear his answer.

GEORGE

Well, I . . .
    (to Annie)
Annie, why don't you draw up a chair? Then you'd be more comfort-able and you could hear everything that's going on.

ANNIE

I would if I thought I'd hear anything worth listening to.

GEORGE

You would, huh?

She gives George a look, and goes on out into the kitchen. Bailey smiles and turns to George.

POP

I know it's soon to talk about it.

GEORGE

Oh, now, Pop, I couldn't. I couldn't face being cooped up for the rest of my life in a shabby little office.

He stops, realizing that he has hurt his father.

GEORGE *(cont'd)*

Oh, I'm sorry, Pop, I didn't mean that remark, but this business of nickels and dimes and spending all your life trying to figure out how to save three cents on a length of pipe . . . I'd go crazy. I want to do something big and something important.

POP

(quietly)
You know, George, I feel that in a small way we are doing something important. Satisfying a fundamental urge. It's deep in the race for a man to want his own roof and walls and fireplace, and we're helping him get those things in our shabby little office.

GEORGE

(unhappily)
I know, Dad. I wish I felt . . . But I've been hoarding pennies like a miser in order to . . . Most of my friends have already finished college. I just feel like if I don't get away, I'd bust.

POP

Yes . . . Yes . . . You're right, son.

GEORGE

You see what I mean, don't you, Pop?

POP

This town is no place for any man unless he's willing to crawl to Potter.

You've got talent, son. I've seen' it. You get yourself an education. Then get out of here.

> GEORGE
> Pop, you want a shock? I think you're a great guy.

To cover his embarrassment, he looks toward the kitchen door and calls:

> GEORGE *(cont'd)*
> Oh, did you hear that, Annie?

CLOSE SHOT — *Annie listening through glass in door.*

> ANNIE
> I heard it. About time one of you lunkheads said it.

CLOSE SHOT — *George and his father at the table.*

> GEORGE
> I'm going to miss old Annie. Pop, I think I'll get dressed and go over to Harry's party.

> POP
> Have a good time, son.

> WIPE TO:

INT. HIGH SCHOOL GYM — NIGHT

MED. CLOSE SHOT — *At one end of the room an orchestra is playing. George wends his way through the dancing couples towards a supper table. He and Harry are carrying plates and pies.*

> GEORGE
> Here you are.

Several of the boys take the plates from him. George looks at them, feeling very grown up and out of place.

> HARRY
> *(introducing George)*
> You know my kid brother, George. I'm going to put him through college.

Sam Wainwright comes in behind Harry, waggles his hands at his ears as he talks.

> SAM
> Here comes George. Hello, hee-haw!

George swings around, delighted to hear a familiar voice.

WIDER ANGLE — *including Sam and Marty Hatch. Sam is assured and breezy, wearing very collegiate clothes.*

> GEORGE
> Oh, oh. Sam Wainwright! How are you? When did you get here?

SAM

Oh, this afternoon. I thought I'd give the kids a treat.

GEORGE

Old college graduate now, huh?

SAM

Yeah — old Joe College Wainwright, they call me. Well, freshman, looks like you're going to make it after all.

GEORGE

Yep.

Sam sees Harry and leaves George in the middle of a gesture.

SAM

(to Harry)

Harry! You're the guy I want to see. Coach has heard all about you.

HARRY

He has?

SAM

Yeah. He's followed every game and his mouth's watering. He wants me to find out if you're going to come along with us.

HARRY

Well, I gotta make some dough first.

SAM

Well, you better make it fast. We need great ends like you — not broken down old guys like this one.

George and Sam wiggle their fingers at their ears, saluting each other.

GEORGE

Hee-haw!

SAM

Hee-haw!

An elderly, fussy school principal comes over to George.

PRINCIPAL

George, welcome back.

GEORGE

Hello, Mr. Partridge, how are you?

PRINCIPAL

Putting a pool under this floor was a great idea. Saved us another building. Now, Harry, Sam, have a lot of fun. There's lots of stuff to eat and drink. Lots of pretty girls around.

Violet Bick comes into the scene and turns to face George. She is waving her dance program at him.

VIOLET
Hey, George . . .

GEORGE
Hello, Violet.

VIOLET
Hello, what am I bid?

Marty Hatch enters scene.

MARTY
George.

GEORGE
Hiya, Marty. Well, it's old home week.

MARTY
Do me a favor, will you, George?

GEORGE

What's that?

MARTY

Well, you remember my kid sister, Mary?

GEORGE

Oh, yeah, yeah.

SAM

"Momma wants you, Marty." "Momma wants you, Marty." Remember?

MARTY

Dance with her, will you?

GEORGE

Oh . . . me? Oh, well, I feel funny enough already, with all these kids.

MARTY

Aw, come on. Be a sport. Just dance with her one time and you'll give her the thrill of her life.

SAM

Aw, go on.

MARTY
(calling off)
Hey, sis.

GEORGE

Well, excuse me, Violet. Don't be long, Marty. I don't want to be a wet nurse for . . .

He stops suddenly as he sees Mary, staring at her.

CLOSEUP — *Mary Hatch. She is standing talking to one of the boys, Freddie, a glass of punch in her hand. For the first time she is wearing an evening gown and she has gained assurance from the admiration of the boy with her. She turns around and for the first time she sees George. For a second she loses her poise, staring at him.*

FREDDIE'S VOICE

And the next thing I know, some guy came up and tripped me. That's the reason why I came in fourth. If it hadn't been for that . . .

CLOSE SHOT — *George, staring at Mary.*

FREDDIE'S VOICE *(cont'd)*

. . . that race would have been a cinch. I tried to find out who it was later . . .

CLOSEUP — *Mary, still staring at George, and smiling.*

FREDDIE'S VOICE *(cont'd)*
. . . but I couldn't find out. Nobody'd ever tell you whoever it was
because they'd be scared. They know . . .

MED. CLOSEUP — *Mary and Freddie. Marty comes into scene, followed by George.*

FREDDIE *(cont'd)*
. . . what kind of . . .

MARTY
(interrupting)
You remember George? This is Mary. Well, I'll be seeing you.

GEORGE
Well . . . Well . . . Well . . .

FREDDIE
Now, to get back to my story, see . . .

Mary hands her punch cup to Freddie, and she and George start dancing.

> FREDDIE *(cont'd)*
> Hey, this is my dance!

> GEORGE
> Oh, why don't you stop annoying people!

> FREDDIE
> Well, I'm sorry. Hey!

MOVING SHOT — *following George and Mary as they dance.*

> GEORGE
> Well, hello.

> MARY
> Hello. You look at me as if you didn't know me.

> GEORGE
> Well, I don't.

> MARY
> You've passed me on the street almost every day.

> GEORGE
> Me?

> MARY
> Uh-huh.

> GEORGE
> Uh-uh. That was a little girl named Mary Hatch. That wasn't you.

A WHISTLE *is heard o.s., and the* MUSIC *stops.*

CLOSE SHOT — *Harry on the orchestra platform, whistle in hand.*

> HARRY
> Oyez — oyez — oyez . . . The big Charleston contest. The prize? A genuine loving cup. Those not tapped by the judges will remain on the floor. Let's go!

CLOSEUP — *George and Mary. As the* MUSIC *starts and couples begin dancing once more, they look at each other.*

> GEORGE
> I'm not very good at this.

> MARY
> Neither am I.

> GEORGE
> Okay — what can we lose?

They start their Charleston. We see a SERIES OF SHOTS *of various couples doing their routines, some good, some bad.*

CLOSEUP — *Freddie leaning against the railing around the dance floor, looking daggers at George. Mickey, a young punk who has had one too many, is beside him.*

> MICKEY
> What's the matter, Othello — jealous? Did you know there's a swimming pool under this floor? And did you know that button behind you causes this floor to open up? And did you further know that George Bailey is dancing right over that crack? And I've got the key?

Freddie needs no more. He takes the key from Mickey and turns the switch. The floor begins to part in the middle, each half sliding under the bleacher seats. Pandemonium starts. Dancers begin to scream as they try to get off. Some are so engrossed in dancing they continue at top speed. Teachers and elders start to scurry off. As the floor opens, it reveals an attractive, lighted swimming pool.

George and Mary are so busy dancing they don't notice the floor opening. Spotlights concentrate on them. They mistake the screams for cheers.

CLOSE SHOT — *George and Mary dancing.*

GEORGE

They're cheering us. We must be good.

MED. CLOSE SHOT — *the crowd watching George and Mary dancing. They move backwards until finally they reach the edge of the floor and fall into the pool below.*

SERIES OF SHOTS — *George and Mary still trying to dance in the water — the crowd on the edge cheering them — some of the crowd leap into the pool — the principal trying to restore order, finally clasps his hands like a diver and leaps in himself.*

FADE OUT

FADE IN

MED. CLOSE SHOT — *George and Mary. The night is warm with a bright moon. George is dressed in jersey sweater and oversize football pants that keep wanting to come down. Mary is in an old white bath robe. Each is carrying their wet clothes tied into a bundle, that leaves a trail of dripping water. As they near the camera we hear them singing:*

> GEORGE AND MARY
> *(singing)*
> Buffalo Gals can't you come out tonight. Can't you come out tonight. Can't you come out tonight. Buffalo Gals can't you come out tonight and dance by the light of the moon.

> GEORGE
> Hot dog! Just like an organ.

> MARY
> Beautiful.

CAMERA MOVES WITH *them as they proceed down the street.*

> GEORGE
> And I told Harry I thought I'd be bored to death. You should have seen the commotion in that locker room. I had to knock down three people to get this stuff we're wearing here. Here, let me hold that old wet dress of yours.

He takes the bundle of clothes from Mary. They stop and look at each other.

> MARY
> Do I look as funny as you do?

> GEORGE
> I guess I'm not quite the football type. You . . . you look wonderful. You know, if it wasn't me talking I'd say you were the prettiest girl in town.

> MARY
> Well, why don't you say it?

> GEORGE
> I don't know. Maybe I will say it. How old are you anyway?

> MARY
> Eighteen.

> GEORGE
> Eighteen! Why, it was only last year you were seventeen.

> MARY
> Too young or too old?

GEORGE

Oh, no. Just right. Your age fits you. Yes, sir, you look a little older without your clothes on.

Mary stops. George, to cover his embarrassment, talks quickly on:

GEORGE *(cont'd)*

I mean, without a dress. You look older . . . I mean, younger. You look just . . .

In his confusion George steps on the end of the belt of Mary's bath robe, which is trailing along behind her. She gathers the robe around her.

GEORGE *(cont'd)*

Oh-oh . . .

MARY

(holding out her hand)

Sir, my train, please.

GEORGE

A pox upon me for a clumsy lout.

He picks up the belt and throws it over her arm.

GEORGE *(cont'd)*

Your . . . your caboose, my lady.

MARY

You may kiss my hand.

GEORGE

Ummmmm . . .

Holding her hand, George moves in closer to Mary.

GEORGE *(cont'd)*

Hey — hey, Mary.

Mary turns away from him, singing "Buffalo Gals":

MARY

(singing)

As I was lumbering down the street . . .

George looks after her, then picks up a rock from the street.

GEORGE

Okay then, I'll throw a rock at the old Granville house.

MARY

Oh, no, don't. I love that old house.

MED. LONG SHOT — *old house. It is a weather-beaten, old-fashioned two-storied house that once was no doubt resplendent.*

GEORGE

No. You see, you make a wish and then try and break some glass. You
got to be a pretty good shot now-a-days, too.

MED. CLOSEUP — *George and Mary.*

MARY

Oh, no, George, don't. It's full of romance, that old place. I'd like to
live in it.

GEORGE

In that place?

MARY

Uh-huh.

GEORGE

I wouldn't live in it as a ghost. Now watch . . . right on the second
floor there.

MED. LONG SHOT — *old house. George hurls the rock at the house. We hear the*
SOUND *of a window breaking.*

EXT. FRONT PORCH OF HOUSE — NIGHT

CLOSE SHOT. *We see a grumpy old man in shirt sleeves in a rocking chair on the
porch. He looks up as he hears the breaking glass.*

EXT. STREET — NIGHT

CLOSEUP — *George and Mary.*

MARY

What'd you wish, George?

GEORGE

Well, not just one wish. A whole hatful, Mary. I know what I'm going
to do tomorrow and the next day and the next year and the year after
that. I'm shaking the dust of this crummy little town off my feet and
I'm going to see the world. Italy, Greece, the Parthenon, the Colos-
eum. Then I'm coming back here and go to college and see what they
know . . . and then I'm going to build things. I'm gonna build air
fields. I'm gonna build skyscrapers a hundred stories high. I'm gonna
build bridges a mile long . . .

*As he talks, Mary has been listening intently. She finally stoops down and picks
up a rock, weighing it in her hand.*

GEORGE *(cont'd)*
Are you gonna throw a rock?

MED. LONG SHOT — *the old deserted house. Mary throws her rock, and once more
we hear the* SOUND *of breaking glass.*

GEORGE (cont'd)

Hey, that's pretty good. What'd you wish, Mary?

Mary looks at him provocatively, then turns, and shuffles off down the street, singing as she goes. George hurries after her.

MARY
(singing)
Buffalo Gals, can't you come out tonight . . .

George joins her in the singing as they proceed down the street.

MARY AND GEORGE
(singing)
. . . can't you come out tonight, can't you come out tonight. Buffalo Gals can't you come out tonight and dance by the light of the moon.

GEORGE
What'd you wish when you threw that rock?

CLOSE SHOT — *man on the porch of house, listening to George and Mary.*

MED. CLOSEUP — *George and Mary have stopped walking and now face one another.*

MARY
Oh, no.

GEORGE
Come on, tell me.

MARY
If I told you it might not come true.

GEORGE
What is it you want, Mary? What do you want? You want the moon? Just say . . .

LONG SHOT — *full moon shining through the trees.*

BACK TO SHOT — *George and Mary.*

GEORGE (cont'd)
. . . the word and I'll throw a lasso around it and pull it down. Hey, that's a pretty good idea. I'll give you the moon, Mary.

MARY
I'll take it. And then what?

GEORGE
Well, then you could swallow it and it'd all dissolve, see? And the moonbeams'd shoot out of your fingers and your toes, and the ends of your hair.
(pauses)
Am I talking too much?

MED. CLOSEUP — *Man on porch of house. As George finishes talking, he jumps up out of his chair:*

> MAN
>
> Yes!! Why don't you kiss her instead of talking her to death?

CLOSE SHOT — *George and Mary.*

> GEORGE
>
> How's that?

MED. CLOSEUP — *man on porch.*

> MAN
>
> Why don't you kiss her instead of talking her to death?

CLOSE SHOT — *George and Mary.*

> GEORGE
>
> Want me to kiss her, huh?

CLOSE SHOT — *porch of house.*

> MAN
>
> Aw, youth is wasted on the wrong people.

As he speaks, the man leaves the porch and goes into his house, slamming the front door.

CLOSE SHOT — *George and Mary.*

> GEORGE
>
> Hey, hey, hold on. Hey, mister, come on back out here, and I'll show you some kissing that'll put hair back on your head. What are you . . .

Mary runs off scene. George has been once more standing on the belt of her bath robe, so as she goes, her robe comes off.

> GEORGE
> *(looking around)*
>
> Mary . . .

He drops his bundle of clothes, and picks up Mary's robe. He cannot see her anywhere.

> GEORGE *(cont'd)*
>
> Okay, I give up. Where are you?

CLOSEUP — *bush at edge of sidewalk. We see Mary's face peering out from the leaves.*

> MARY
>
> Over here in the hydrangea bushes.

MED. CLOSE SHOT — *George and Mary. George walks towards the bush.*

GEORGE
Here you are. Catch.

He is about to throw her the robe, when a thought strikes him.

GEORGE *(cont'd)*
Wait a minute. What am I doing? This is a very interesting situation.

MARY
(from the bushes)
Please give me my robe.

GEORGE
Hmm . . . A man doesn't get in a situation like this every day.

MARY
(impatiently)
I'd like to have my robe.

GEORGE
Not in Bedford Falls, anyway.

Mary thrashes around in the bushes. We hear her say:

MARY

Ouch!

GEORGE

Gesundheit. This requires a little thought here.

MARY
(getting mad)
George Bailey! Give me my robe!

GEORGE

I've heard about things like this, but I've never . . .

MARY
(interrupting)
Shame on you. I'm going to tell your mother on you.

GEORGE

Oh, my mother's way up the corner there.

MARY
(desperate)
I'll call the police.

GEORGE

They're way downtown. They'd be on my side, too.

MARY

I'm going to scream!

GEORGE
(thoughtfully)
Maybe I could sell tickets. Let's see. No, the point is, in order to get this robe . . . I've got it! I'll make a deal with you, Mary.

Headlights flash into the scene, and the old Bailey automobile drives in, with Harry at the wheel, and Uncle Billy beside him.

UNCLE BILLY
George! George! Come on home, quick! Your father's had a stroke!

George throws Mary's robe over the bush, and gets into the car.

GEORGE
Mary . . . Mary, I'm sorry. I've got to go.

HARRY
Come on, George, let's hurry.

GEORGE
Did you get a doctor?

UNCLE BILLY
Yes, Campbell's there now.

CLOSEUP — *the hydrangea bush. As the car drives off, Mary, now wearing the robe, rises up from the bush, and follows the car with her eyes.*

FADE OUT

FADE IN

EXT. BAILEY BUILDING AND LOAN SIGN OVER ENTRANCE

INT. BAILEY BUILDING AND LOAN OFFICE — DAY

CLOSE SHOT — *Directors Meeting. There are about twelve directors seated around a long table. They are the substantial citizens of Bedford Falls: Doctor Campbell, a lawyer, an insurance agent, a real estate salesman, etc. Prominently seated among them is Henry F. Potter, his goon beside his wheelchair. Uncle Billy and George are seated among the directors. The Chairman of the Board is Doctor Campbell. They have folders and papers before them, on which they have been reporting. Before each of the directors there are individual reports for them to study.*

> DR. CAMPBELL
> I think that's all we'll need you for, George. I know you're anxious to make a train.

> GEORGE
> *(rising)*
> I have a taxi waiting downstairs.

> DR. CAMPBELL
> I want the Board to know that George gave up his trip to Europe to help straighten things out here these past few months. Good luck to you at school, George.

> GEORGE
> Thanks.

> DR. CAMPBELL
> Now we come to the real purpose of this meeting — to appoint a successor to our dear friend, Peter Bailey.

> POTTER
> Mr. Chairman, I'd like to get to my real purpose.

> MAN
> Wait just a minute now.

> POTTER
> Wait for what? I claim this institution is not necessary to this town. Therefore, Mr. Chairman, I make a motion to dissolve this institution and turn its assets and liabilities over to the receiver.

> UNCLE BILLY
> *(angrily)*
> George, you hear what that buzzard . . .

LAWYER

Mr. Chairman, it's too soon after Peter Bailey's death to discuss chloroforming the Building and Loan.

MAN

Peter Bailey died three months ago. I second Mr. Potter's motion.

DR. CAMPBELL

Very well. In that case I'll ask the two executive officers to withdraw.

Dr. Campbell rises from his seat. George and Uncle Billy start to collect their papers and leave the table.

DR. CAMPBELL *(cont'd)*

But before you go, I'm sure the whole board wishes to express its deep sorrow at the passing of Peter Bailey.

GEORGE

Thank you very much.

DR. CAMPBELL

It was his faith and devotion that are responsible for this organization.

POTTER

I'll go further than that. I'll say that to the public Peter Bailey *was* the Building and Loan.

Everyone looks at him surprised.

UNCLE BILLY
(trying to control himself)
Oh, that's fine, Potter, coming from you, considering that you probably drove him to his grave.

POTTER

Peter Bailey was not a business man. That's what killed him. Oh, I don't mean any disrespect to him, God rest his soul. He was a man of high ideals, so called, but ideals without common sense can ruin this town.
(picking up papers from table)
Now, you take this loan here to Ernie Bishop . . . You know, that fellow that sits around all day on his brains in his taxi. You know . . . I happen to know the bank turned down this loan, but he comes here and we're building him a house worth five thousand dollars. Why?

George is at the door of the office, holding his coat and papers, ready to leave.

GEORGE

Well, I handled that, Mr. Potter. You have all the papers there. His salary, insurance. I can personally vouch for his character.

POTTER
(sarcastically)
A friend of yours?

163

Yes, sir.

POTTER

You see, if you shoot pool with some employee here, you can come and borrow money. What does that get us? A discontented, lazy rabble instead of a thrifty, working class. And all because a few starry-eyed dreamers like Peter Bailey stir them up and fill their heads with a lot of impossible ideas. Now, I say . . .

George puts down his coat, and comes around to the table, incensed by what Potter is saying about his father.

GEORGE

Just a minute — just a minute. Now, hold on, Mr. Potter. You're *right* when you say my father was no *business* man. I know that. Why he ever started this cheap, penny-ante Building and Loan, I'll *never* know. But neither you nor anybody else can say anything against his character, because his whole life was . . . Why, in the twenty-five years since he and Uncle Billy started this thing, he never once thought of himself. Isn't that right, Uncle Billy? He didn't save enough money to send *Harry* to school, let alone me. But he *did* help a few people get out of your slums, Mr. Potter. And what's wrong with that? Why . . . Here, you're all businessmen here. Doesn't it make them better citizens? Doesn't it make them better customers? You . . . you said . . . What'd you say just a minute ago? . . . They had to wait and save their money before they even ought to think of a decent home. Wait! Wait for what? Until their children grow up and leave them? Until they're so old and broken-down that they . . . Do you know how long it takes a working man to save five thousand dollars? Just remember this, Mr. Potter, that this rabble you're talking about . . . they do most of the working and paying and living and dying in this community. Well, is it too much to have them work and pay and live and die in a couple of decent rooms and a bath? Anyway, my *father* didn't think so. People were human beings to him, but to you, a warped, frustrated old man, they're cattle. Well, in my book he died a much richer man than you'll ever be!

POTTER

I'm not interested in your book. I'm talking about the Building and Loan.

GEORGE

I know very well what you're talking about. You're talking about something you can't get your fingers on, and it's galling you. That's what you're talking about, I know.
    (to the Board)
Well, I've said too much. I . . . You're the Board here. You do what you want with this thing. Just one thing more, though. This town needs this measly one-horse institution if only to have some place

where people can come without crawling to Potter. Come on, Uncle Billy!

George leaves the room, followed by the jubilant Uncle Billy. Potter's face is grim with hatred. The "frustrated old man" remark was gall in his veins.

POTTER
Sentimental hogwash! I want my motion . . .

He is interrupted by a babble of talk, as the directors take up the argument.

INT. OUTER OFFICE — BUILDING AND LOAN — DAY

MED. CLOSE SHOT — *George, visibly shaken, is busy with his bag, his papers. He is worried about the outcome of the meeting. Dissolving the Building and Loan will alter all his plans. Uncle Billy follows him around, chattering.*

UNCLE BILLY

Boy, oh, boy, that was telling him, George, old boy. You shut his big mouth.

(to Cousin Tilly and Cousin Eustace)

You should have heard him.

COUSIN EUSTACE

What happened? We heard a lot of yelling.

UNCLE BILLY

Well, we're being voted out of business after twenty-five years. Easy come, easy go.

COUSIN TILLY

(reading newspaper)

Here it is, "Help Wanted — Female."

MED. CLOSE SHOT — DOORWAY TO OFFICE. *Ernie is in the doorway.*

ERNIE

You still want me to hang around, George?

MED. CLOSE SHOT — *George and the others.*

GEORGE

(looking at his watch)

Yeah, I'll be right down.

UNCLE BILLY

Hey, you'll miss your train. You're a week late for school already. Go on.

GEORGE

(indicating Board room)

I wonder what's going on in there?

UNCLE BILLY

Oh, never mind. Don't worry about that. They're putting us out of business. So what? I can get another job. I'm only fifty-five.

COUSIN TILLY

Fifty-six!

UNCLE BILLY

Go on — go on. Hey, look, you gave up your boat trip, now you don't want to miss college too, do you?

Dr. Campbell comes running out, all excited.

DR. CAMPBELL

George! George! They voted Potter down! They want to keep it going!

Cousin Eustace, Cousin Tilly and Uncle Billy cheer wildly, Dr. Campbell and George shake hands.

UNCLE BILLY

Whoopee!

DR. CAMPBELL

But they've got one condition — only one condition.

GEORGE

What's that?

DR. CAMPBELL

That's the best part of it. They've appointed George here as executive secretary to take his father's place.

GEORGE

Oh, no! But, Uncle Billy . . .

DR. CAMPBELL

You can keep him on. That's all right. As secretary you can hire anyone you like.

GEORGE
(emphatically)
Dr. Campbell, now let's get this thing straight. I'm leaving. I'm leaving right now. I'm going to school. This is my last chance. Uncle Billy here, he's your man.

DR. CAMPBELL
But, George, they'll vote with Potter otherwise.

LAP DISSOLVE

EXT. SKY — NIGHT

The same stars we saw in the opening sequence are once more twinkling as we hear the voices from Heaven:

CLARENCE'S VOICE
I know, I know. He didn't go.

JOSEPH'S VOICE
That's right. Not only that, but he gave his school money to his brother Harry, and sent him to college. Harry became a football star — made second team All American.

CLARENCE'S VOICE
Yes, but what happened to George?

LAP DISSOLVE

EXT. RAILROAD STATION — DAY — FOUR YEARS LATER

MED. SHOT — *Characteristic activity; a number of people waiting for the train. Uncle Billy is seated on a baggage wagon eating peanuts as George paces up and down in front of him.*

JOSEPH'S VOICE
George got four years older, waiting for Harry to come back and take over the Building and Loan.

GEORGE
Oh, there are plenty of jobs around for somebody that likes to travel. Look at this.
(takes some folders from his pocket)
There . . . Venezuela oil fields — wanted, man with construction experience. Here's the Yukon, right here — wanted, man with engineering experience.

The WHISTLE *of the approaching train is heard.*

GEORGE *(cont'd)*
Thar she blows. You know what the three most exciting sounds in the world are?

168

UNCLE BILLY

Uh-huh. Breakfast is served; lunch is served, dinner . . .

GEORGE

No, no, no, no! Anchor chains, plane motors, and train whistles.

UNCLE BILLY

Peanut?

WIPE TO:

EXT. TRAIN — DAY

MED. SHOT — *The train comes to a stop, and Harry is among the first to get off, followed by an attractive girl about the same age as he is. George rushes into the shot, and as the brothers embrace:*

GEORGE
(joyously)

There's the professor now! Old professor, Phi Beta Kappa Bailey! All American!

HARRY

Well, if it isn't old George Geographic Explorer Bailey! What? No husky dogs? No sled?
(to Uncle Billy)
Uncle Billy, you haven't changed a bit.

UNCLE BILLY

Nobody ever changes around here. You know that.

GEORGE

Oh, am I glad to see you.

HARRY

Say, where's Mother?

GEORGE

She's home cooking the fatted calf. Come on, let's go.

HARRY

Oh, wait. Wait . . . Wait a minute.

CLOSE SHOT — *the group, including Ruth Dakin. This is the young lady who came off the train with Harry. In the excitement of greetings she has been momentarily forgotten. She stands, smiling, waiting.*

GEORGE

Hello.

UNCLE BILLY

How do you do.

HARRY

Ruth Dakin.

RUTH
Ruth Dakin Bailey, if you don't mind.

George and Uncle Billy stare, astounded.

UNCLE BILLY
Huh?

HARRY
Well, I wired you I had a surprise. Here she is. Meet the wife.

George is thunderstruck. He takes Ruth's hand.

UNCLE BILLY
Well, what do you know — wife.

GEORGE
Well, how do you do. Congratulations. Congratulations. What am I
doing?

He kisses Ruth. CAMERA MOVES WITH *them down the platform.*

> GEORGE
> Harry, why didn't you tell somebody?
> *(to Ruth)*
> What's a pretty girl like you doing marrying this two-headed brother
> of mine?

> RUTH
> *(smiling)*
> Well, I'll tell you. It's purely mercenary. My father offered him a job.

George stops, with a sinking feeling. Uncle Billy and Ruth continue out of shot.
Harry stops with George.

> UNCLE BILLY
> *(as he moves off)*
> Oh, he gets you and a job? Well, Harry's cup runneth over.

HARRY

George . . . About that job. Ruth spoke out of turn. I never said I'd take it. You've been holding the bag here for four years, and . . . well, I won't let you down, George. I would like to . . . Oh, wait a minute, I forgot the bags. I'll be right back.

He runs out of shot, George watching him.

CLOSE SHOT — *George slowly moves after Uncle Billy and Ruth. He is thinking deeply.*

UNCLE BILLY'S VOICE

It was a surprise to me. This is the new Mrs. Bailey, my nephew's wife. Old, old friend of the family.

RUTH'S VOICE

Oh, of course. I've heard him speak of you.

UNCLE BILLY'S VOICE

And I want to tell you, we're going to give the biggest party this town ever saw.

CAMERA MOVES WITH *George as he comes into the scene. Ruth detaches herself from the group, and offers George some popcorn.*

RUTH
(to George)
Here, have some popcorn. George, George, George . . . that's all Harry ever talks about.

GEORGE
(quietly)
Ruth, this . . . what about this job?

RUTH

Oh, well, my father owns a glass factory in Buffalo. He wants to get Harry started in the research business.

GEORGE

Is it a good job?

RUTH

Oh, yes, very. Not much money, but a good future, you know. Harry's a genius at research. My father fell in love with him.

GEORGE

And you did, too?

Ruth nods, smiling.

WIPE TO:

EXT. FRONT PORCH — BAILEY HOME — NIGHT

MED. CLOSE SHOT — *Cousin Eustace is taking a photograph of the family group assembled on the porch. Flash bulbs go off, and the group breaks up. The crowd enters the front door of the house, leaving George and Uncle Billy on the porch.*

CLOSE SHOT — *George and Uncle Billy. The latter is tipsy. He feels very high.*

> UNCLE BILLY
>
> Oh, boy, oh boy, oh boy. I feel so good I could spit in Potter's eye. I think I will. What did you say, huh? Oh, maybe I'd better go home.

He looks around for his hat, which is on his head.

> UNCLE BILLY *(cont'd)*
>
> Where's my hat? Where's my . . .

George takes the hat from Uncle Billy's head and hands it to him.

> UNCLE BILLY *(cont'd)*
>
> Oh, thank you, George. Which one is mine?

> GEORGE
> *(laughing)*
> The middle one.

> UNCLE BILLY
>
> Oh, thank you, George, old boy, old boy. Now, look — if you'll point me in the right direction . . . would you do that? George?

GEORGE

Right down here.

They descend the porch steps, and George turns his uncle around and heads him down the street.

UNCLE BILLY

Old Building and Loan pal, huh . . .

GEORGE

Now you just turn this way and go right straight down.

UNCLE BILLY

That way, huh?

He staggers out of the scene, and as George turns away, we hear Uncle Billy singing "My Wild Irish Rose." There is a CRASH *of cans and bottles, then:*

UNCLE BILLY'S VOICE

I'm all right. I'm all right. ". . . the sweetest flower that grows . . ."

EXT. HOUSE — NIGHT

MED. CLOSE SHOT. *George is standing at the garden gate. He takes some travel folders from his pocket, looks at them and throws them away. He is obviously disturbed about the latest turn of events. His mother comes out of the house and kisses him.*

GEORGE

Hello, Mom.

MRS. BAILEY

(as she kisses him)

That's for nothing. How do you like her?

She nods toward the house, where Harry and Ruth, among a crowd of other couples, are dancing to the MUSIC *of a phonograph, and can be seen through the front door.*

GEORGE

She's swell.

MRS. BAILEY

Looks like she can keep Harry on his toes.

GEORGE

Keep him out of Bedford Falls, anyway.

MRS. BAILEY

Did you know that Mary Hatch is back from school?

GEORGE

Uh-huh.

MRS. BAILEY

Came back three days ago.

GEORGE

Hmmmm . . .

MRS. BAILEY

Nice girl, Mary.

GEORGE

Hmmmm . . .

MRS. BAILEY

Kind that will help you find the answers, George.

GEORGE

Hmmm . . .

MRS. BAILEY

Oh, stop that grunting.

GEORGE

Hmmm . . .

MRS. BAILEY

Can you give me one good reason why you shouldn't call on Mary?

GEORGE

Sure — Sam Wainwright.

MRS. BAILEY

Hmmm?

GEORGE

Yes, Sam's crazy about Mary.

MRS. BAILEY

Well, she's not crazy about him.

GEORGE

Well, how do you know? Did she discuss it with you?

MRS. BAILEY

No.

GEORGE

Well then, how do you know?

MRS. BAILEY

Well, I've got eyes, haven't I? Why, she lights up like a firefly whenever you're around.

GEORGE

Oh . . .

MRS. BAILEY

And besides, Sam Wainwright's away in New York, and you're here in Bedford Falls.

GEORGE

And all's fair in love and war?

MRS. BAILEY

(primly)

I don't know about war.

GEORGE

Mother, you know, I can see right through you — right to your back collar button . . . trying to get rid of me, huh?

MOTHER

Uh-huh.

They kiss. Mrs. Bailey puts George's hat on his head.

GEORGE

Well, here's your hat, what's your hurry? All right, mother, old Building and Loan pal, I think I'll go out and find a girl and do a little passionate necking.

MRS. BAILEY

Oh, George!

GEORGE

Now if you'll just point me in the right direction . . . This direction?
(as he leaves)
Good night, Mrs. Bailey.

WIPE TO:

EXT. MAIN STREET BEDFORD FALLS — NIGHT

CLOSE SHOT — *George is standing in the middle of the street, hands in his pockets. As a girl passes, he turns and watches her for a moment. He is obviously undecided as to what he wants to do.*

EXT. VIOLET BICK'S BEAUTY SHOP — NIGHT

MED. SHOT — *Violet is locking up for the night. A couple of men are crowding around her, each one bent on taking her out. There is laughter, kidding and pawing. She looks up and sees George standing there.*

VIOLET

(to the two men)

Excuse me . . .

MAN

Now, wait a minute.

VIOLET
I think I got a date. But stick around fellows, just in case, huh?

MAN
We'll wait for you, baby.

CAMERA PANS WITH *Violet as she crosses the street to George.*

MED. CLOSE SHOT — *George and Violet.*

VIOLET
Hello, Georgie-Porgie.

GEORGE
Hello, Vi.

He looks her over. Violet takes her beauty shop seriously and she's an eyeful. She senses the fact that George is far from immune to her attractions. She links her arm in his and continues on down the street with him.

> VIOLET
>
> What gives?

> GEORGE
>
> Nothing.

> VIOLET
>
> Where are you going?

> GEORGE
>
> Oh, I'll probably end up down at the library.

They stop walking and face one another.

> VIOLET
>
> Georgie, don't you ever get tired of just reading about things?

Her eyes are seductive and guileful as she looks up at him. He is silent for a moment, then blurts out:

> GEORGE
>
> Yes . . . what are you doing tonight?

> VIOLET
> *(feigned surprise)*
>
> Not a thing.

> GEORGE
>
> Are you game, Vi? Let's make a night of it.

> VIOLET
> *(just what she wanted)*
>
> Oh, I'd love it, Georgie. What'll we do?

> GEORGE
>
> Let's go out in the fields and take off our shoes and walk through the grass.

> VIOLET
>
> Huh?

> GEORGE
>
> Then we can go up to the falls. It's beautiful up there in the moonlight, and there's a green pool up there, and we can swim in it. Then we can climb Mt. Bedford, and smell the pines, and watch the sunrise against the peaks, and . . . we'll stay up there the whole night, and everybody'll be talking and there'll be a terrific scandal . . .

> VIOLET
> *(interrupting)*
>
> George, have you gone crazy? Walk in the grass in my bare feet? Why it's ten miles up to Mt. Bedford.

GEORGE
Shhh . . .

VIOLET
(angrily)
You think just because you . . .

By this time a small crowd has collected to watch the above scene. Violet is furious, and talking in a loud voice, and George is trying to quiet her. Finally:

GEORGE
Okay, just forget about the whole thing.

As George stalks off, the crowd breaks into laughter, and we:

WIPE TO:

182

EXT. RESIDENTIAL STREET — NIGHT

CLOSE SHOT — *George is walking slowly past the Hatch home. He stares medi-tatively at the simple dwelling, then he starts walking ahead. But after a few steps he turns around and starts back. He walks past the house a few yards, turns, and starts back again.*

INT. BEDROOM WINDOW — HATCH HOME — NIGHT

CLOSE SHOT — *Mary is looking out the window, watching George walk back and forth.*

MARY
What are you doing, picketing?

George stops, startled, and looks up.

GEORGE
Hello, Mary. I just happened to be passing by.

MARY
Yes, so I noticed. Have you made up your mind?

GEORGE
How's that?

                    MARY

Have you made up your mind?

                    GEORGE

About what?

                    MARY

About coming in. Your mother just phoned and said you were on your
way over to pay me a visit.

EXT. STREET — NIGHT

MED. LONG SHOT — *George looks surprised at this.*

                    GEORGE

My mother just called you? Well, how did she know?

                    MARY

Didn't you tell her?

GEORGE

I didn't tell anybody. I just went for a walk and happened to be passing by . . .

But Mary has disappeared from the window.

GEORGE *(cont'd)*
(to himself)
What do you . . . went for a walk, that's all.

INT. HATCH HOME — NIGHT

MED. CLOSE SHOT — *stairway to upper hall. Mary is running down the stairs.*

MARY
(calling out)
I'll be downstairs, mother.

MRS. HATCH'S VOICE
All right, dear.

Mary looks in a mirror at the bottom of the stairs, and fixes her hair. She is plainly excited at George's visit. She runs into the parlor and puts a sketch on an easel.

INSERT: THE SKETCH. *It is a caricature of George throwing a lasso around the moon. Lettering on the drawing says: "George Lassos The Moon."*

BACK TO SHOT — *Mary runs into the hall, opens the phonograph and puts on a record of "Buffalo Gals." Then she opens the front door and stands there waiting for George.*

INT. DOORWAY — NIGHT

MED. CLOSE SHOT — *George is struggling with the gate — he finally kicks it open and starts slowly up the path toward Mary.*

MARY
Well, are you coming in or aren't you?

GEORGE
Well, I'll come in for a minute, but I didn't tell anybody I was coming over here.

CLOSE SHOT — *Mary and George are in the entrance hall.*

GEORGE
When did you get back?

MARY
Tuesday.

GEORGE
Where'd you get that dress?

MARY

Do you like it?

GEORGE

It's all right. I thought you'd go back to New York like Sam and Ingie, and the rest of them.

MARY

Oh, I worked there a couple of vacations, but I don't know . . . I guess I was homesick.

GEORGE
(shocked)
Homesick? For Bedford Falls?

MARY

Yes, and my family and . . . oh, everything. Would you like to sit down?

They go through the doorway into the parlor.

GEORGE

All right, for a minute. I still can't understand it though. You know I didn't tell anybody I was coming here.

MARY

Would you rather leave?

GEORGE

No, I don't want to be rude.

MARY

Well, then, sit down.

George sees the cartoon on the easel, and bends down for a close look at it.

GEORGE
(indicating cartoon)
Some joke, huh?

CLOSE SHOT — *George and Mary sitting on the divan. He is uncomfortable, and she tries desperately to keep the conversation alive.*

GEORGE

Well, I see it still smells like pine needles in here.

MARY

Thank you.

There is silence for a moment, then Mary joins in singing with the phonograph record which has been playing all through the above scene:

MARY
(singing)
"And dance by the light . . ."

GEORGE

What's the matter? Oh, yeah . . . yeah . . .

He looks at his watch, as though about to leave.

GEORGE *(cont'd)*

Well, I . . .

MARY

(desperately)

It was nice about your brother Harry, and Ruth, wasn't it?

GEORGE

Oh . . . yeah, yeah. That's all right.

MARY

Don't you like her?

GEORGE

Well, of course I like her. She's a peach.

MARY

Oh, it's just marriage in general you're not enthusiastic about, huh?

GEORGE

No. Marriage is all right for Harry, and Marty, and Sam and you.

INT. STAIRS

MED. CLOSE SHOT — *Mrs. Hatch, in a bathrobe, and with her hair in curlers, is leaning over the bannister as she calls:*

MRS. HATCH

Mary! Mary!

INT. PARLOR — NIGHT

CLOSE SHOT — *George and Mary seated on the divan.*

MRS. HATCH'S VOICE

Who's down there with you?

MARY

It's George Bailey, mother.

MRS. HATCH'S VOICE

George Bailey! What's he want?

MARY

I don't know.
      (to George)
What do you want?

GEORGE

(indignant)

Me? Not a thing. I just came in to get warm.

MARY
(to Mother)
He's making violent love to me, mother.

George is aghast.

MRS. HATCH'S VOICE
You tell him to go right back home, and don't you leave the house, either. Sam Wainwright promised to call you from New York tonight.

GEORGE
(heatedly)
But your mother needn't . . . you know I didn't come here to . . . to . . . to . . .

MARY
(rising)
What did you come here for?

GEORGE
I don't know. You tell me. You're supposed to be the one that has all the answers. You tell me.

MARY
(terribly hurt)
Oh, why don't you go home?

GEORGE
(almost shouting)
That's where I'm going. I don't know why I came here in the first place! Good night!

As George leaves the room, the telephone in the hall starts ringing.

MARY
(to George)
Good night!

MRS. HATCH'S VOICE
Mary! Mary! The telephone! It's Sam!

INT. HALL — NIGHT

MED. CLOSE SHOT — *Mary comes into the hall.*

MARY
(almost weeping)
I'll get it.

MRS. HATCH
(from stairway)
Whatever were you doing that you couldn't hear?

As Mary comes into the hall, she stops by the phonograph, which is still playing "Buffalo Gals," takes off the record with a jerk, and smashes it against the machine. The phone is still ringing.

MRS. HATCH

Mary, he's waiting!

MARY

Hello.

As Mary picks up the phone, George comes in from the front porch.

GEORGE

I forgot my hat.

MARY
(overly enthusiastic)

Hee-haw! Hello, Sam, how are you?

SAM'S VOICE

Aw, great. Gee, it's good to hear your voice again.

George has stopped, hat in hand, to hear the first greetings.

MARY

Oh, well, that's awfully sweet of you, Sam.
(glances toward door, sees George still there)
There's an old friend of yours here. George Bailey.

SAM'S VOICE

You mean old moss-back George?

MARY

Yes, old moss-back George.

SAM'S VOICE

Hee-haw! Put him on.

MARY

Wait a minute. I'll call him.
(calling)
George!

MRS. HATCH

He doesn't want to speak to George, you idiot!

MARY

He does so. He asked for him.
(calling)
Geo . . . George, Sam wants to speak to you.

She hands the instrument to George.

GEORGE

Hello, Sam.

INT. SAM'S NEW YORK OFFICE — NIGHT

MED. CLOSE SHOT — *Sam is seated at his desk, while a couple of his friends are nearby, with highballs in their hands.*

192

> SAM
> *(into phone)*
> Well, George Baileyoffski! Hey, a fine pal you are. What're you trying
> to do? Steal my girl?

INT. HATCH HALL — NIGHT

MED. CLOSEUP — *George and Mary.*

> GEORGE
> *(into phone)*
> What do you mean? Nobody's trying to steal your girl. Here . . . here's
> Mary.

> SAM'S VOICE
> No, wait a minute. Wait a minute. I want to talk to both of you. Tell
> Mary to get on the extension.

> GEORGE
> *(to Mary)*
> Here. You take it. You tell him.

MARY

Mother's on the extension.

INT. UPPER HALLWAY — NIGHT

CLOSE SHOT — *Mrs. Hatch. As she hears this, she hastily hangs up the extension phone on which she has been listening.*

BACK TO SHOT — *George and Mary.*

MARY

We can both hear. Come here.

Mary takes the telephone from George and holds it so that of necessity George's cheek is almost against hers. He is very conscious of her proximity.

MARY *(cont'd)*
(on phone)
We're listening, Sam.

SAM'S VOICE

I have a big deal coming up that's going to make us all rich. George, you remember that night in Martini's bar when you told me you read someplace about making plastics out of soybeans?

GEORGE

Huh? Yeah-yeah-yeah . . . soybeans. Yeah.

SAM'S VOICE

Well, Dad snapped up the idea. He's going to build a factory outside of Rochester. How do you like that?

Mary is watching George interestedly. George is very conscious of her, close to him.

GEORGE

Rochester? Well, why Rochester?

gSAM'S VOICE

Well, why not? Can you think of anything better?

GEORGE

Oh, I don't know . . . why not right here? You remember that old tool and machinery works? You tell your father he can get that for a song. And all the labor he wants, too. Half the town was thrown out of work when they closed down.

SAM'S VOICE

That so? Well, I'll tell him. Hey, that sounds great. Oh, baby, I knew you'd come through. Now, here's the point. Mary, Mary, you're in on this too. Now listen. Have you got any money?

GEORGE

Money? Yeah . . . well, a little.

SAM'S VOICE

Well, now listen. I want you to put every cent you've got into our stock, you hear? And George, I may have a job for you, that is, unless you're still married to that broken-down Building and Loan. This is the biggest thing since radio, and I'm letting you in on the ground floor. Oh, Mary . . . Mary . . .

MARY
(nervously)
I'm here.

SAM'S VOICE

Would you tell that guy I'm giving him the chance of a lifetime, you hear? The chance of a lifetime.

As Mary listens, she turns to look at George, her lips almost on his lips.

> MARY
> *(whispering)*
> He says it's the chance of a lifetime.

George can stand it no longer. He drops the phone with a crash, grabs Mary by the shoulders and shakes her. Mary begins to cry.

> GEORGE
> *(fiercely)*
> Now you listen to me! I don't want any plastics! I don't want any ground floors, and I don't want to get married — ever — to anyone! You understand that? I want to do what *I* want to do. And you're . . . and you're . . .

He pulls her to him in a fierce embrace. Two meant for each other find themselves in tearful ecstasy.

GEORGE (cont'd)

Oh, Mary . . . Mary . . .

MARY

George . . . George . . . George . . .

GEORGE

Mary . . .

CLOSE SHOT — *Mrs. Hatch at the top of the stairs. She practically faints at what she sees.*

WIPE TO:

INT. FRONT HALL BAILEY HOME — DAY — SEVERAL MONTHS LATER

CLOSEUP — *Cousin Tilly's face fills the screen as she cries:*

COUSIN TILLY

Here they come!

CAMERA PULLS BACK, *and we hear the* SOUND *of the Wedding March. People are crowded into the rooms: family, friends, neighbors. There is a din of conversation. Mary and George appear at the top of the stairs in travelling clothes, with Mrs. Hatch, red-eyed behind them. Mary throws her bouquet, which is caught by Violet Bick. As they come out onto the porch, we see that it is raining. Nevertheless, Cousin Eustace has his camera equipment set up and is taking pictures of the group. George and Mary dodge through the rain and a shower of rice, and get into Ernie's taxicab, which pulls away from the curb.*

EXT. PORCH OF BAILEY HOUSE — DAY

CLOSE SHOT — *Mrs. Bailey and Annie, the colored maid.*

MRS. BAILEY

First Harry, now George. Annie, we're just two old maids now.

ANNIE

You speak for yourself, Mrs. B.

INT. ERNIE'S CAB — DAY

CLOSE SHOT — *George, Mary and Ernie. George and Mary are in each other's arms.*

ERNIE

If either of you two see a stranger around here, it's me.

GEORGE

Hey, look! Somebody's driving this cab.

Ernie reaches over and hands George a bottle of champagne done up in gift wrappings.

ERNIE

Bert, the cop, sent this over. He said to float away to Happy Land on the bubbles.

GEORGE

Oh, look at this. Champagne!

MARY

Good old Bert.

ERNIE

By the way, where are you two going on this here now honeymoon?

GEORGE

Where we going?
(takes out a fat roll of bills)
Look at this. There's the kitty, Ernie. Here, come on, count it, Mary.

MARY

I feel like a bootlegger's wife.
            (holding up the money)
Look!

GEORGE

You know what we're going to do? We're going to shoot the works. A whole week in New York. A whole week in Bermuda. The highest hotels — the oldest champagne — the richest caviar — the hottest music, and the prettiest wife!

ERNIE

That does it! Then what?

GEORGE

            (to Mary)
Then what, honey?

MARY

After that, who cares?

GEORGE

That does it — come here.

The cab passes the bank, and Ernie sees a crowd of people around the door. He stops the cab.

LONG SHOT — *scurrying people under umbrellas, swarming around the bank doors. Panic is in the air. Attendants are trying to close down. Several people come running past the cab.*

INT. CAB

CLOSE SHOT — *George, Mary and Ernie.*

> ERNIE
> Don't look now, but there's something funny going on over there at the bank, George. I've never really seen one, but that's got all the earmarks of a run.

> PASSERBY
> Hey, Ernie, if you got any money in the bank, you better hurry.

                    MARY
            George, let's not stop. Let's go!

George gets out of the cab and looks down the street.

                    GEORGE
            Just a minute, dear. Oh-oh . . .

                    MARY
            Please, let's not stop, George.

                    GEORGE
            I'll be back in a minute, Mary.

George runs off up the street, toward the Building and Loan.

EXT. BUILDING AND LOAN — DAY

CLOSE SHOT — *sidewalk. An iron grill blocks the street entrance to the Building and Loan. It has been locked. A crowd of men and women are waiting around the grill. They are simply dressed people, to whom their savings are a matter of life and death.*

George comes in, with an assumed cheerful manner. The people look at him silently, half shamefaced, but grimly determined on their rights. In their hearts there is panic and fear.

                    GEORGE
            Hello, everybody. Mrs. Thompson, how are you? Charlie? What's the matter here, can't you get in?

No one answers. He quickly unlocks the grill door and pushes it open. Followed by the crowd, George runs upstairs and into the outer offices of the Building and Loan.

INT. OUTER OFFICE — BUILDING AND LOAN — DAY

MED. CLOSE SHOT — *George, followed by the still silent people, comes in. Uncle Billy is standing in the doorway to his private office, taking a drink from a bottle. He motions to George to join him.*

                    GEORGE
            What is this, Uncle Billy? A holiday?

                    UNCLE BILLY
            George . . .

He points to George's office. George turns back cheerfully to the crowd.

                    GEORGE
            Come on in, everybody. That's right, just come in.

George vaults over the counter.

GEORGE *(cont'd)*

Now look, why don't you all sit down. There are a lot of seats over there. Just make yourselves at home.

UNCLE BILLY

George, can I see you a minute.

The people ignore George and remain standing in front of the teller's window. They all have their passbooks out. George hurries into his office where Uncle Billy is waiting for him.

INT. GEORGE'S OFFICE — DAY

CLOSE SHOT — *George and Uncle Billy.*

GEORGE

Why didn't you call me?

UNCLE BILLY

I just did, but they said you left. This is a pickle, George, this is a pickle.

GEORGE

All right now, what happened? How did it start?

UNCLE BILLY

How does anything like this ever start? All I know is the bank called our loan.

GEORGE

When?

UNCLE BILLY

About an hour ago. I had to hand over all our cash.

GEORGE

All of it?

UNCLE BILLY

Every cent of it, and it still was less than we owe.

GEORGE

Holy mackerel!

UNCLE BILLY

And then I got scared, George, and closed the doors. I . . . I . . .
I . . .

GEORGE

The whole town's gone crazy.

The telephone rings. Uncle Billy picks it up.

UNCLE BILLY

Yes, hello? George . . . it's Potter.

GEORGE

Hello?

INT. POTTER'S LIBRARY — DAY

MED. SHOT — *Potter seated behind his desk, his goon alongside him. Standing in front of the desk is a distinguished-looking man, obviously the president of the bank. He is mopping his brow with his handkerchief.*

> POTTER
> George, there is a rumor around town that you've closed your doors. Is that true? Oh, well, I'm very glad to hear that. . . . George, are you all right? Do you need any police?

INT. GEORGE'S OFFICE — DAY

CLOSE SHOT — *George and Uncle Billy.*

> GEORGE
> *(on phone)*
> Police? What for?

INT. POTTER'S OFFICE — DAY

MED. CLOSE SHOT — *Potter talking on phone.*

> POTTER
> Well, mobs get pretty ugly sometimes, you know. George, I'm going all out to help in this crisis. I've just guaranteed the bank sufficient funds to meet their needs. They'll close up for a week, and then re-open.

INT. GEORGE'S OFFICE — DAY

CLOSE SHOT — *George and Uncle Billy.*

> GEORGE
> *(to Uncle Billy)*
> He just took over the bank.

INT. POTTER'S OFFICE — DAY

CLOSE SHOT — *Potter on phone.*

> POTTER
> I may lose a fortune, but I'm willing to guarantee your people too. Just tell them to bring their shares over here and I will pay them fifty cents on the dollar.

INT. GEORGE'S OFFICE — DAY

CLOSE SHOT — *George and Uncle Billy.*

> GEORGE
> *(furiously)*
> Aw, you never miss a trick, do you, Potter? Well, you're going to miss this one.

George bangs the receiver down, and turns to meet Uncle Billy's anxious look.

INT. POTTER'S OFFICE

CLOSEUP — *Potter on phone.*

> POTTER
> If you close your doors before six P.M. you will never reopen.

He realizes George has hung up, and clicks the phone furiously.

INT. GEORGE'S OFFICE — DAY

CLOSE SHOT — *George and Uncle Billy.*

> UNCLE BILLY
> George, was it a nice wedding? Gosh, I wanted to be there.

> GEORGE
> Yeah . . .
> *(looks at string on Uncle Billy's finger)*
> . . . you can take this one off now.

An ominous SOUND *of angry voices comes from the other room. George and Uncle Billy exit from George's office.*

INT. OUTER OFFICE — BLDG. AND LOAN — DAY

MED. CLOSE SHOT — *More people have crowded around the counter. Their muttering stops and they stand silent and grim. There is panic in their faces.*

> GEORGE
> *(from behind counter)*
> Now, just remember that this thing isn't as black as it appears.

As George speaks, sirens are heard passing in the street below. The crowd turn to the windows, then back to George.

> GEORGE *(cont'd)*
> I have some news for you, folks. I've just talked to old man Potter, and he's guaranteed cash payments at the bank. The bank's going to reopen next week.

> ED
> But, George, I got *my* money here.

> CHARLIE
> Did he guarantee this place?

> GEORGE
> Well, no, Charlie. I didn't even ask him. We don't need Potter over here.

Mary and Ernie have come into the room during this scene. Mary stands watching silently.

CHARLIE

I'll take mine now.

GEORGE

No, but you . . . you . . . you're thinking of this place all wrong. As
if I had the money back in a safe. The money's not here. Your money's
in Joe's house . . .
                    (to one of the men)
. . . right next to yours. And in the Kennedy house, and Mrs. Mack-
lin's house, and a hundred others. Why, you're lending them the
money to build, and then, they're going to pay it back to you as best
they can. Now what are you going to do? Foreclose on them?

TOM

I got two hundred and forty-two dollars in here, and two hundred and
forty-two dollars isn't going to break anybody.

MED. CLOSE SHOT — ANOTHER ANGLE

GEORGE
                    (handing him a slip)
Okay, Tom. All right. Here you are. You sign this. You'll get your
money in sixty days.

TOM

Sixty days?

GEORGE

Well, now that's what you agreed to when you bought your shares.

*There is a commotion at the outer doors. A man (Randall) comes in and makes
his way up to Tom.*

RANDALL

Tom . . . Tom, did you get your money?

TOM

No.

RANDALL

Well, I did. Old man Potter'll pay fifty cents on the dollar for every
share you got.
                    (shows bills)

CROWD
                    (ad lib)
Fifty cents on the dollar!

RANDALL

Yes, cash!

TOM
                    (to George)
Well, what do you say?

206

GEORGE

Now, Tom, you have to stick to your original agreement. Now give us sixty days on this.

TOM
(turning to Randall)
Okay, Randall.

He starts out.

MRS. THOMPSON

Are you going to go to Potter's?

TOM

Better to get half than nothing.

A few other people start for the door. CAMERA PANS WITH *George as he vaults over the counter quickly, speaking to the people.*

GEORGE

Tom! Tom! Randall! Now wait . . . now listen . . . now listen to me. I beg of you not to do this thing. If Potter gets hold of this Building and Loan there'll never be another decent house built in this town. He's already got charge of the bank. He's got the bus line. He's got the department stores. And now he's after us. Why? Well, it's very simple. Because we're cutting in on his business, that's why. And because he wants to keep you living in his slums and paying the kind of rent he decides.

The people are still trying to get out, but some of them have stood still, listening to him. George has begun to make an impression on them.

GEORGE *(cont'd)*

Joe, you lived in one of his houses, didn't you? Well, have you forgotten? Have you forgotten what he charged you for that broken-down shack?

(to Ed)

Here, Ed. You know, you remember last year when things weren't going so well, and you couldn't make your payments. You didn't lose your house, did you? Do you think Potter would have let you keep it?

(turns to address the room again)

Can't you understand what's happening here? Don't you see what's happening? Potter isn't selling. Potter's buying! And why? Because we're panicky and he's not. That's why. He's picking up some bargains. Now, we can get through this thing all right. We've got to stick together, though. We've got to have faith in each other.

MRS. THOMPSON

But my husband hasn't worked in over a year, and I need money.

WOMAN

How am I going to live until the bank opens?

MAN

I got doctor bills to pay.

MAN

I need cash.

MAN

Can't feed my kids on faith.

During this scene Mary has come up behind the counter. Suddenly, as the people once more start moving towards the door, she holds up a roll of bills, and calls out:

MARY

How much do you need?

George jumps over the counter and takes the money from Mary.

GEORGE

Hey! I got two thousand dollars! Here's two thousand dollars. This'll tide us over until the bank reopens.

    (to Tom)

All right, Tom, how much do you need?

TOM

    (doggedly)

Two hundred and forty-two dollars!

GEORGE

    (pleading)

Aw, Tom, just enough to tide you over till the bank reopens.

TOM

I'll take two hundred and forty-two dollars.

George starts rapidly to count out the money. Tom throws his passbook on the counter.

GEORGE

There you are.

TOM

That'll close my account.

GEORGE

Your account's still here. That's a loan.

Mary turns and slips out through the crowd, followed by Ernie. George hands the two hundred and forty-two dollars to Tom, and speaks to Ed, the next in line.

GEORGE *(cont'd)*

Okay. All right, Ed?

ED

I got three hundred dollars here, George.

Uncle Billy takes out his wallet and takes out all the cash he's got.

GEORGE

Aw, now, Ed . . . what'll it take till the bank reopens? What do you need?

ED

Well, I suppose twenty dollars.

210

GEORGE

Twenty dollars. Now you're talking. Fine. Thanks, Ed.
        (to Mrs. Thompson, next in line)
All right, now, Mrs. Thompson. How much do you want?

MRS. THOMPSON

But it's your own money, George.

GEORGE

Never mind about that. How much do you want?

MRS. THOMPSON

I can get along with twenty, all right.

GEORGE
        (counting it out)
Twenty dollars.

MRS. THOMPSON

And I'll sign a paper.

GEORGE

You don't have to sign anything. I know you'll pay it back when you
can. That's okay.
        (to woman next in line)
All right, Mrs. Davis.

MRS. DAVIS

Could I have seventeen-fifty?

GEORGE

Seven . . .
        (he kisses her)
Bless your heart. Of course you can have it. You got fifty cents?
        (counting)
Seven . . .

WIPE TO:

INT. OUTER OFFICE BUILDING AND LOAN — NIGHT

CLOSE SHOT — *George, Uncle Billy and Cousin Tilly are behind the counter,
watching the minute hand of a clock on the wall as George counts off the seconds.
Cousin Eustace is ready to close the door.*

UNCLE BILLY
        (excitedly)
We're going to make it, George. They'll never close us up today!

GEORGE
        (counting)
Six . . . five . . . four . . . three . . . two . . . one . . . Bingo!

*Cousin Eustace slams and locks the door, and scurries around the counter to join
the others.*

GEORGE *(cont'd)*
We made it! Look . . .
    (holds up bills)
. . . look, we're still in business! We've still got two bucks left!

Uncle Billy is taking a drink out of his bottle.

GEORGE *(cont'd)*
Well, let's have some of that. Get some glasses, Cousin Tilly.
    (to Uncle Billy)
We're a couple of financial wizards.

UNCLE BILLY
Those Rockefellers!

GEORGE
Get a tray for these great big important simoleons.

UNCLE BILLY
We'll save them for seed. A toast!

They raise their glasses.

> GEORGE

A toast! A toast to Papa Dollar and to Mama Dollar, and if you want the old Building and Loan to stay in business, you better have a family real quick.

> COUSIN TILLY

I wish they were rabbits.

> GEORGE

I wish they were too. Okay, let's put them in the safe and see what happens.

The four of them parade through the office; George puts the two dollars in the safe.

CLOSE SHOT — *group around the safe door. As George comes out:*

> COUSIN EUSTACE
> *(handing out cigars)*

Folks, folks, wedding cigars!

> GEORGE
> *(startled)*

Oh-oh . . . wedding! Holy mackerel, I'm married! Where's Mary? Mary . . .
> *(he runs around looking for her)*

Poor Mary. Look I've got a train to catch.
> *(looks at his watch)*

Well, the train's gone. I wonder if Ernie's still here with his taxicab?

George rushes into his office to look out the window.

> COUSIN TILLY
> *(on telephone)*

George, there's a call for you.

> GEORGE

Look, will you get my wife on the phone? She's probably over at her mother's.

> COUSIN TILLY

Mrs. Bailey is on the phone.

INT. GEORGE'S OFFICE

MED. CLOSEUP — *George is thoroughly rattled.*

> GEORGE

I don't want Mrs. Bailey. I want my wife. Mrs. Bailey! Oh, that's my wife! Here, I'll take it in here.
> *(picks up phone)*

Mary? Hello. Listen, dear, I'm sorry . . . What? Come home? What home? Three-twenty Sycamore? Well, what . . . whose home is that? The Waldorf Hotel, huh?

WIPE TO:

EXT. OLD GRANVILLE HOUSE — NIGHT

MED. LONG SHOT — *An old-fashioned, run-down house, unpainted and warped by the weather. It once had class but has not been lived in for years. This is the house that George and Mary will live in from now on. The rain is pouring down. A faint glow of light shines out from bottom windows. George hurries into scene. He stops to make sure it is the right number before going up the steps.*

EXT. SIDE OF HOUSE — NIGHT

CLOSE SHOT — *Bert and man working in rain, sorting through travel posters.*

> MAN
>
> Hey, this is the company's posters, and the company won't like this.

> BERT
>
> How would you like to get a ticket next week? Haven't you any romance in you?

> MAN
>
> Sure I have, but I got rid of it.

> BERT
> *(reading poster)*
>
> Liver pills! Who wants to see liver pills on their honeymoon? What? They want romantic places, beautiful places . . . places George wants to go.

A sharp whistle is heard.

CLOSE SHOT — *window of house. Ernie is leaning from the window.*

> ERNIE
>
> Hey, Bert, here he comes.

CLOSE SHOT — *Bert and man.*

> BERT
>
> Come on, we got to get this up. He's coming.

> MAN
>
> Who?

> BERT
>
> The groom, idiot. Come on, get that ladder.

> MAN
> *(disgustedly)*
>
> What are they — ducks?

CLOSE SHOT — *side porch of house. Bert and the man are putting up travel posters to cover up the broken windows.*

BERT

Get that ladder up here.

MAN

All right — all right.

BERT

Hurry up . . . hurry up . . . hurry up.

MAN

I'm hurrying.

MED. CLOSE SHOT — *George is approaching the front door of the house, on which a sign is hanging: "Bridal Suite." Ernie looks out through the curtain covering the broken glass of the front door.*

ERNIE

Hiya . . . Good evening, sir.

Ernie opens the door, revealing himself as a home-made butler. This has been accomplished by rolling up his pants, and putting on an old coachman's hat. George enters.

ERNIE
Entray, monsieur, entray.

INT. GRANVILLE HOUSE — NIGHT

CLOSE SHOT — *George enters. The house is carpetless, empty — the rain and wind cause funny noises upstairs. A huge fire is burning in the fireplace. Near the fireplace a collection of packing boxes are heaped together in the shape of a small table and covered with a checkered oil cloth. It is set for two. A bucket with ice and a champagne bottle sit on the table as well as a bowl of caviar. Two small chickens are impaled on a spit over the fire. A phonograph is playing on a box, and a string from the phonograph is turning the chickens on the spit. The phonograph is playing "Song of the Islands." Mary is standing near the fireplace looking as pretty as any bride ever looked. She is smiling at George, who has been slowly taking in the whole set-up. Through a door he sees the end of a cheap bed, over the back of which is a pair of pajamas and a nightie. Ernie exits and closes the door.*

MARY
(tears in her eyes)
Welcome home, Mr. Bailey.

216

GEORGE
(overcome)
Well, I'll be . . . Mary, Mary, where did you . . .

They rush into each other's arms, and hold each other in ecstasy.

EXT. SIDE OF HOUSE — NIGHT

CLOSE SHOT — *Bert and Ernie, standing in the pouring rain, start singing "I Love You Truly."*

INT. HOUSE — NIGHT

CLOSE SHOT — *George and Mary. They remain embraced.*

GEORGE
Oh, Mary . . .

MARY
Remember the night we broke the windows in this old house? This is what I wished for.

GEORGE
Darling, you're wonderful.

EXT. SIDE OF HOUSE — NIGHT

CLOSE SHOT — *Bert and Ernie. They finish their song, and Ernie kisses Bert on the forehead. Bert slams Ernie's hat on his head.*

FADE OUT

FADE IN

EXT. SLUM STREET BEDFORD FALLS — DAY — TWO YEARS LATER

MED. CLOSE SHOT — *In front of one of the miserable shacks that line the street are two vehicles. One of them is George Bailey's rickety car, and the other is an even more rickety truck piled high with household goods. The Martini family is moving. The family consists of Martini, his wife and four kids of various ages, from two to ten. George and Mary are helping the Martinis move. About a dozen neighbors crowd around. Martini and George, assisted by three of the Martini children, are carrying out the last of the furniture. As they emerge from the house, one of the neighbors, Schultz, calls out:*

SCHULTZ
Martini, you rented a new house?

MARTINI
Rent?
(to George)
You hear what he say, Mr. Bailey?

GEORGE
What's that?

MARTINI

I own the house. Me, Giuseppe Martini, I own my own house. No more we live like pigs in thisa Potter's Field. Hurry, Maria.

MARIA

Yes . . .

GEORGE

Come on . . .
    (to Mary)
Bring the baby.
    (to Martini)
I'll take the kids in the car.

MARTINI

Oh, thank you, Mr. Bailey.

Mary gets in the front seat of the car, with the baby in her arms.

GEORGE

All right, kids — here — get in here. Now get right up on the seat there. Get the . . . get the goat!

The family goat gets in the back seat with the three kids.

MARTINI

Goodbye, everybody!

GEORGE

All in . . .

The rickety caravan starts off down the street, to the cheers of the neighbors.

WIPE TO:

EXT. BAILEY PARK — DAY

CLOSE SHOT — *Sign hanging from a tree: "Welcome to Bailey Park."* CAMERA PANS TO *follow George's car and the old truck laden with furniture as they pass — we hear Martini's voice singing "O Sole Mio." Bailey Park is a district of new small houses, not all alike, but each individual. New lawns here and there, and young trees. It has the promise when built up of being a pleasant little middle class section.*

WIPE TO:

EXT. MARTINI'S NEW HOUSE — DAY

MED. CLOSE SHOT — *George and Mary are on the porch of the new house, with the Martinis lined up before them.*

GEORGE

Mr. and Mrs. Martini, welcome home.

The Martinis cross themselves.

EXT. STREET — BAILEY PARK — DAY

CLOSE SHOT — *Sam Wainwright is standing in front of his big black town car. Sam is the epitome of successful, up and coming businessman. His wife, in the car, is a very attractive, sophisticated-looking lady, dripping with furs and jewels. Sam is watching George across the street.*

> SAM
> That old George . . . he's always making a speech.
> *(to George)*
> Hee-haw!
> *(wiggles his hands)*

EXT. NEW HOUSE — DAY

CLOSE SHOT — *Mary and George on porch.*

GEORGE
(to Mary)
Sam Wainwright!

MARY
Oh, who cares.
(to Mrs. Martini, giving her loaf of bread)
Bread! That this house may never know hunger.

Mrs. Martini crosses herself.

MARY
(giving her salt)
Salt! That life may always have flavor.

GEORGE
(handing bottle to Martini)
And wine! That joy and prosperity may reign forever. Enter the Martini castle!

The Martinis cross themselves, shaking hands all around. The kids enter with screams of delight. Mrs. Martini kisses Mary.

INT. POTTER'S OFFICE IN BANK — DAY

CLOSE SHOT — *Potter seated in his wheelchair at his desk, with his goon beside him. His rent-collector, Reineman, is talking, pointing to maps spread out on the desk:*

REINEMAN

Look, Mr. Potter, it's no skin off my nose. I'm just your little rent collector. But you can't laugh off this Bailey Park any more. Look at it.

A buzzer is heard, and Potter snaps on the dictaphone on his desk.

SECRETARY'S VOICE

Congressman Blatz is here to see you.

POTTER
(to dictaphone)
Oh, tell the congressman to wait.
(to Reineman)
Go on.

REINEMAN

Fifteen years ago, a half-dozen houses stuck here and there.
(indicating map)
There's the old cemetery, squirrels, buttercups, daisies. Used to hunt rabbits there myself. Look at it today. Dozens of the prettiest little homes you ever saw. Ninety per cent owned by suckers who used to pay rent to you. Your Potter's Field, my dear Mr. Employer, is becoming just that. And are the local yokels making with those David and Goliath wisecracks!

POTTER

Oh, they are, are they? Even though they know the Baileys haven't made a dime out of it.

REINEMAN

You know very well why. The Baileys were all chumps. Every one of these homes is worth twice what it cost the Building and Loan to build. If I were you, Mr. Potter . . .

POTTER
(interrupting)
Well, you are not me.

REINEMAN
(as he leaves)
As I say, it's no skin off my nose. But one of these days this bright young man is going to be asking George Bailey for a job.

Reineman exits.

POTTER

The Bailey family has been a boil on my neck long enough.

He flips the switch on the dictaphone.

Yes, sir?

POTTER

Come in here.

EXT. STREET IN BAILEY PARK — DAY

CLOSE SHOT — *George and Mary are talking to Sam Wainwright in front of the latter's car. His wife, Jane, is now out of the car.*

SAM

We just stopped in town to take a look at the new factory, and then we're going to drive on down to Florida.

GEORGE

Oh . . .

JANE

Why don't you have your friends join us?

SAM

Why sure. Hey, why don't you kids drive down with us, huh?

GEORGE

Oh, I'm afraid I couldn't get away, Sam.

SAM

Still got the nose to the old grindstone, eh? Jane, I offered to let George in on the ground floor in plastics, and he turned me down cold.

GEORGE

Oh, now, don't rub it in.

SAM

I'm not rubbing it in. Well, I guess we better run along.

There is handshaking all around as Sam and Jane get into their car.

JANE

Awfully glad to have met you, Mary.

MARY

Nice meeting you.

GEORGE

Goodbye.

JANE

Goodbye, George.

SAM

So long, George. See you in the funny papers.

GEORGE

Goodbye, Sam.

MARY

Have fun.

GEORGE

Thanks for dropping around.

SAM
(to chauffeur)
Florida!
(to George)
Hee-haw!

GEORGE

Hee-haw.

The big black limousine glides away, leaving George standing with his arm around Mary, gazing broodingly after it. They slowly walk over to George's old car and look at it silently.

WIPE TO:

INT. POTTER'S OFFICE — DAY

CLOSE SHOT — *Potter is lighting a big cigar which he has just given George. The goon is beside Potter's chair, as usual.*

> GEORGE
>
> Thank you, sir. Quite a cigar, Mr. Potter.

> POTTER
>
> You like it? I'll send you a box.

> GEORGE
> *(nervously)*
>
> Well, I . . . I suppose I'll find out sooner or later, but just what exactly did you want to see me about?

> POTTER
> *(laughs)*
>
> George, now that's just what I like so much about you.
> *(pleasantly and smoothly)*
> George, I'm an old man, and most people hate me. But I don't like them either, so that makes it all even. You know just as well as I do, that I run practically everything in this town but the Bailey Building and Loan. You know, also, that for a number of years I've been trying to get control of it . . . or kill it. But I haven't been able to do it. You have been stopping me. In fact, you have beaten me, George, and as anyone in this county can tell you, that takes some doing. Take during the depression, for instance. You and I were the only ones that kept our heads. You saved the Building and Loan, and I saved all the rest.

> GEORGE
>
> Yes. Well, most people say you *stole* all the rest.

> POTTER
>
> The envious ones say that, George, the suckers. Now, I have stated my side very frankly. Now, let's look at your side. Young man, twenty-seven, twenty-eight . . . married, making say . . . forty a week.

> GEORGE
> *(indignantly)*
>
> Forty-five!

> POTTER
>
> Forty-five. Forty-five. Out of which, after supporting your mother, and paying your bills, you're able to keep, say ten, if you skimp. A child or two comes along, and you won't even be able to save the ten. Now, if this young man of twenty-eight was a common, ordinary yokel, I'd say he was doing fine. But, George Bailey is *not* a common, ordinary yo-

kel. He's an intelligent, smart, ambitious young man — who hates his job — who hates the Building and Loan, almost as much as I do. A young man who's been dying to get out on his own ever since he was born. A young man . . . the smartest one of the crowd, mind you, a young man who has to sit by and watch his friends go places, because he's trapped. Yes, sir, trapped into frittering his life away playing nursemaid to a lot of garlic-eaters. Do I paint a correct picture, or do I exaggerate?

GEORGE
(*mystified*)
Now what's your point, Mr. Potter?

POTTER
My point? My point is, I want to hire you.

GEORGE
(*dumbfounded*)
Hire me?

POTTER

I want you to manage my affairs, run my properties. George, I'll start you out at twenty thousand dollars a year.

George drops his cigar on his lap. He nervously brushes off the sparks from his clothes.

GEORGE
(flabbergasted)
Twenty thou . . . twenty thousand dollars a year?

POTTER

You wouldn't mind living in the nicest house in town, buying your wife a lot of fine clothes, a couple of business trips to New York a year, maybe once in a while Europe. You wouldn't mind that, would you, George?

GEORGE

Would I?
(looking around skeptically)
You're not talking to somebody else around here, are you? You know, this is me, you remember me? George Bailey.

POTTER

Oh, yes, George Bailey. Whose ship has just come in — providing he has brains enough to climb aboard.

GEORGE

Well, what about the Building and Loan?

POTTER

Oh, confound it man, are you afraid of success? I'm offering you a three year contract at twenty thousand dollars a year, starting today. Is it a deal or isn't it?

GEORGE

Well, Mr. Potter, I . . . I . . . I know I ought to jump at the chance, but I . . . I just . . . I wonder if it would be possible for you to give me twenty-four hours to think it over?

POTTER

Sure, sure, sure. You go on home and talk about it to your wife.

GEORGE

I'd like to do that.

POTTER

In the meantime, I'll draw up the papers.

GEORGE

All right, sir.

POTTER
(offers hand)
Okay, George?

GEORGE
(taking his hand)
Okay, Mr. Potter.

As they shake hands, George feels a physical revulsion. Potter's hand feels like a cold mackerel to him. In that moment of physical contact he knows he could never be associated with this man. George drops his hand with a shudder. He peers intently into Potter's face.

GEORGE *(cont'd)*
(vehemently)
No . . . no . . . no . . . no, now wait a minute, here! I don't have to talk to anybody! I know right now, and the answer is no! NO! Dog-gone it!
(getting madder all the time)

You sit around here and you spin your little webs and you think the whole world revolves around you and your money. Well, it doesn't, Mr. Potter! In the . . . in the whole vast configuration of things, I'd say you were nothing but a scurvy little spider. You . . .

He turns and shouts at the goon, impassive as ever beside Potter's wheelchair.

> GEORGE *(cont'd)*
> . . . and that goes for you too!

As George opens the office door to exit, he shouts at Mr. Potter's secretary in the outer office:

> GEORGE *(cont'd)*
> And it goes for you too!

WIPE TO:

INT. BEDROOM — GEORGE AND MARY'S HOUSE — NIGHT

CLOSE SHOT — *George enters the bedroom. The room is modestly furnished with just a cheap bed, a chair or two, and a dresser. Mary is asleep in the bed. As George comes in, his head is filled with many confusing thoughts, relating to incidents in his past life.*

> POTTER'S VOICE
> You wouldn't mind living in the nicest house in town. Buying your wife a lot of fine clothes, going to New York on a business trip a couple of times a year. Maybe to Europe once in a while.

George takes off his hat and coat, moves over to the dresser and stares at his reflection in the mirror.

> GEORGE'S VOICE
> I know what I'm going to do tomorrow and the next day and next year and the year after that. I'm shaking the dust of this crummy little town off my feet, and I'm going to see the world. . . . And I'm going to build things. I'm going to build air fields. I'm going to build skyscrapers a hundred stories high. I'm going to build a bridge a mile long.

While the above thoughts are passing through George's head, his attention is caught by a picture on the wall near the dresser.

INSERT: *Picture on the wall. It is the sketch of George lassoing the moon that we first saw in Mary's living room. The lettering reads: "George Lassos The Moon."*

> GEORGE'S VOICE
> What is it you want, Mary? You want the moon? If you do, just say the word, I'll throw a lasso around it and pull it down for you.

Mary is now awake, and starts singing their theme-song:

MARY
(singing)
Buffalo Gals, won't you come out tonight, won't you come out tonight, won't you come out tonight.

George crosses over and sits on the edge of the bed.

GEORGE
Hi.

MARY
Hi.

GEORGE
Mary Hatch, why in the world did you ever marry a guy like me?

MARY
To keep from being an old maid.

GEORGE
You could have married Sam Wainwright or anybody else in town.

MARY
I didn't want to marry anybody else in town. I want my baby to look like you.

GEORGE
You didn't even have a honeymoon. I promised you . . .
(does a double take)
. . . Your what?

MARY
My baby.

                                GEORGE
                            (incredulously)
            You mean . . . Mary, you on the nest?

                                MARY
            George Bailey lassoes stork.

                                GEORGE
            Lassoes the stork! You mean you . . . What is it, a boy or a girl?

Mary nods her head happily.

                                                        FADE OUT

FADE IN

MONTAGE SEQUENCE: *Over the following* SERIES OF SHOTS *we hear the voices of Joseph and Clarence in Heaven.*

EXT. MAIN STREET BEDFORD FALLS — NIGHT

MED. SHOT — *George is crossing the street, heading for the offices of the Building and Loan.*

                          JOSEPH'S VOICE
            Now, you've probably already guessed that George never leaves Bedford Falls.

                          CLARENCE'S VOICE
            No!

INT. HOSPITAL — DAY

CLOSE SHOT — *nurse holding newborn baby.*

                          JOSEPH'S VOICE
            Mary had her baby, a boy.

INT. SITTING ROOM — DAY

CLOSE SHOT — *Mary sitting on the floor playing with a baby. A little boy is in a play-pen nearby.*

                          JOSEPH'S VOICE
            Then she had another one — a girl.

INT. GRANVILLE HOUSE — DAY

CLOSE SHOT — *Mary is busy hanging wallpaper and painting the old place.*

                          JOSEPH'S VOICE
            Day after day she worked away remaking the old Granville house into a home.

INT. GRANVILLE HOUSE — NIGHT

CLOSE SHOT — *George has just come into the hall. He is obviously tired and discouraged as he starts up the stairs. The knob on the bannister comes off in his hand.*

> JOSEPH'S VOICE
> Night after night George came back late from the office. Potter was bearing down hard.

WIPE TO:

EXT. RECRUITING GROUNDS — DAY

MED. LONG SHOT — *A group of men, obviously just drafted, marching along in a camp.*

> JOSEPH'S VOICE
> Then came a war.

INT. RED CROSS WORKROOM — DAY

CLOSE SHOT — *Mrs. Bailey and other women in Red Cross uniforms busily sewing, etc.*

> JOSEPH'S VOICE
> Ma Bailey and Mrs. Hatch joined the Red Cross and sewed.

EXT. TRAIN IN RAILROAD STATION — DAY

CLOSE SHOT — *Mary, with portable U.S.O. pushcart, is serving coffee and doughnuts to men leaning from the train.*

> JOSEPH'S VOICE
> Mary had two more babies, but still found time to run the U.S.O.

INT. FACTORY — DAY

CLOSE SHOT — *Sam Wainwright showing set of blueprints to two Army officers.*

> JOSEPH'S VOICE
> Sam Wainwright made a fortune in plastic hoods for planes.

INT. DRAFT BOARD OFFICE — DAY

CLOSE SHOT — *Potter is wheeled in toward a long table around which several men are seated.*

JOSEPH'S VOICE
Potter became head of the draft board.

POTTER
(reading from papers)
One-A . . . One-A . . . One-A . . .

EXT. STREET IN BEDFORD FALLS — DAY

MED. CLOSE SHOT — *Gower and Uncle Billy are conducting a bond rally from the top of an Army tank.*

JOSEPH'S VOICE
Gower and Uncle Billy sold war bonds.

EXT. BATTLEFIELD — NIGHT

MED. CLOSEUP — *Bert, in uniform, moving cautiously with fixed bayonet. Smoke and flashes of gunfire in b.g.*

JOSEPH'S VOICE
Bert the cop was wounded in North Africa. Got the Silver Star.

EXT. SKY — DAY

LONG SHOT — *Hundreds of planes flying overhead, with parachutes dropping from them.*

JOSEPH'S VOICE
Ernie, the taxi driver, parachuted into France.

EXT. REMAGEN BRIDGE OVER THE RHINE — DAY

CLOSE SHOT — *Marty in the foreground, beckoning to soldiers to come on.*

JOSEPH'S VOICE
                Marty helped capture the Remagen Bridge.

INT. READY ROOM ON AIRCRAFT CARRIER — NIGHT

CLOSE SHOT — *Harry is fastening the helmet of his flying clothes. He waves as he exits through the door.*

JOSEPH'S VOICE
                Harry . . . Harry Bailey topped them all. A Navy flier, he shot down fifteen planes.

EXT. OCEAN FROM DECK OF CARRIER — NIGHT

LONG SHOT — *A flaming plane crashes into the sea.*

JOSEPH'S VOICE
                . . . two of them as they were about to crash into a transport full of soldiers.

CLARENCE'S VOICE
                Yes, but George . . .

INT. RATION OFFICE — DAY

CLOSE SHOT — *George, behind the counter, is trying to quiet a crowd of people all clamoring for more ration points.*

JOSEPH'S VOICE
                George? Four-F on account of his ear, George fought the battle of Bedford Falls.

George shouts.

GEORGE
                Hold on . . . hold on . . . hold on now. Don't you know there's a war on?

EXT. STREET — NIGHT

CLOSE SHOT — *George, in the uniform of an air raid warden, is patrolling his beat.*

JOSEPH'S VOICE
                Air raid Warden . . .

EXT. HOUSE — NIGHT

CLOSE SHOT — *man beside lighted window pulls down the shade as George blows his whistle.*

EXT. STREET — DAY

CLOSE SHOT — *George is helping load his old car with scrap paper.*

JOSEPH'S VOICE
. . . paper drives . . .

EXT. DUMP — DAY

CLOSE SHOT — *Wheelbarrow full of junk being dumped onto pile.*

JOSEPH'S VOICE
. . . scrap drives . . .

EXT. STREET — DAY

MED. CLOSE SHOT — *children wheeling old tires.*

JOSEPH'S VOICE
. . . rubber drives . . .

INT. CHURCH — DAY

MED. SHOT — *people praying in church.*

JOSEPH'S VOICE
Like everybody else, on V-E Day he wept and prayed.

EXT. CHURCH — ANOTHER ANGLE

MED. CLOSE SHOT — *people entering church.*

JOSEPH'S VOICE
On V-J Day he wept and prayed again.

FRANKLIN'S VOICE
Joseph, now show him what happened today.

JOSEPH'S VOICE
Yes, sir.

(END OF MONTAGE)

EXT. BEDFORD FALLS STREET — WINTER — DAY

George is walking along the sidewalk, reading a newspaper. It is a raw, gusty day, and his overcoat and muffler flap in the breeze. Draped around one arm is a large Christmas wreath. Under his other arm are several more copies of the paper.

JOSEPH'S VOICE
This morning, day before Christmas, about ten A.M. Bedford Falls time . . .

George comes to where Ernie, the taxi driver, is standing on the sidewalk.

GEORGE
(holding out paper)
Hi, Ernie, look at that.

237

INSERT: NEWSPAPER. *The front page of the paper, the Bedford Falls Sentinel. The headline reads:* PRESIDENT DECORATES HARRY BAILEY — LOCAL BOY WINS CONGRESSIONAL MEDAL OF HONOR. *The subhead tells of a plan for a giant jubilee and parade, to be followed by a banquet, in honor of Commander Harry Bailey, U.S.N. on his way home from Washington after receiving the Congressional Medal of Honor. There's a large picture of President Truman pinning the coveted medal on Harry's bosom, in the midst of dignitaries; a picture of the transport which Harry saved. Practically the whole front page is devoted to the story.*

CLOSE SHOT — *George and Ernie.*

ERNIE
(kidding)
Gonna snow again.

GEORGE
(outraged)
What do you mean — it's gonna snow again? Look at the headlines.

ERNIE
I know — I know — I know. I think it's marvelous.

Gower comes running across the street from his drugstore and joins them.

GEORGE
(reading)
Commander Harry Bailey. Mr. Gower, look at this — the second page.
(gives them papers)
Now look, this is for you. This is for you, this is for you.
(as he leaves)
See you again.

EXT. STREET — DAY

MED. LONG SHOT — *Uncle Billy is walking along the street, humming happily to himself. He sees some men decorating the Court House with banners and bunting — there is a huge sign reading: Welcome Home Harry Bailey.*

UNCLE BILLY
(calls out)
Be sure you spell the name right.

INT. OUTER OFFICE BUILDING AND LOAN — DAY

FULL SHOT — *The offices are unchanged, still small-time and old-fashioned. The same office force, albeit a few years older: Cousin Tilly and Cousin Eustace. Seated on a chair is a middle-aged man with a brief case. The outer door opens and George enters:*

GEORGE
Extra! Extra! Read all about it!

Cousin Tilly and Cousin Eustace are talking on the phone.

COUSIN EUSTACE
George! George! It's Harry now on long distance from Washington!

GEORGE
Harry! What do you know about that?

COUSIN EUSTACE
He reversed the charges. It's okay, isn't it?

GEORGE
What do you mean it's okay? For a hero?
(takes the phone)
Harry! Oh, you old seven kinds of a son of a gun. Congratulations! How's mother standing it? . . . She did? What do you know . . .

(to Eustace)
Mother had lunch with the President's wife.

COUSIN TILLY
Wait till Martha hears about this.

COUSIN EUSTACE
What did they have to eat?

GEORGE
(on phone)
What did they have to eat? Harry, you should see what they're cooking up in the town for you. . . . Oh, are they?
(to Eustace)
The Navy's going to fly mother home this afternoon.

COUSIN EUSTACE
In a plane?

GEORGE
(on phone)
What? Uncle Billy?
(to Eustace)
Has Uncle Billy come in yet?

COUSIN TILLY
No, he stopped at the bank first.

GEORGE
(on phone)
He's not here right now, Harry.

Cousin Eustace has turned away from George and caught a glimpse of the man waiting in the chair. This is Carter, the bank examiner, come for his annual audit of the books of the Building and Loan.

GEORGE *(cont'd)*
(on phone)
But look . . .

COUSIN EUSTACE
(interrupting)
George . . .

GEORGE
(on phone)
. . . now tell me about it.

COUSIN EUSTACE
(interrupting)
. . . George, that man's here again.

GEORGE
What man?

COUSIN EUSTACE
(nervously)
Bank . . . bank examiner.

GEORGE
Oh . . .
(on phone)
Talk to Eustace a minute, will you. I'll be right back.

He gives the phone to Eustace, puts down his wreath and goes over to Carter.

CLOSE SHOT — *George and Carter. They shake hands.*

GEORGE
Good morning, sir.

CARTER
Carter — bank examiner.

                    GEORGE
Mr. Carter, Merry Christmas.

                    CARTER
Merry Christmas.

                    GEORGE
We're all excited around here.
          (shows him paper)
My brother just got the Congressional Medal of Honor. The President
just decorated him.

                    CARTER
Well, I guess they do those things. Well, I trust you had a good year.

                    GEORGE
Good year? Well, between you and me, Mr. Carter, we're broke.

                    CARTER
Yeah, very funny.

                    GEORGE
Well . . .
          (leading him into office)
. . . now, come right in here, Mr. Carter.

                    CARTER
          (as they go)
Although I shouldn't wonder when you okay reverse charges on personal long distance calls.

                    COUSIN TILLY
George, shall we hang up?

                    GEORGE
No, no. He wants to talk to Uncle Billy. You just hold on.

                    CARTER
          (in doorway)
Now, if you'll cooperate, I'd like to finish with you by tonight. I want
to spend Christmas in Elmira with my family.

                    GEORGE
I don't blame you at all, Mr. Carter. Just step right in here. We'll fix
you up.

INT. BANK — DAY

CLOSE SHOT — *Uncle Billy is filling out a deposit slip at one of the desks.*

                    UNCLE BILLY
          (writing)
December twenty-fourth . . .

He takes a thick envelope from his inside pocket and thumbs through the bills it contains. It is evidently a large sum of money.

UNCLE BILLY *(cont'd)*
(writing)
Eight thousand . . .

MED. SHOT — *door to street. Potter is being wheeled in by his goon. Various bank officials run over to greet him — he is reading a newspaper. Uncle Billy has finished filling out his slip, and comes over to taunt Potter, the envelope containing the money in his hand.*

UNCLE BILLY
Well, good morning, Mr. Potter. What's the news?

He grabs the paper from Potter's hand.

UNCLE BILLY *(cont'd)*
Well, well, well, Harry Bailey wins Congressional Medal. That couldn't be one of the Bailey boys? You just can't keep those Baileys down, now can you, Mr. Potter?

POTTER
How does slacker George feel about that?

UNCLE BILLY
Very jealous, very jealous. He only lost three buttons off his vest. Of course, slacker George would have gotten two of those medals if he had gone.

POTTER
Bad ear.

UNCLE BILLY
Yes.

Uncle Billy folds Potter's paper over the envelope containing his money, and flings his final taunt at the old man.

UNCLE BILLY *(cont'd)*
After all, Potter, some people like George *had* to stay home. Not every heel was in Germany and Japan!

In a cold rage, Potter grabs his paper and wheels off toward his office. Uncle Billy smiles triumphantly and goes toward deposit window with his deposit slip.

CLOSE SHOT — *Uncle Billy and bank teller at the window.*

TELLER
Good morning, Mr. Bailey.

UNCLE BILLY
(still chuckling)
Good morning, Horace.

Uncle Billy hands the bank book over. The teller opens it, starts to punch it with rubber stamps.

TELLER
I guess you forgot something.

UNCLE BILLY
Huh?

TELLER
You forgot something.

UNCLE BILLY
What?

TELLER
Well, aren't you going to make a deposit?

UNCLE BILLY
Sure, sure I am.

TELLER
Well, then . . . it's usually customary to bring the money with you.

UNCLE BILLY
Oh, shucks . . .

Uncle Billy searches through every pocket he has.

UNCLE BILLY *(cont'd)*
(looks bewildered)
I know I had . . .

The teller, knowing the old man's vagaries, points to one of the numerous strings tied around his fingers.

TELLER
How about that one there?

UNCLE BILLY
Hmm? Well, I . . .

INT. POTTER'S OFFICE — DAY

CLOSE SHOT — *Potter is now behind his desk. He spreads the newspaper out in front of him, muttering as he does so.*

POTTER
Bailey . . .

He sees the envelope, looks inside at the money. Then, to his goon, indicating the office door:

POTTER *(cont'd)*
Take me back there. Hurry up.
(as they go)
Come on, look sharp.

Potter opens the door just a little, and peers through into the bank.

INT. BANK — DAY

CLOSE SHOT — *deposit slip desk. Uncle Billy looks around for the money envelope. It is not there. He looks puzzled, thinks hard, then a look of concern creeps into his eyes. He starts thumping his pockets, with increasing panic, and looks in the waste paper basket on the floor. He finally rushes through the door and out onto the street.*

INT. POTTER'S OFFICE — DAY

CLOSE SHOT — *Potter watching through the door.*

POTTER
(to goon)
Take me back.

The goon wheels him back to his desk. He is deep in thought, with a crafty expression on his face.

EXT. STREET — DAY

MED. CLOSE SHOT — *Uncle Billy running across the street in the direction of the Building and Loan.*

INT. OUTER OFFICE — BUILDING AND LOAN — DAY

CLOSE SHOT — *George coming from room where he has just left the bank examiner.*

GEORGE
Just make yourself at home, Mr. Carter. I'll get those books for you.

He sees Violet Bick standing there.

GEORGE *(cont'd)*
Oh, hello, Vi.

VIOLET
George, can I see you for a second?

GEORGE
Why, of course you can. Come on in the office here.

He hears a noise, and sees Uncle Billy entering the office.

GEORGE *(cont'd)*
Uncle Billy, talk to Harry. He's on the telephone.

George and Violet enter his private office. Uncle Billy comes hurrying in.

COUSIN TILLY
Hurry, Uncle Billy, hurry. Long distance, Washington.

COUSIN EUSTACE
Hey, here's Harry on the phone.

COUSIN TILLY
Harry, your nephew, remember?

COUSIN EUSTACE
(on phone)
Here he is.

Uncle Billy picks up the phone and speaks distractedly, without knowing what he is saying.

UNCLE BILLY
(on phone)
Hello . . . hello . . . Yes, Harry — yes . . . everything . . . everything's fine.

He hangs up agitatedly, muttering to himself as he goes into his own office. Cousin Tilly and Cousin Eustace look after him, dumbfounded.

UNCLE BILLY *(cont'd)*
I should have my head examined. Eight thousand dollars. It's got to be somewhere.

INT. GEORGE'S OFFICE — DAY

CLOSE SHOT — *George and Violet. George has just finished writing something, and is slipping the paper into an envelope.*

GEORGE
(hands it to her)
Here you are.

VIOLET
(bitterly)
Character? If I had any character, I'd . . .

GEORGE
It takes a lot of character to leave your home town and start all over again.

He pulls some money from his pocket, and offers it to her.

VIOLET
No, George, don't . . .

GEORGE
Here, now, you're broke, aren't you?

VIOLET
I know, but . . .

GEORGE
What do you want to do, hock your furs, and that hat? Want to walk to New York? You know, they charge for meals and rent up there just the same as they do in Bedford Falls.

VIOLET
(taking money)
Yeah — sure . . .

GEORGE
It's a loan. That's my business. Building and Loan. Besides, you'll get a job. Good luck to you.

She looks at him, then says a strange thing.

                    VIOLET
        I'm glad I know you, George Bailey.

She reaches up and kisses him on the cheek, leaving lipstick. George opens the door for her.

INT. OUTER OFFICE — DAY

CLOSE SHOT — *As George and Violet come through the door, they are being watched by Cousin Tilly, Cousin Eustace and the bank examiner, who is still waiting to go to work on the books.*

                    GEORGE
                  (to Violet)
        Say hello to New York for me.

                    VIOLET
        Yeah — yeah . . . sure I will.

GEORGE

Now, let's hear from you.

Violet sees the lipstick on George's cheek, and dabs at it with her handkerchief.

GEORGE *(cont'd)*

What's the matter? Merry Christmas, Vi.

VIOLET

Merry Christmas, George.

She exits.

MR. CARTER

Mr. Bailey . . .

GEORGE

Oh, Mr. Carter, I'm sorry. I'll be right with you.
     (to Cousin Tilly)
Uncle Billy in?

COUSIN TILLY

Yeah, he's in his office.

INT. DOORWAY TO UNCLE BILLY'S OFFICE — DAY

CLOSE SHOT — *As George opens the door he sees Uncle Billy frantically looking for the missing envelope. The office is in a mess, drawers are opened, and papers scattered on the floor and on the desk.*

GEORGE

Unc . . . What's going on? The bank examiner's here, and I . . .

UNCLE BILLY
     (in dismay)
He's here?

GEORGE

Yeah, yeah. He wants the accounts payable . . .

George stops short, suddenly aware of the tragic old eyes looking up at him.

GEORGE *(cont'd)*

What's the matter with you?

Uncle Billy gestures nervously for George to come in. He does so and closes the door.

INT. OUTER OFFICE — DAY

MED. SHOT — *Cousin Tilly is at her switchboard, and Cousin Eustace standing beside her. Carter is still waiting in the doorway to his office. Suddenly the door opens and George comes striding out. He goes directly to the safe and starts searching, but doesn't find the money. Then he goes to the cash drawer in the counter, and looks through it.*

GEORGE

Eustace . . .

EUSTACE

Yeah?

GEORGE

Come here a minute.

Cousin Eustace runs over to George.

GEORGE *(cont'd)*

Did you see Uncle Billy with any cash last night?

COUSIN EUSTACE

He had it on his desk counting it before he closed up.

EXT. MAIN STREET BEDFORD FALLS — DAY

MED. SHOT — *Uncle Billy and George are retracing the former's steps through the snow, looking everywhere for the missing money. They pause for a moment on the sidewalk.*

GEORGE

Now look, did you buy anything?

UNCLE BILLY

Nothing. Not even a stick of gum.

GEORGE

All right. All right. Now we'll go over every step you took since you left the house.

UNCLE BILLY

This way.

They continue on down the street on their search.

EXT. WINDOW OF POTTER'S OFFICE IN BANK — DAY

CLOSE SHOT — *Potter is peering through the slats of the Venetian blind, watching them as they go.*

EXT. MAIN STREET BEDFORD FALLS — DAY

MOVING SHOT — *George and Uncle Billy continue their search.*

WIPE TO:

INT. UNCLE BILLY'S LIVING ROOM

CLOSE SHOT — *A shabby, old-fashioned, gas-lit room which has been turned almost inside out and upside down in an effort to locate the missing money. Drawers of an old secretary have been pulled out and are on the floor. Every conceivable place which might have been used by Uncle Billy to put the money has been searched. George, his hair rumpled, is feverishly pursuing the search. Uncle Billy is seated behind the desk, his head on his hands.*

GEORGE

And did you put the envelope in your pocket?

UNCLE BILLY

Yeah . . . yeah . . . maybe . . . maybe . . .

GEORGE

(shouts)

Maybe — maybe! I don't want any maybe. Uncle Billy, we've got to find that money!

UNCLE BILLY

(piteously)

I'm no good to you, George. I . . .

GEORGE

Listen to me. Do you have any secret hiding place here in the house? Someplace you could have put it? Someplace to hide the money?

UNCLE BILLY
(exhausted)
I've gone over the whole house, even in rooms that have been locked ever since I lost Laura.

Uncle Billy starts sobbing hysterically. George grabs him by the lapels and shakes him.

GEORGE
(harshly)
Listen to me! Listen to me! Think! Think!

UNCLE BILLY
(sobbing)
I can't think any more, George. I can't think any more. It hurts . . .

George jerks him to his feet, and shakes him. Uncle Billy stands before him like a frisked criminal, all his pockets hanging out, empty. George's eyes and manner are almost maniacal.

> GEORGE
> *(screaming at him)*
> Where's that money, you stupid, silly old fool? Where's the money? Do you realize what this means? It means bankruptcy and scandal, and prison!

He throws Uncle Billy down into his chair, and still shouts at him:

> GEORGE *(cont'd)*
> That's what it means! One of us is going to jail! Well, it's not going to be me!

George turns and heads for the door, kicking viciously at a waste basket on the floor as he goes. Uncle Billy remains sobbing at the table, his head in his arms.

WIPE TO:

INT. GEORGE'S LIVING ROOM — NIGHT

CLOSE SHOT — *Janie (aged eight) is seated at the piano playing "Hark, the Herald Angels Sing," which she practices during the remainder of this scene. There is a Christmas tree all decorated near the fireplace. At a large table Mary is busy putting cellophane bows and decorations on gift packages. At a small table Pete (aged nine) is seated with pad and pencil in the throes of composition. On the floor Tommy (aged three) is playing with a toy vacuum cleaner. We hear the SOUND of a door open and close. Mary turns and sees George enter the hall, a slight powdering of snow on his head and shoulders.*

INT. HALL — NIGHT

CLOSE SHOT — *As George comes into the house.*

> MARY
> Hello darling.

> CHILDREN
> Hello daddy, hello daddy.

> MARY
> *(indicating tree)*
> How do you like it?

George sneezes violently.

> MARY AND CHILDREN
> Bless you!

> MARY
> Did you bring the wreath?

PETE

Daddy, did you bring the Christmas wreath?

GEORGE

Wreath? What wreath?

MARY

The Merry Christmas wreath for the window.

GEORGE

(gruffly)

No. I left it at the office.

MARY

Is it snowing?

GEORGE

Yeah, just started.

MARY

Where's your coat and hat?

GEORGE

Left them at the office.

Mary stares at him, aware that something unusual has happened.

MARY

What's the matter?

GEORGE

(bitterly)

Nothing's the matter. Everything's all right.

INT. LIVING ROOM — NIGHT

CLOSE SHOT — *George slumps into an armchair and lifts Tommy onto his lap. Mary is helping Pete decorate the Christmas tree.*

MARY

Go on, Pete, you're a big boy. You can put the star up. Way up at the top. That's it. Fill in that little bare spot right there. That's it.
(to George)
Isn't it wonderful about Harry? We're famous, George. I'll bet I had fifty calls today about the parade, the banquet. Your mother's so excited, she . . .

During this scene, George has been sitting in the chair, hugging Tommy to him, and crying quietly. Mary realizes that something is seriously wrong, and breaks off. Janie is thumping away at the piano.

GEORGE

(sharply)

Must she keep playing that?

254

JANIE
(hurt)
I have to practice for the party tonight, daddy.

PETE
Mommy says we can stay up till midnight and sing Christmas Carols.

TOMMY
Can you sing, Daddy?

MARY
(to George)
Better hurry and shave. The families will be here soon.

GEORGE
(rising from chair)
Families! I don't want the families over here!

Mary leads him out toward the kitchen.

MARY
Come on out in the kitchen with me while I finish dinner.

They exit with Tommy hanging onto George's coat-tails, and pulling at him. CAMERA PANS WITH *them.*

TOMMY
(to George)
Excuse me . . . excuse me . . .

INT. HALL — NIGHT

CLOSE SHOT — *as they go toward kitchen.*

MARY
Have a hectic day?

GEORGE
(bitterly)
Oh, yeah, another big red letter day for the Baileys.

PETE
Daddy, the Browns next door have a new car. You should see it.

GEORGE
(turns on him)
Well, what's the matter with our car? Isn't it good enough for you?

PETE
Yes, daddy.

TOMMY
(tugging at coat)
Excuse me, excuse me . . .

256

INT. KITCHEN — NIGHT

CLOSE SHOT — *They come through the door.*

> GEORGE
> *(annoyed)*
> Excuse you for what?

> TOMMY
> I burped!

> MARY
> All right, darling, you're excused. Now go upstairs and see what little
> Zuzu wants.

Tommy leaves, and Mary turns to the stove.

> GEORGE
> Zuzu! What's the matter with Zuzu?

> MARY
> Oh, she's got a cold. She's in bed. Caught it coming home from
> school. They gave her a flower for a prize and she didn't want to crush
> it so she didn't button up her coat.

> GEORGE
> What is it, a sore throat or what?

> MARY
> Just a cold. The doctor says it's nothing serious.

> GEORGE
> The doctor? Was the doctor here?

> MARY
> Yes, I called him right away. He says it's nothing to worry about.

> GEORGE
> Is she running a temperature? What is it?

> MARY
> Just a teensie one — ninety-nine, six. She'll be all right.

George paces about the kitchen, worried.

> GEORGE
> Gosh, it's this old house. I don't know why we don't all have pneu-
> monia. This drafty old barn! Might as well be living in a refrigerator!
> Why did we have to live here in the first place and stay around this
> measly, crummy old town?

> MARY
> *(worried)*
> George, what's wrong?

GEORGE
Wrong? Everything's wrong! You call this a happy family? Why did we have to have all these kids?

PETE

(coming in)

Dad, how do you spell frankincense?

GEORGE

(shouts)

I don't know. Ask your mother.

George goes toward doorway.

MARY

Where're you going?

GEORGE

Going up to see Zuzu.

We hear his footsteps as he leaves. Mary looks after him, puzzled and concerned, then comes over to Pete.

PETE

He told me to write a play for tonight.

MARY

F-R-A-N-K-I-N . . .

INT. HALL — NIGHT

MED. CLOSE SHOT — *George starts up the stairs. The knob on the bannister comes off in his hand, and for a moment he has an impulse to hurl it into the living room. Then, he replaces the knob, and goes on up the stairs.*

INT. ZUZU'S BEDROOM — NIGHT

FULL SHOT — *The* SOUND *of Janie at the piano can be heard, the same monotonous rhythm over and over. Zuzu (aged six) is sitting up in her bed, the lamp burning beside her. She is holding her prize flower. George tiptoes in. Then, as he sees she's awake, he comes over, sitting on the edge of her bed.*

ZUZU

Hi, daddy.

GEORGE

Well, what happened to you?

ZUZU

I won a flower.

She starts to get out of bed.

GEORGE

Wait now. Where do you think you're going?

ZUZU

Want to give my flower a drink.

GEORGE
All right, all right. Here, give daddy the flower. I'll give it a drink.

She shakes her head and presses the flower to her. A few petals fall off. She picks them up.

ZUZU
Look, daddy . . . paste it.

GEORGE
Yeah, all right. Now, I'll paste this together.

She hands him the fallen petals and the flower. He turns his back to Zuzu, pretending to be tinkering with the flower. He sticks the fallen petals in his watch pocket, re-arranges the flower, and then turns back to Zuzu.

GEORGE
There it is, good as new.

ZUZU
Give the flower a drink.

George puts the flower in a glass of water on the table beside her bed.

GEORGE

Now, will you do something for me?

CLOSEUP — *George and Zuzu. They whisper.*

ZUZU

What?

GEORGE

Will you try to get some sleep?

ZUZU

I'm not sleepy. I want to look at my flower.

GEORGE

I know — I know, but you just go to sleep, and then you can dream about it, and it'll be a whole garden.

ZUZU

It will?

GEORGE

Uh-huh.

She closes her eyes, and relaxes on the bed. George pulls the covers over her. He bends down and his lips touch a tendril of the child's hair. Then he gets up and tiptoes out of the room.

INT. LIVING ROOM — NIGHT

CLOSE SHOT — *Janie is still pounding with grim determination at the piano, Pete is seated at the table writing, Tommy is playing with his toy vacuum cleaner. The telephone rings.*

JANIE AND PETE

Telephone.

INT. HALL — NIGHT

CLOSE SHOT — *Mary comes in and picks up the phone.*

MARY

I'll get it.
    (on phone)
Hello. Yes, this is Mrs. Bailey.

George enters shot, and stands listening to her.

MARY (cont'd)

Oh, thank you, Mrs. Welch. I'm sure she'll be all right. The doctor says that she ought to be out of bed in time to have her Christmas dinner.

GEORGE

Is that Zuzu's teacher?

MARY
(hand over mouthpiece)
Yes.

GEORGE
Let me speak to her.

He snatches the phone from Mary.

GEORGE *(cont'd)*
(on phone)
Hello. Hello, Mrs. Welch? This is George Bailey. I'm Zuzu's father. Say, what kind of a teacher are you anyway? What do you mean sending her home like that, half naked? Do you realize she'll probably end up with pneumonia on account of you?

MARY
(shocked)
George!

She puts a restraining hand on his arm. He shakes it off. She cannot know that George's tirade against Mrs. Welch is really a tirade against the world, against life itself, against God. Over the phone we hear Mrs. Welch's voice sputtering with protest.

GEORGE
Is this the sort of thing we pay taxes for — to have teachers like you? Silly, stupid, careless people who send our kids home without any clothes on? You know, maybe my kids aren't the best dressed kids, maybe they don't have any decent clothes . . .

Mary succeeds in wresting the phone from George's hand.

GEORGE *(cont'd)*
Aw, that stupid . . .

Mary speaks quickly into the phone.

MARY
Hello, Mrs. Welch. I want to apologize . . . hello . . . hello . . .
(to George)
She's hung up.

GEORGE
(savagely)
I'll hang her up!

But the telephone is suddenly alive with a powerful male voice calling:

MR. WELCH'S VOICE
Now, who do you think you are?

George hears this and grabs the receiver from Mary.

GEORGE
(to Mary)
Wait a minute.
(on phone)
Hello? Who is this? Oh, Mr. Welch! Okay, that's fine Mr. Welch.
Gives me a chance to tell you what I really think of your wife.

Mary once more tries to take the phone from him.

MARY
George . . .

GEORGE
(raving at her)
Will you get out and let me handle this?
(into phone — shouting)
Hello? Hello? What? Oh, you will, huh? Okay, Mr. Welch, any time
you think you're man enough . . . Hello? Any . . .

But before he can think of an insult to top Welch's, we hear a click on the phone.

GEORGE
Oh . . .

*He hangs up the receiver, and turns toward the living room. His face is flushed
and wet.*

PETE
Daddy, how do you spell "Hallelujah?"

GEORGE
(shouts)
How should I know? What do you think I am, a dictionary?

He yells at Tommy, noisily playing with his vacuum cleaner.

GEORGE *(cont'd)*
Tommy, stop that! Stop it!

Janie is still practicing at the piano, monotonously.

GEORGE *(cont'd)*
(savagely)
Janie, haven't you learned that silly tune yet? You've played it over and
over again. Now stop it! Stop it!

INT. LIVING ROOM — NIGHT

CLOSE SHOT — *The room has suddenly become ominously quiet, the only* SOUND
*being George's labored breathing. George goes over to a corner of the room where
his workshop is set up — a drawing table, several models of modern buildings,
bridges, etc. Savagely he kicks over the models, picks up some books and hurls
them into the corner. Mary and the children watch, horrified. George looks*

around, and sees them staring at him as if he were some unknown wild animal. The three children are crying.

> GEORGE
> *(gasping for breath)*
> I'm sorry, Mary. Janie, I'm sorry. I didn't mean . . . you go on and practice. Pete, I owe you an apology, too. I'm sorry. What do you want to know.

> PETE
> *(holding back his tears)*
> Nothing, daddy.

Mary and the children stare at him, stunned by his furious outburst. There is silence in the room.

> GEORGE
> What's the matter with everybody? Janie, go on. I told you to practice.
> *(shouts)*
> Now, go on, play!

Janie breaks into sobs.

> JANIE
> Oh, daddy . . .

> MARY
> *(in an outburst)*
> George, why must you torture the children? Why don't you . . .

The sight of Mary and the children suffering is too much for George.

> GEORGE
> Mary . . .

He looks around him, then quickly goes out the front door of the house. Mary goes to the phone, picks it up.

> MARY
> Bedford two-four-seven, please.

> PETE
> Is daddy in trouble?

> MARY
> Yes, Pete.

> JANIE
> Shall I pray for him?

> MARY
> Yes, Janie, pray very hard.

> TOMMY
> Me, too?

MARY
You too, Tommy.
(on phone)
Hello, Uncle Billy?

WIPE TO:

INT. POTTER'S OFFICE IN BANK — NIGHT — 8:00 P.M.

MED. CLOSEUP — *Potter is seated at his desk, his goon beside him. He is signing some papers. George is seated in a chair before the desk, without a hat or coat, covered lightly with snow.*

GEORGE
I'm in trouble, Mr. Potter. I need help. Through some sort of an

265

accident my company's short in their accounts. The bank examiner's up there today. I've got to raise eight thousand dollars immediately.

POTTER
(casually)
Oh, so that's what the reporters wanted to talk to you about?

GEORGE
(incredulous)
The reporters?

POTTER
Yes. They called me up from your Building and Loan. Oh, there's a man over there from the D.A.'s office, too. He's looking for you.

GEORGE
(desperate)
Please help me, Mr. Potter. Help me, won't you, please? Can't you see what it means to my family? I'll pay you any sort of a bonus on the loan . . . any interest. If you still want the Building and Loan, why I . . .

POTTER
(interrupting)
George, could it possibly be there's a slight discrepancy in the books?

GEORGE
No, sir. There's nothing wrong with the books. I've just misplaced eight thousand dollars. I can't find it anywhere.

POTTER
(looking up)
You misplaced eight thousand dollars?

GEORGE
Yes, sir.

POTTER
Have you notified the police?

GEORGE
No, sir. I didn't want the publicity. Harry's homecoming tomorrow . . .

POTTER
(snorts)
They're going to believe that one. What've you been doing, George? Playing the market with the company's money?

GEORGE
No, sir. No, sir. I haven't.

POTTER
What is it — a woman then? You know, it's all over town that you've been giving money to Violet Bick.

GEORGE
(incredulous)
What?

POTTER
Not that it makes any difference to me, but why did you come to me? Why don't you go to Sam Wainwright and ask him for the money?

GEORGE
I can't get hold of him. He's in Europe.

POTTER
Well, what about all your other friends?

GEORGE
They don't have that kind of money, Mr. Potter. You know that. You're the only one in town that can help me.

POTTER
I see. I've suddenly become quite important. What kind of security would I have, George? Have you got any stocks?

GEORGE
(shaking his head)
No, sir.

POTTER
Bonds? Real estate? Collateral of any kind?

GEORGE
(pulls out policy)
I have some life insurance, a fifteen thousand dollar policy.

POTTER
Yes . . . how much is your equity in it?

GEORGE
Five hundred dollars.

POTTER
(sarcastically)
Look at you. You used to be so cocky! You were going to go out and conquer the world! You once called me a warped, frustrated old man. What are you but a warped, frustrated young man? A miserable little clerk crawling in here on your hands and knees and begging for help. No securities — no stocks — no bonds — nothing but a miserable little five hundred dollar equity in a life insurance policy. You're worth more dead than alive. Why don't you go to the riff-raff you love so much and ask them to let you have eight thousand dollars? You know why? Because they'd run you out of town on a rail. . . . But I'll tell you what I'm going to do for you, George. Since the state examiner is still here, as a stockholder of the Building and Loan, I'm going to swear out a warrant for your arrest. Misappropriation of funds — manipulation — malfeasance . . .

George turns and starts out of the office as Potter picks up the phone and dials.

POTTER *(cont'd)*
All right, George, go ahead. You can't hide in a little town like this.

George is out of the door by now. CAMERA MOVES CLOSER *to Potter.*

POTTER *(cont'd)*
(on phone)
Bill? This is Potter.

EXT. MAIN STREET BEDFORD FALLS — NIGHT

MED. CLOSE SHOT. *George comes out of the bank into the falling snow. He crosses the street, tugs at the door of his old car, finally steps over the door, and drives off.*

EXT. MARTINI'S BAR — NIGHT

MED. CLOSE SHOT — *An attractive little roadside tavern, with the name "Martini's" in neon lights on the front wall.*

INT. MARTINI'S BAR — NIGHT

CLOSE SHOT — *The place is an Italian restaurant with bar. The bottles sparkle. There are Christmas greens and holly decorating the place. It has a warm, welcoming spirit, like Martini himself, who is welcoming new arrivals. The booths and the checkered cloth covered tables are full. There is an air of festivity and friendliness, and more like a party than a public drinking place. George is seated at the bar — he has had a great deal to drink, far more than he's accustomed to.*

MARTINI'S VOICE
(to new customers)
Merry Christmas. Glad you come.

MAN'S VOICE
How about some of that good spaghetti?

MARTINI'S VOICE
We got everything.

During this, CAMERA MOVES CLOSER *to George. Nick, the bartender, is watching him solicitously. Seated on the other side of George is a burly individual, drinking a glass of beer. George is mumbling:*

GEORGE
(mumbling)
God . . . God . . . Dear Father in Heaven, I'm not a praying man, but if you're up there and you can hear me, show me the way. I'm at the end of my rope. Show me the way, God.

NICK
(friendly)
Are you all right, George? Want someone to take you home?

George shakes his head. Martini comes over to his side.

> MARTINI
> *(worried)*
> Why you drink so much, my friend? Please go home, Mr. Bailey. This is Christmas Eve.

The ugly man next to George, who has been listening, reacts sharply to the name "Bailey."

> MAN
> Bailey? Which Bailey?

> NICK
> This is Mr. George Bailey.

Without any warning, the burly man throws a vicious punch at George who goes down and out. Martini, Nick and several others rush to pick him up.

MAN
(to George)
And the next time you talk to my wife like that you'll get worse. She cried for an hour. It isn't enough she slaves teaching your stupid kids how to read and write, and you have to bawl her out. . . .

MARTINI
(furious)
You get out of here, Mr. Welch!

Mr. Welch reaches in his pocket for money.

WELCH
Now wait . . . I want to pay for my drink.

MARTINI
Never mind the money. You get out of here quick.

WELCH
All right.

MARTINI
You hit my best friend. Get out!

Nick and Martini shove Welch out the door, then run back to help George to his feet. George's mouth is cut and bleeding.

NICK
You all right, George?

GEORGE
(stunned)
Who was that?

MARTINI
He gone. Don't worry. His name is Welch. He don't come in to my place no more.

GEORGE
Oh — Welch. That's what I get for praying.

MARTINI
The last time he come in here. You hear that, Nick?

NICK
Yes, you bet.

GEORGE
Where's my insurance policy?
(finds it in pocket)
Oh, here. . . .

He starts for the door.

MARTINI

Oh, no, please, don't go out this way, Mr. Bailey.

GEORGE

I'm all right.

Nick and Martini try to stop him, but he shrugs them off.

MARTINI

Oh, no — you don't feel so good.

GEORGE

I'm all right.

MARTINI

Please don't go away — please!

George opens the door and exits to the street.

WIPE TO:

EXT. RESIDENTIAL STREET — NIGHT

MED. SHOT — *George's car comes along the empty street, through the falling snow, suddenly swerves and crashes into a tree near the sidewalk of a house. George gets out to look at the damage, and savagely kicks at the open door of the car, trying to shut it. The noise brings the owner of the house running out.*

OWNER

What do you think you're doing?

CLOSE SHOT — *George stands unsteadily near the car, shaken by the accident. The front lights are broken and the fender is ripped. George stands dully looking at the damage. The owner comes up, looking at his tree. He leans over to examine the damages.*

OWNER
(indignation)
Now look what you did. My great-grandfather planted this tree.

George staggers off down the street, paying no attention to the man.

OWNER *(cont'd)*
Hey, you . . . Hey, you! Come back here, you drunken fool! Get this car out of here!

EXT. BRIDGE OVER RIVER — NIGHT

MED. LONG SHOT — *George is crossing the approach to the bridge when a truck swings around the corner and nearly hits him.*

DRIVER

Hey, what's the matter with you? Look where you're going!

The truck turns onto the bridge, and George takes a narrow catwalk at the railing.

CLOSE SHOT — *George has stopped by the railing at the center of the bridge. The snow is now falling hard.*

EXT. RIVER — NIGHT

MED. CLOSE SHOT — CAMERA SHOOTING DOWN *from George's angle* TO *the water, dotted with floating ice, passing under the bridge.*

273

EXT. BRIDGE AT RAILING — NIGHT

CLOSEUP — *George. He stares down at the water, desperate, trying to make up his mind to act. He leans over looking at the water, fascinated, glances furtively around him, hunches himself as though about to jump.*

MED. CLOSE SHOT — *From above George a body hurtles past and lands in the water with a loud splash. George looks down, horrified.*

> VOICE
> *(from river)*
> Help! Help!

George quickly takes off his coat, and dives over the railing into the water.

CLOSER ANGLE — *George comes up, sees the man flailing about in the water, and* CAMERA PANS WITH *him as he swims toward the man.*

> MAN
> Help! Help! Help!

EXT. TOLL HOUSE ON BRIDGE — NIGHT

CLOSE SHOT — *The toll house keeper, hearing the cries for help, comes running out on the bridge with a flashlight, which he shines on the two figures struggling in the water below.*

EXT. RIVER — NIGHT

CLOSE SHOT — *The man in the water is Clarence, the angel whose voice we have heard speaking from Heaven. George reaches him, grabs hold of him, and starts swimming for shore.*

WIPE TO:

INT. TOLL HOUSE ON BRIDGE — NIGHT

MED. SHOT — *George, Clarence, and the tollkeeper. George is seated before a wood burning stove before which his clothes are drying on a line. He is in his long winter underwear. He is sipping a mug of hot coffee, staring at the stove, cold, gloomy and drunk, ignoring Clarence and the tollkeeper, preoccupied by his near suicide and his unsolved problems. Clarence is standing on the other side of the stove, putting on his undershirt. This is a ludicrous seventeenth century garment which looks like a baby's night shirt — with embroidered cuffs and collar, and gathered at the neck with a drawstring. It falls below his knees.*

The tollkeeper is seated against the wall eyeing them suspiciously. Throughout the scene he attempts to spit, but each time is stopped by some amazing thing Clarence does or says. Clarence becomes aware that his garment is amazing the tollkeeper.

> CLARENCE
> I didn't have time to get some stylish underwear. My wife gave me this on my last birthday. I passed away in it.

The tollkeeper, about to spit, is stopped in the middle of it by this remark. Clarence, secretly trying to get George's attention, now picks up a copy of "Tom Sawyer" which is hanging on the line, drying. He shakes the book.

> CLARENCE *(cont'd)*
> Oh, Tom Sawyer's drying out, too. You should read the new book Mark Twain's writing now.

The tollkeeper stares at him incredulously.

> TOLLKEEPER
> How'd you happen to fall in?

> CLARENCE
> I didn't fall in. I jumped in to save George.

George looks up, surprised.

> GEORGE
> You what? To save me?

> CLARENCE
> Well, I did, didn't I? You didn't go through with it, did you?

> GEORGE
> Go through with what?

> CLARENCE
> Suicide.

George and the tollkeeper react to this.

> TOLLKEEPER
> It's against the law to commit suicide around here.

> CLARENCE
> Yeah, it's against the law where I come from, too.

> TOLLKEEPER
> Where do you come from?

He leans forward to spit, but is stopped by Clarence's next statement.

> CLARENCE
> Heaven.
> *(to George)*
> I had to act quickly, that's why I jumped in. I knew if I were drowning you'd try to save me. And you see, you did, and that's how I saved you.

The tollkeeper becomes increasingly nervous. George casually looks at the strange smiling little man a second time.

> GEORGE
> *(offhand)*
> Very funny.

CLARENCE
Your lip's bleeding, George.

George's hand goes to his mouth.

GEORGE
Yeah, I got a bust in the jaw in answer to a prayer a little bit ago.

CLARENCE
(comes around to George)
Oh, no — no — no, George. *I'm* the answer to your prayer. That's why I was sent down here.

GEORGE
(casually interested)
How do you know my name?

CLARENCE
Oh, I know all about you. I've watched you grow up from a little boy.

GEORGE
What are you, a mind reader or something?

CLARENCE
Oh, no.

GEORGE
Well, who are you, then?

CLARENCE
Clarence Odbody, A–S–2.

GEORGE
Odbody . . . A–S–2. What's that A–S–2?

CLARENCE
Angel Second Class.

The tollkeeper's chair slips out from under him with a crash. He has been leaning against the wall on it, tipped back on two legs. Tollkeeper rises and makes his way warily out the door. From his expression he looks like he'll call the nearest cop.

CLARENCE *(cont'd)*
(to tollkeeper)
Cheerio, my good man.

George rubs his head with his hand, to clear his mind.

GEORGE
Oh, brother. I wonder what Martini put in those drinks?

He looks up at Clarence standing beside him.

GEORGE *(cont'd)*
Hey, what's with you? What did you say just a minute ago? Why'd you want to save me?

CLARENCE

That's what I was sent down for. I'm your guardian angel.

GEORGE

I wouldn't be a bit surprised.

CLARENCE

Ridiculous of you to think of killing yourself for money. Eight thousand dollars.

GEORGE
(bewildered)

Yeah . . . just things like that. Now how'd you know that?

CLARENCE

I told you — I'm your guardian angel. I know everything about you.

GEORGE

Well, you look about like the kind of an angel I'd get. Sort of a fallen angel, aren't you? What happened to your wings?

CLARENCE

I haven't won my wings yet. That's why I'm an angel Second Class.

GEORGE

I don't know whether I like it very much being seen around with an angel without any wings.

CLARENCE

Oh, I've got to earn them, and you'll help me, won't you?

GEORGE
(humoring him)

Sure, sure. How?

CLARENCE

By letting me help you.

GEORGE

Only one way you can help me. You don't happen to have eight thousand bucks on you?

CLARENCE

Oh, no, no. We don't use money in Heaven.

GEORGE

Oh, that's right, I keep forgetting. Comes in pretty handy down here, bub.

CLARENCE

Oh, tut, tut, tut.

GEORGE

I found it out a little late. I'm worth more dead than alive.

CLARENCE

Now look, you mustn't talk like that. I won't get my wings with that attitude. You just don't know all that you've done. If it hadn't been for you . . .

GEORGE

(interrupts)

Yeah, if it hadn't been for me, everybody'd be a lot better off. My wife, and my kids and my friends.

(annoyed with Clarence)

Look, little fellow, go off and haunt somebody else, will you?

CLARENCE

No, you don't understand. I've got my job. . . .

GEORGE

(savagely)

Aw, shut up, will you.

Clarence is not getting far with George. He glances up, paces across the room, thoughtfully.

CLARENCE

(to himself)

Hmmm, this isn't going to be so easy.

(to George)

So you still think killing yourself would make everyone feel happier, eh?

GEORGE

(dejectedly)

Oh, I don't know. I guess you're right. I suppose it would have been better if I'd never been born at all.

CLARENCE

What'd you say?

GEORGE

I said I wish I'd never been born.

CLARENCE

Oh, you mustn't say things like that. You . . .

(gets an idea)

. . . wait a minute. Wait a minute. That's an idea.

(glances up toward Heaven)

What do *you* think? Yeah, that'll do it. All right.

(to George)

You've got your wish. You've never been born.

As Clarence speaks this line, the snow stops falling outside the building, a strong wind springs up which blows open the door to the shack. Clarence runs to close the door.

CLARENCE *(cont'd)*
(looking upward)
You don't have to make all that fuss about it.

As Clarence speaks, George cocks his head curiously, favoring his deaf ear, more interested in his hearing than in what Clarence has said.

GEORGE
What did you say?

CLARENCE
You've never been born. You don't exist. You haven't a care in the world.

George feels his ear as Clarence talks.

CLARENCE *(cont'd)*
No worries — no obligations — no eight thousand dollars to get — no Potter looking for you with the Sheriff.

CLOSEUP — *George and Clarence. George indicates his bad ear.*

GEORGE
Say something else in that ear.

CLARENCE
(bending down)
Sure. You can hear out of it.

GEORGE
Well, that's the doggonedest thing . . . I haven't heard anything out of that ear since I was a kid. Must have been that jump in the cold water.

CLARENCE
Your lip's stopped bleeding, too, George.

George feels his lip, which shows no sign of the recent cut he received from Welch. He is now thoroughly confused.

GEORGE
What do you know about that. . . . What's happened?

MED. CLOSE SHOT — *George looks around, as though to get his bearings.*

GEORGE
It's stopped snowing out, hasn't it? What's happened here?
(standing up)
Come on, soon as these clothes of ours are dry . . .

CLARENCE
Our clothes *are* dry.

George feels the clothes on the line.

GEORGE
What do you know about that? Stove's hotter than I thought. Now, come on, get your clothes on, and we'll stroll up to my car and get . . .

They start dressing. George interrupts himself.

GEORGE *(cont'd)*
Oh, I'm sorry. I'll stroll. You fly.

CLARENCE
I can't fly. I haven't got my wings.

GEORGE
You haven't got your wings. Yeah, that's right.

WIPE TO:

EXT. STREET — NIGHT

MED. SHOT — *This is the same empty street where George's car swerved into the tree near the sidewalk. George and Clarence come into shot and up to the spot where George had left his car smashed against the tree. George looks around, but his car is nowhere to be seen, and the tree is undamaged.*

> CLARENCE
>
> What's the matter?

> GEORGE
> *(puzzled)*
> Well, this is where I left my car and it isn't here.

> CLARENCE
>
> You have no car.

> GEORGE
>
> Well, I had a car, and it was right here. I guess somebody moved it.

CLOSE SHOT — *at curb. The owner of the house passes with some Christmas packages under his arm.*

> OWNER
> *(politely)*
> Good evening.

> GEORGE
>
> Oh, say . . . Hey . . . where's my car?

> OWNER
>
> I beg your pardon?

> GEORGE
>
> My car, my car. I'm the fellow that owns the car that ran into your tree.

> OWNER
>
> What tree?

> GEORGE
>
> What do you mean, what tree? This tree. Here, I ran into it. Cut a big gash in the side of it here.

The owner bends down to examine the trunk of the tree, then straightens up and smells George's breath. He backs away.

> OWNER
>
> You must mean two other trees. You had me worried. One of the oldest trees in Pottersville.

> GEORGE
> *(blankly)*
> Pottersville? Why, you mean Bedford Falls.

> OWNER
>
> I mean Pottersville.

> (sharply)
> Don't you think I know where I live? What's the matter with you?

The owner proceeds towards his house. George is completely bewildered.

> GEORGE
> Oh, I don't know. Either I'm off my nut, or he is . . .
> (to Clarence)
> . . . or you are!

> CLARENCE
> It isn't me!

> GEORGE
> Well, maybe I left the car up at Martini's. Well, come on, Gabriel.

He puts his arm around Clarence, and they start off up the road.

> CLARENCE
> (as they go)
> Clarence!

GEORGE

Clarence! Clarence!

WIPE TO:

INT. NICK'S BAR — NIGHT

CLOSE SHOT — *It is Martini's place, but almost unrecognizable. The cheerful Italian feeling is gone. It is now more of a hard-drinking joint, a honky-tonk. Same bar, tables have no covers. People are lower down and tougher. Nick the bartender is behind the bar. George and Clarence come in. George does not notice the difference, but Clarence is all eyes and beaming. They go up to the bar.*

GEORGE
(as they come in)
That's all right. Go on in. Martini's a good friend of mine.

Two people leave the bar as they approach.

GEORGE *(cont'd)*
There's a place to sit down. Sit down.

MED. CLOSEUP — *Nick is wiping off the bar as they sit down.*

GEORGE *(cont'd)*
Oh, hello, Nick. Hey, where's Martini?

NICK
You want a martini?

GEORGE
No, no, Martini. Your boss. Where is he?

NICK
(impatient)
Look, I'm the boss. You want a drink or don't you?

GEORGE
Okay — all right. Double bourbon, quick, huh?

NICK
Okay.
(to Clarence)
What's yours?

CLARENCE
I was just thinking . . .
(face puckers up with delicious anticipation)
It's been so long since I . . .

NICK
(impatient)
Look, mister, I'm standing here waiting for you to make up your mind.

CLARENCE
(appreciatively)

That's a good man. I was just thinking of a flaming rum punch. No, it's not cold enough for that. Not nearly cold enough. . . . Wait a minute . . . wait a minute . . . I got it. Mulled wine, heavy on the cinnamon and light on the cloves. Off with you, me lad, and be lively!

NICK

Hey, look mister, we serve hard drinks in here for men who want to get drunk fast. And we don't need any characters around to give the joint atmosphere. Is that clear? Or do I have to slip you my left for a convincer?

As he says this, Nick leans over the counter, and puts his left fist nearly in Clarence's eye. Clarence is puzzled by this conduct.

CLARENCE
(to George)
What's he talking about?

GEORGE
    (soothingly)
Nick — Nick, just give him the same as mine. He's okay.

NICK
Okay.

Nick turns away to get the drinks.

GEORGE
What's the matter with him? I never saw Nick act like that before.

CLARENCE
You'll see a lot of strange things from now on.

GEORGE
Oh, yeah. Hey, little fellow — you worry me. You got someplace to sleep?

CLARENCE
No.

GEORGE
You don't, huh? Well, you got any money?

Nick is listening suspiciously to this conversation.

CLARENCE
No.

GEORGE
No wonder you jumped in the river.

CLARENCE
I jumped in the river to save you so I could get my wings.

Nick stops pouring the drinks, bottle poised in his hand.

GEORGE
Oh, that's right.

A cash register bell rings off stage. Clarence reacts to the SOUND *of the bell.*

CLARENCE
Oh — oh. Somebody's just made it.

GEORGE
Made what?

CLARENCE
Every time you hear a bell ring, it means that some angel's just got his wings.

George glances up at Nick.

GEORGE
Look, I think maybe you better not mention getting your wings around here.

CLARENCE

Why? Don't they believe in angels?

GEORGE
(looking at Nick)
A . . . Yeah, but . . . you know . . .

CLARENCE

Then why should they be surprised when they see one?

GEORGE
(to Nick)
He never grew up. He's . . .
(to Clarence)
How old are you, anyway, Clarence?

CLARENCE

Two hundred and ninety-three . . .
(thinks)
. . . next May.

Nick slams the bottle down on the counter.

NICK

That does it! Out you two pixies go, through the door or out the
window!

GEORGE

Look, Nick. What's wrong?

NICK
(angrily)
And that's another thing. Where do *you* come off calling me Nick?

GEORGE

Well, Nick, that's your name, isn't it?

NICK

What's that got to do with it? I don't know you from Adam's off ox.
(sees someone come in)
Hey, you! Rummy! Come here! Come here!

CLOSE SHOT — *a small wreck of a man, with weak, watery eyes. Obviously a
broken-down panhandler, his hat in his hand.*

CLOSEUP — *George. He can hardly believe his eyes. It is Gower, the druggist.*

BACK TO SHOT — *Nick at the bar.*

NICK
(to Gower)
Didn't I tell you never to come panhandling around here?

*Nick picks up a seltzer bottle, and squirts Gower in the face with it. The crowd
laugh brutally. Gower smiles weakly, as the soda runs off his face.*

CLOSE SHOT — *George, horrified, leaps up and goes over to Gower.*

> GEORGE
>
> Mr. Gower! Mr. Gower! This is George Bailey! Don't you know me?

> GOWER
>
> No. No.

> NICK
> *(to his bouncers)*
> Throw him out. Throw him out.

The bouncers throw Gower out the front door. George rushes back to the bar.

> GEORGE
> *(bewildered)*
> Hey, what is . . . Hey, Nick, Nick . . . Isn't that Mr. Gower, the drug-
> gist?

NICK

You know, that's another reason for me not to like you. That rum-
head spent twenty years in jail for poisoning a kid. If you know him,
you must be a jail-bird yourself.
   (to his bouncers)
Would you show these gentlemen to the door.

BOUNCER

Sure. This way, gentlemen.

EXT. NICK'S BAR — NIGHT

CLOSE SHOT — *George and Clarence come flying through the door and land in
the snow.*

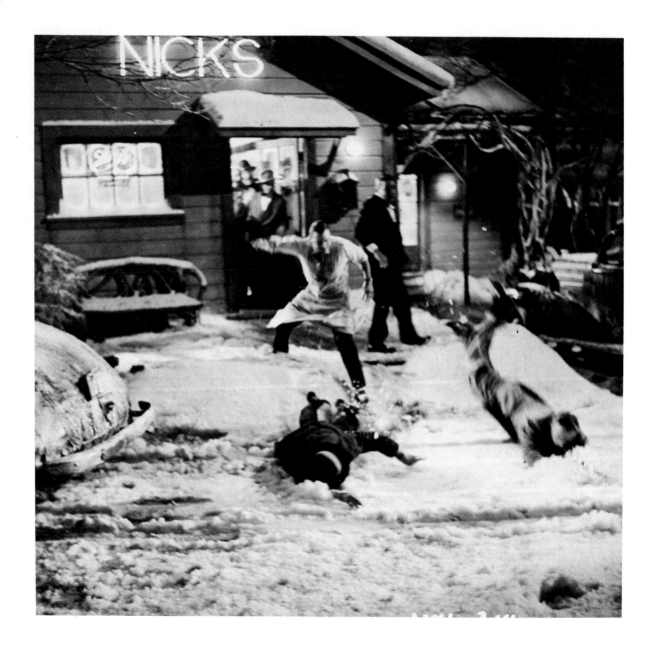

INT. NICK'S BAR — NIGHT

CLOSE SHOT — *Nick at the cash register, busily ringing the bell.*

> NICK
> Hey! Get me! I'm giving out wings!

EXT. NICK'S BAR — NIGHT

CLOSE SHOT — *George and Clarence lying in the snow. George has a strange, puzzled look on his face. They remain for a moment as they landed, looking at each other.*

> CLARENCE
> You see, George, you were not there to stop Gower from putting that poison into the . . .

> GEORGE
> What do you mean, I wasn't there? I remember distinctly . . .

George catches a glimpse of the front of the building with the neon sign over the door. It now reads "NICK'S PLACE" *instead of* "MARTINI'S."

George and Clarence get to their feet.

> GEORGE
> *(exasperated)*
> What the . . . hey, what's going on around here? Why, this ought to be Martini's place.

He points to the sign, and looks at Clarence. Clarence sort of hangs his head. George fixes him with a very interested look.

> GEORGE *(cont'd)*
> Look, who are you?

> CLARENCE
> *(patiently)*
> I told you, George. I'm your guardian angel.

George, still looking at him, goes up to him and pokes his arm. It's flesh.

> GEORGE
> Yeah, yeah, I know. You told me that. What else are you? What . . . are you a hypnotist?

> CLARENCE
> No, of course not.

> GEORGE
> Well then, why am I seeing all these strange things?

> CLARENCE
> Don't you understand, George? It's because you were not born.

GEORGE

Then if I wasn't born, who am I?

CLARENCE

You're nobody. You have no identity.

George rapidly searches his pockets for identification, but without success.

GEORGE

What do you mean, no identity? My name's George Bailey.

CLARENCE

There is no George Bailey. You have no papers, no cards, no driver's license, no 4-F card, no insurance policy . . .
(*he says these things as George searches for them*)

George looks in his watch pocket.

CLARENCE (*cont'd*)

They're not there, either.

GEORGE

What?

CLARENCE

Zuzu's petals.

George feverishly continues to turn his pockets inside out.

CLARENCE (*cont'd*)

You've been given a great gift, George. A chance to see what the world would be like without you.

George is completely befuddled.

GEORGE
(*shaking his head*)

Now wait a minute, here. Wait a minute here. Aw, this is some sort of a funny dream I'm having here. So long, mister, I'm going home.

He starts off. Clarence rises.

CLARENCE

Home? What home?

GEORGE
(*furious*)

Now shut up! Cut it out! You're . . . you're . . . you're crazy! That's what I think . . . you're screwy, and you're driving me crazy, too! I'm seeing things. I'm going home and see my wife and family. Do you understand that? And I'm going home alone!

George strides off hurriedly. Clarence slowly follows him, glancing up toward Heaven as he goes.

CLARENCE

How'm I doing, Joseph? Thanks.
(*pause*)
No, I didn't have a drink!

WIPE TO:

EXT. STREET — NIGHT

MED. SHOT — *George moves into the scene. The sign bearing the name of the town reads: "*POTTERSVILLE.*" George looks at it in surprise, then starts up the street*

toward the main part of town. As he goes, CAMERA MOVES WITH *him. The character of the place has completely changed. Where before it was a quiet, orderly small town, it has now become in nature like a frontier village. We see a* SERIES OF SHOTS *of night clubs, cafes, bars, liquor stores, pool halls and the like, with blaring jazz* MUSIC *issuing from the majority of them. The motion picture theatre has become a burlesque house, Gower's drugstore is now a pawnbroker's establishment, and so on.*

CLOSE SHOT — *George stops before what used to be the offices of the Building and Loan. There is a garish electric sign over the entrance reading: "Welcome Jitterbugs." A crowd of people are watching the police, who are raiding the place, and dragging out a number of screaming women, whom they throw into a patrol wagon. George talks to one of the cops:*

GEORGE

Hey . . . hey. Where did the Building and Loan move to?

COP

The Building and what?

GEORGE

The Bailey Building and Loan. It was up there.

COP

They went out of business years ago.

MED. CLOSEUP — *George sees the struggling figure of Violet Bick, arrayed as a tart, being dragged into the patrol wagon.*

GEORGE

Hey, Violet!
            (to the cop)
Hey, listen — that's Violet Bick!

COP

I know. I know.

GEORGE

I know that girl!

The cop shoves George to one side. He looks around and sees Ernie's taxi cruising slowly by.

GEORGE *(cont'd)*

Hey, Ernie — Ernie!

EXT. STREET — NIGHT

CLOSE SHOT — *Ernie stops the cab, and George enters it.*

GEORGE

Ernie, take me home. I'm off my nut!

ERNIE

            (a much harder Ernie)
Where do you live?

GEORGE

Aw, now, doggone it, Ernie, don't you start pulling that stuff. You know where I live. Three-twenty Sycamore. Now hurry up.

ERNIE

Okay. Three-twenty Sycamore? . . .

GEORGE

Yeah — yeah — hurry up. Zuzu's sick.

ERNIE

All right.

He pulls down the flag on the meter and starts the cab.

INT. CAB — NIGHT

MED. CLOSEUP — *George and Ernie. Ernie is puzzled by the stranger.*

> GEORGE
>
> Look here, Ernie, straighten me out here. I've got some bad liquor or
> something. Listen to me now. Now, you are Ernie Bishop, and you live
> in Bailey Park with your wife and kid? That's right, isn't it?

> ERNIE
> *(suspiciously)*
> You seen my wife?

> GEORGE
> *(exasperated)*
> Seen your wife! I've been to your house a hundred times.

ERNIE

Look, bud, what's the idea? I live in a shack in Potter's Field and my wife ran away three years ago and took the kid. . . . And I ain't never seen you before in my life.

GEORGE

Okay. Just step on it. Just get me home.

Ernie turns to driving, but he's worried about his passenger. As he passes the burlesque house he sees Bert the cop standing beside his police car. Attracting his attention, he motions to Bert to follow him, indicating he has a nut in the back. Bert gets into his car and follows.

WIPE TO:

EXT. GEORGE'S HOUSE — NIGHT

MED. LONG SHOT — *The taxi pulls up to the curb and stops.*

MED. CLOSE SHOT — *The cab is parked. George gets out and looks at the house.*

ERNIE

Is this the place?

GEORGE

Of course it's the place.

ERNIE

Well, this house ain't been lived in for twenty years.

EXT. HOUSE — NIGHT

MED. SHOT — *George is stopped momentarily by the appearance of the house. Windows are broken, the porch sags, one section of the roof has fallen, doors and shutters hang askew on their hinges. Like a doomed man, George approaches the house.*

EXT. CAB — NIGHT

MED. CLOSE SHOT — *The police car has pulled up beside the cab, and Bert and Ernie stand watching George's actions.*

BERT

What's up, Ernie?

ERNIE

I don't know, but we better keep an eye on this guy. He's bats.

Ernie switches on the spotlight on his cab, and turns the beam toward the old house.

INT. HALLWAY GEORGE'S HOUSE — NIGHT

CLOSE SHOT — *The interior of the house is lit up here and there, ghostlike, by Ernie's spotlight. No furniture, cobwebs, wallpaper hanging and swinging —*

stairs are broken and collapsed. In a voice that sounds like a cry for help, George yells out:

> GEORGE
> Mary! Mary! Tommy! Pete! Janie! Zuzu! Where are you?

Clarence suddenly appears leaning against a wall.

> CLARENCE
> They're not here, George. You have no children.

> GEORGE
> *(ignoring him)*
> Where are you?
> *(then, to Clarence)*
> What have you done with them?

INT. DOORWAY — NIGHT

CLOSE SHOT — *Bert is standing in the entrance, with his gun in his hand. Ernie is a few feet behind him, ready to run.*

> BERT
> All right, put up your hands. No fast moves. Come on out here, both of you.

> GEORGE
> Bert! Thank heaven you're here!

He rushes toward Bert.

> BERT
> Stand back!

> GEORGE
> Bert, what's happened to this house? Where's Mary? Where's my kids?

> ERNIE
> *(warningly)*
> Watch him, Bert.

> BERT
> Come on, come on.

> GEORGE
> *(bewildered)*
> Bert — Ernie! What's the matter with you two guys? You were here on my wedding night. You, both of you, stood out here on the porch and sung to us, don't you remember?

> ERNIE
> *(nervously)*
> Think I'd better be going.

BERT

Look, now why don't you be a good kid and we'll take you in to a doctor. Everything's going to be all right.

Bert tries to lead George away by the arm, but George struggles with him, trying to explain.

GEORGE

Bert, now listen to me. Ernie, will you take me over to my mother's house? Bert, listen!
          (gesturing to Clarence)
It's that fellow there — he says he's an angel — he's tried to hypnotize me.

BERT

I hate to do this, fella.

Bert raises his gun to hit George on the head. As he does so, Clarence darts in and fixes his teeth in Bert's wrist, forcing him to let George go.

CLARENCE

Run . . . George! Run, George!

George dashes out of the house, and down the street, as Bert grapples with Clarence, and they fall to the ground, wrestling. We see Bert kneeling, trying to put handcuffs on Clarence.

CLARENCE *(cont'd)*

Help! Joseph, help!

BERT

Oh, shut up!

CLARENCE

Help, Oh Joseph, help! Joseph!

Suddenly Clarence disappears from under Bert's hands. Bert gets up, amazed by his vanishing.

BERT

Where'd he go? Where'd he go? I had him right here.

Ernie's hair is now standing on end with fright.

ERNIE
(stammering)
I need a drink.

He runs out of the scene.

BERT

Well, which way'd they go? Help me find 'em.

EXT. BAILEY HOME — NIGHT

MED. SHOT — *George runs up the path to the front door of the house, and raps on the door. He rings the bell and taps on the glass, when his attention is caught by a sign on the wall reading: "Ma Bailey's Boarding House."*

MED. CLOSEUP — *George at the door. The door opens and a woman appears. It is Mrs. Bailey, but she has changed amazingly. Her face is harsh and tired. In her eyes, once kindly and understanding, there is now cold suspicion. She gives no sign that she knows him.*

MA BAILEY

Well?

GEORGE

Mother . . .

MA BAILEY

Mother? What do you want?

It is a cruel blow to George.

GEORGE

Mother, this is George. I thought sure you'd remember me.

MA BAILEY
(coldly)
George who? If you're looking for a room there's no vacancy.

She starts to close the door, but George stops her.

GEORGE
Oh, mother, mother, please help me. Something terrible's happened
to me. I don't know what it is. Something's happened to everybody.
Please let me come in. Keep me here until I get over it.

MA BAILEY
Get over what? I don't take in strangers unless they're sent here by
somebody I know.

GEORGE
(desperate)
Well, I know everybody you know. Your brother-in-law, Uncle Billy.

MA BAILEY
(suspiciously)
You know him?

GEORGE
Well, sure I do.

MA BAILEY

When'd you see him last?

GEORGE

Today, over at his house.

MA BAILEY

That's a lie. He's been in the insane asylum ever since he lost his business. And if you ask me, that's where you belong.

She slams the door shut in George's face.

EXT. HOUSE — NIGHT

MED. CLOSE SHOT — *George stands a moment, stunned. Then he turns and runs out to the sidewalk, until his face fills the screen. His features are distorted by the emotional chaos within him. We see Clarence leaning on the mail box at the curb, holding his volume of "Tom Sawyer" in his hand.*

CLARENCE

Strange, isn't it? Each man's life touches so many other lives, and when he isn't around he leaves an awful hole, doesn't he?

GEORGE
(quietly, trying to use logic)
I've heard of things like this. You've got me in some kind of a spell, or something. Well, I'm going to get out of it. I'll get out of it. I know how, too. I . . . the last man I talked to before all this stuff started happening to me was Martini.

CLARENCE

You know where he lives?

GEORGE

Sure I know where he lives. He lives in Bailey Park.

They walk out of scene.

WIPE TO:

EXT. CEMETERY — NIGHT

MED. SHOT — *George and Clarence approach the tree from which the "Bailey Park" sign once hung. Now it is just outside a cemetery, with graves where the houses used to be.*

CLARENCE

Are you sure this is Bailey Park?

GEORGE

Oh, I'm not sure of anything anymore. All I know is this should be Bailey Park. But where are the houses?

The two walk into the cemetery.

CLARENCE
(as they go)
You weren't here to build them.

CLOSE MOVING SHOT — *George wandering like a lost soul among the tombstones, Clarence trotting at his heels. Again George stops to stare with frightened eyes at:*

CLOSE SHOT — *a tombstone. Upon it is engraved a name, Harry Bailey. Feverishly George scrapes away the snow covering the rest of the inscription, and we read:*
IN MEMORY OF OUR BELOVED SON — HARRY BAILEY — 1911–1919.

CLOSE SHOT — *George and Clarence.*

CLARENCE
Your brother, Harry Bailey, broke through the ice and was drowned at the age of nine.

George jumps up.

GEORGE
That's a lie! Harry Bailey went to war! He got the Congressional Medal of Honor! He saved the lives of every man on that transport.

CLARENCE
(sadly)
Every man on that transport died. Harry wasn't there to save them because you weren't there to save Harry. You see, George, you really had a wonderful life. Don't you see what a mistake it would be to throw it away?

CLOSEUP — *George and Clarence.*

GEORGE
Clarence . . .

CLARENCE
Yes, George?

GEORGE
Where's Mary?

CLARENCE
Oh, well, I can't . . .

GEORGE
I don't know how you know these things, but tell me — where is she?

George grabs Clarence by the coat collar and shakes him.

CLARENCE
I . . .

GEORGE
If you know where she is, tell me where my wife is.

CLARENCE

I'm not supposed to tell.

GEORGE
(becoming violent)
Please, Clarence, tell me where she is.

CLARENCE
You're not going to like it, George.

GEORGE
(shouting)
Where is she?

CLARENCE
She's an old maid. She never married.

GEORGE
(choking him)
Where's Mary? Where is she?

CLARENCE
She's . . .

GEORGE
Where is she?

CLARENCE
(in self-defense)
She's just about to close up the library!

George lets Clarence go, and runs off. Clarence falls to the ground, where he rubs his neck.

CLARENCE
(to himself)
There must be some easier way for me to get my wings.

WIPE TO:

EXT. LIBRARY — NIGHT

CLOSE SHOT — *Mary comes out the door, then turns and locks it. We see George watching her from the sidewalk. Mary is very different — no buoyancy in her walk, none of Mary's abandon and love of life. Glasses, no make-up, lips compressed, elbows close to body. She looks flat and dried up, and extremely self-satisfied and efficient.*

CLOSEUP — *George, as he watches her.*

CLOSE SHOT — *George and Mary, on the sidewalk.*

GEORGE
Mary!

She looks up, surprised, but, not recognizing him, continues on.

GEORGE *(cont'd)*
Mary!

Mary starts to run away from him, and he follows, desperately.

GEORGE *(cont'd)*
Mary! Mary!

He catches up to her, grabs her by the arms, and keeps a tight grip on her. She struggles to free herself.

GEORGE *(cont'd)*
Mary, it's George! Don't you know me? What's happened to us?

MARY
(struggling)
I don't know you! Let me go!

GEORGE
Mary, please! Oh, don't do this to me. Please, Mary, help me. Where's our kids? I need you, Mary! Help me, Mary!

Mary breaks away from him, and dashes into the first door she comes to, the Blue Moon Bar.

INT. BLUE MOON — NIGHT

CLOSE SHOT — *Small tables, booths, perhaps a counter. It is crowded. Many of the people are the same who were present during the run on the Building and Loan. Mary comes running in, screaming. The place goes into an uproar. George comes in, practically insane. Some of the men grab and hold on to him.*

GEORGE
(shouting)
Mary . . .
(to men holding him)
Let me go! Mary, don't run away!

MAN
Somebody call the police!

ANOTHER MAN
Hit him with a bottle!

ANOTHER MAN
He needs a straight jacket!

MARY
(from back of room)
That man — stop him!

GEORGE
(recognizing some of them)
Tom! Ed! Charlie! That's my wife!

Mary lets out a final scream, then faints into the arms of a couple of women at the bar.

GEORGE *(cont'd)*
Mary!

MAN
Oh, no you don't!

GEORGE
(screaming)
Mary!

George can't fight through the men holding him. Desperately he thinks of Clarence, and heads for the door.

GEORGE *(cont'd)*
Clarence! Clarence! Where are you!

EXT. SIDEWALK — NIGHT

CLOSE SHOT — *Just as George breaks through the door, Bert arrives in his police car. He gets out and heads for the door, to run into George as he comes out.*

BERT
Oh, it's you!

He grabs for George, who lets him have one square on the button, knocking him down, then continues running down the street yelling for Clarence. Bert gets up, takes out his gun and fires several shots after the fleeing figure.

                    BERT
              (to crowd)
          Stand back!

Bert gets into the police car, and, siren screaming, sets off in pursuit of George.

WIPE TO:

EXT. BRIDGE OVER RIVER — NIGHT

MED. SHOT — *The same part of the bridge where George was standing before Clarence jumped in. The wind is blowing as it has all through this sequence. George comes running into shot. He is frantically looking for Clarence.*

                  GEORGE
          Clarence! Clarence! Help me, Clarence. Get me back. Get me back. I don't care what happens to me. Only get me back to my wife and kids. Help me, Clarence, please. Please! I want to live again!

CLOSEUP — *George leaning on the bridge railing, praying.*

                  GEORGE
          I want to live again. I want to live again. Please, God, let me live again.

George sobs. Suddenly, toward the end of the above, the wind dies down. A soft, gentle snow begins to fall.

CLOSE SHOT — *George sobbing at the railing. The police car pulls up on the roadway behind him, and Bert comes into scene.*

                    BERT
          Hey, George! George! You all right?

George backs away and gets set to hit Bert again.

                  BERT *(cont'd)*
          Hey, what's the matter?

                  GEORGE
              (warningly)
          Now get out of here, Bert, or I'll hit you again! Get out!

                    BERT
          What the Sam Hill you yelling for, George.

                  GEORGE
          Don't . . . George?

George talks hopefully — George touches Bert unbelievingly — George's mouth is bleeding again.

                  GEORGE *(cont'd)*
          Bert, do you know me?

                    BERT
          Know you? Are you kiddin'? I've been looking all over town trying to

find you. I saw your car piled into that tree down there, and I thought maybe . . . Hey, your mouth's bleeding, are you sure you're all right?

> GEORGE
>
> What did . . .

George touches his lips with his tongue, wipes his mouth with his hand, laughs happily. His rapture knows no bounds.

> GEORGE *(cont'd)*
> *(joyously)*
> My mouth's bleeding, Bert! My mouth's bleed . . .
> *(feeling in watch pocket)*
> Zuzu's petals! Zuzu's . . . they're . . . they're here Bert! What do you know about that! Merry Christmas!

He practically embraces the astonished Bert, then runs at top speed toward town.

LONG SHOT — *George runs away from camera yelling:*

> GEORGE
>
> Mary! Mary!

WIPE TO:

EXT. RESIDENTIAL STREET — NIGHT

CLOSE SHOT — *George's wrecked car is smashed against the tree. He comes running into shot, sees the car, lets out a triumphant yell, pats the car, and dashes on.*

EXT. MAIN STREET BEDFORD FALLS — NIGHT

CLOSE SHOT — *George sees that the* POTTERSVILLE *sign is now replaced by the original* YOU ARE NOW IN BEDFORD FALLS *sign.*

> GEORGE
>
> Hello, Bedford Falls!

He turns and runs through the falling snow up the main street of the town. As he runs, he notices that the town is back in its original appearance. He passes some late shoppers on the street:

> GEORGE *(cont'd)*
> Merry Christmas!

> PEOPLE
> *(ad lib)*
> Merry Christmas! Merry Christmas, George!

EXT. THEATRE — NIGHT

PAN SHOT — *As George runs by:*

> GEORGE
>
> Merry Christmas, movie house!

EXT. BEDFORD FALLS EMPORIUM — NIGHT

PAN SHOT — *As George runs by:*

GEORGE
Merry Christmas, emporium!

EXT. BUILDING AND LOAN OFFICES — NIGHT

PAN SHOT — *As George runs by:*

GEORGE
Merry Christmas, you wonderful old Building and Loan!

EXT. BANK — NIGHT

CLOSE SHOT — *George notices a light in Potter's office window, and races across the street.*

INT. POTTER'S OFFICE — NIGHT

CLOSE SHOT — *Potter is seated working at his desk, his goon by his side. George pounds on the window.*

GEORGE
(from outside)
Merry Christmas, Mr. Potter!

George runs off as Potter looks up from his work.

POTTER
Happy New Year to you — in jail! Go on home — they're waiting for you!

INT. GEORGE'S HOME — NIGHT

The lights are on. There is a fire in the fireplace. The Christmas tree is fully decorated with presents stacked around.

INT. ENTRANCE HALL — NIGHT

CLOSE SHOT — *Carter, the bank examiner, a newspaper reporter and photographer, and a sheriff, are waiting in the hall for George. George comes dashing in the front door.*

GEORGE
(excitedly)
Mary . . .
(sees the men)
Well, hello, Mr. Bank Examiner!

He grabs his hand and shakes it.

CARTER
(surprised)
Mr. Bailey, there's a deficit!

GEORGE
I know. Eight thousand dollars.

SHERIFF
(reaching in coat)
George, I've got a little paper here.

GEORGE
(happily)
I'll bet it's a warrant for my arrest. Isn't it wonderful? Merry Christmas!

The photographer sets off a flash bulb.

GEORGE
Reporters? Where's Mary?
(calling)
Mary!

George runs to the kitchen. He gets no answer. As he goes:

GEORGE *(cont'd)*
Oh, look at this wonderful old drafty house! Mary! Mary!

He comes running back to the hall.

GEORGE *(cont'd)*
Have you seen my wife?

CHILDREN'S VOICES
Merry Christmas, daddy! Merry Christmas, daddy!

INT. STAIRS — NIGHT

MED. SHOT — *The three children are standing at the top of the stairs. They are in their pajamas.*

GEORGE
Kids!

George starts to run up the stairs, and the old familiar knob on the bannister comes off in his hand. He kisses it lovingly and puts it back, then continues up the stairs.

GEORGE *(cont'd)*
Pete — kids — Janie — Tommy.
(takes them in his arms)
I could eat you up!

INT. TOP OF STAIRS — NIGHT

CLOSE SHOT — *George and the kids. He is hugging them.*

GEORGE
Where's your mother?

JANIE
She went looking for you with Uncle Billy.

Zuzu comes running out of her bedroom. George crushes her to him.

ZUZU
Daddy!

GEORGE
Zuzu — Zuzu. My little gingersnap! How do you feel?

ZUZU
Fine.

JANIE
And not a smitch of temperature.

GEORGE
(laughing)
Not a smitch of temp . . .

INT. HALL — NIGHT

CLOSE SHOT — *As Mary comes through the door, breathless and excited. The four men are watching with open mouths.*

GEORGE'S VOICE
Hallelujah!

MARY
(to the men)
Hello.
(sees George)
George! Darling!

INT. STAIRS — NIGHT

CLOSE SHOT — *Mary races up the stairs, where George meets her in a fierce embrace.*

GEORGE
Mary! Mary!

MARY
George, darling! Where have you been?

George and Mary embrace tearfully.

MARY *(cont'd)*
Oh, George, George, George.

GEORGE
Mary! Let me touch you! Oh, you're real!

MARY
Oh, George, George!

GEORGE
You have no idea what's happened to me.

MARY
You have no idea what happened . . .

He stops her with a kiss. She leads him excitedly down the stairs.

MARY *(cont'd)*
Well, come on, George, come on downstairs quick. They're on their way.

GEORGE
All right.

INT. LIVING ROOM — NIGHT

CLOSE SHOT — *Mary leads George, who is carrying a couple of the kids on his back, to a position in front of the Christmas tree.*

MARY
Come on in here now. Now, you stand right over here, by the tree. Right there, and don't move, don't move. I hear 'em now, George, it's a miracle! It's a miracle!

She runs toward front door and flings it open. Ad lib SOUNDS of an excited crowd can be heard. Uncle Billy, face flushed, covered with snow, and carrying a clothes basket filled with money, bursts in. He is followed by Ernie, and about twenty more townspeople.

MARY *(cont'd)*
Come in, Uncle Billy! Everybody! In here!

Uncle Billy, Mary and the crowd come into the living room. A table stands in front of George. George picks up Zuzu to protect her from the mob. Uncle Billy dumps the basketful of money out onto the table — the money overflows and falls all over.

UNCLE BILLY
Isn't it wonderful?

The rest of the crowd all greet George with greetings and smiles. Each one comes forward with money. In their pockets, in shoe boxes, in coffee pots. Money pours onto the table — pennies, dimes, quarters, dollar bills — small money, but lots of it. Mrs. Bailey and Mrs. Hatch push toward George. More people come in. The place becomes a bedlam. Shouts of "Gangway — gangway" as a new bunch comes

*in and pours out its money. Mary stands next to George, watching him. George
stands there overcome and speechless as he holds Zuzu. As he sees the familiar
faces, he gives them sick grins. Tears course down his face. His lips frame their
names as he greets them.*

UNCLE BILLY *(cont'd)*
(emotionally at the breaking point)
Mary did it, George! Mary did it! She told a few people you were in
trouble and they scattered all over town collecting money. They didn't
ask any questions — just said: "If George is in trouble — count on
me." You never saw anything like it.

Tom comes in, digging in his purse as he comes.

TOM
What is this, George? Another run on the bank?

Charlie adds his money to the pile.

CHARLIE
Here you are, George. Merry Christmas.

Ernie is trying to get some system into the chaos.

319

ERNIE
The line forms on the right.

Mr. Martini comes in bearing a mixing bowl overflowing with cash.

ERNIE *(cont'd)*
Mr. Martini! Merry Christmas! Step right up here.

Martini dumps his money on the table.

MARTINI
I busted the juke-box, too!

Mr. Gower enters with a large glass jar jammed full of notes.

ERNIE
Mr. Gower!

GOWER
(to George)
I made the rounds of my charge accounts.

Violet Bick arrives, and takes out the money George had given her for her trip to New York.

GEORGE
Violet Bick!

VIOLET
I'm not going to go, George. I changed my mind.

Annie, the colored maid, enters, digging money out of a long black stocking.

ANNIE
I've been saving this money for a divorce, if ever I get a husband.

Mr. Partridge, the high school principal, is the next donor.

PARTRIDGE
There you are, George. I got the faculty all up out of bed.
(hands his watch to Zuzu)
And here's something for you to play with.

MAN
(giving money)
I wouldn't have a roof over my head if it wasn't for you, George.

Ernie is reading a telegram he has just received.

ERNIE
Just a minute. Quiet, everybody. Quiet — quiet. Now, this is from London.
(reading)
Mr. Gower cables you need cash. Stop. My office instructed to advance you up to twenty-five thousand dollars. Stop. Hee-haw and Merry Christmas. Sam Wainwright.

The crowd breaks into a cheer as Ernie drops the telegram on top of the pile of money on the table.

MARY
(calling out)
Mr. Martini. How about some wine?

As various members of the family bring out a punch bowl and glasses, Janie sits down at the piano and strikes a chord. She starts playing "Hark the Herald Angels Sing," and the entire crowd joins in the singing. We see a SERIES OF SHOTS of the various groups singing the hymn, and some people are still coming in and dropping their money on the table. Carter, the bank examiner, makes a donation, the sheriff sheepishly looks at George and tears his warrant in small pieces. In the midst of this scene, Harry, in Naval uniform, enters, accompanied by Bert, the cop.

HARRY
Hello, George, how are you?

GEORGE

Harry . . . Harry . . .

HARRY
(as he sees the money)
Mary — looks like I got here too late.

BERT

Mary, I got him here from the airport as quickly as I could. The fool flew all the way up here in a blizzard.

Mrs. Bailey enters scene.

MRS. BAILEY

Harry, how about your banquet in New York?

HARRY

Oh, I left right in the middle of it as soon as I got Mary's telegram.

Ernie hands Harry a glass of wine.

HARRY *(cont'd)*

Good idea, Ernie. A toast . . . to my big brother, George. The richest man in town!

Once more the crowd breaks into cheering and applause. Janie at the piano and Bert on his accordion start playing "Auld Lang Syne," and everyone joins in.

CLOSE SHOT — *George, still holding Zuzu in his arms, glances down at the pile of money on the table. His eye catches something on top of the pile, and he reaches down for it. It is Clarence's copy of "Tom Sawyer." George opens it and finds an inscription written in it: "Dear George, remember no man is a failure who has friends. Thanks for the wings, Love Clarence."*

MARY
(looking at book)
What's that?

GEORGE

That's a Christmas present from a very dear friend of mine.

At this moment, perhaps because of the jostling of some of the people on the other side of the tree, a little silver bell on the Christmas tree swings to and fro with a silvery tinkle. Zuzu closes the cover of the book, and points to the bell.

ZUZU

Look daddy. Teacher says, every time a bell rings an angel gets his wings.

GEORGE
(smiling)
That's right, that's right.

He looks up toward the ceiling and winks.

GEORGE *(cont'd)*
Attaboy, Clarence.

The voices of the people singing swell into a final crescendo for the

FADE OUT

THE END

FRANK CAPRA AT WORK

The Original Opening Sequence

The estimating script contains an opening sequence that Frank Capra cut in half when he made the movie. Comparing the original with the final script reveals the full extent of Capra's influence on changes. The handwritten notes contain some of Capra's original dialogue and his production notes, which indicate his directorial skill at delineating character, planning camera angles and shots, writing natural dialogue, and adding small touches that deepen the realism of the film.

CREDITS AND TITLES *are* SUPERIMPOSED OVER *beautiful moving clouds,* CAMERA MOVEMENT *to give impression of* RISING UP FROM *the earth.* OVER THIS, *full symphonic strength, the* MUSIC *of Beethoven's Ninth, which, since its theme is the Brotherhood of Man, might very well form the motif of the overall score, winding up at the end with the choral section of the final movement of the symphony.*

FADE IN

INT. BEN FRANKLIN'S OFFICE AND WORKSHOP — HEAVEN

1 CAMERA OPENS *at entrance to this workshop. Joseph, a sourpuss, flat-speaking, Ned Sparks type, enters. He is dressed in smart business suit and carries a rather large looseleaf folder. On his left breast is a pair of shining, heavenly wings.*

CAMERA TRUCKS AND PANS *with Joseph as he goes by arbor effect with openings in between through which can be seen sunlit fields and heavenly vistas. The keynote of these heavenly sets are no roofs, no walls, no windows, no*

doors. It is eternally day and eternally pleasant. The people, props, furniture, etc., are all familiar to us. What little we see of Heaven must want to make us go there.

Joseph comes into Ben Franklin's workshop and office. Radio parts and various electronic devices are scattered around. In the middle is a large, glass-topped table at which Franklin (dressed and looking as before he died) is examining some delicate electrical device. The props and furniture are all familiar ones but the office has no roof or walls. Arches or columns serve for this purpose. Vines and flowers are in between and distant vistas can be seen. Birds fly in and out.

Next to the table is a device with many dials and also something that resembles a loudspeaker.

2 MED. SHOT. *Joseph walks up to Franklin, who notices him as he stops.*

> FRANKLIN
> Oh, hello, Joseph. New radar equipment from down below —
> *(chuckling)*
> They're not far behind us down there.

> JOSEPH
> *(drily)*
> Yeah.

Joseph is deferential to Franklin, but his manner is definitely tired, disillusioned and cynical.

> FRANKLIN
> Trouble, Joseph?

> JOSEPH
> Looks like we'll have to send someone

down — a lot of people asking for help for a man named George.

FRANKLIN
George who?

JOSEPH
Don't know, Mr. Franklin. The prayers are coming from Bedford Falls, New York.

FRANKLIN
Bedford Falls —

He switches on under-lighting on glass top table. Another switch brings forth New York, lighted up. Franklin looks for Bedford Falls.

FRANKLIN *(cont'd)*
Bedford Falls — yes, here it is — our territory all right. Are the prayers sincere, or are they the "gimme" type?

JOSEPH
I'm getting so I can't tell. Why don't you listen in, sir?

Franklin turns to mechanism alongside, that looks like loud-speaker, and revolves a dial until he comes to Bedford Falls. An overlapping murmur of prayers are heard.

VOICES
Oh Lord, please help my son, George — he needs You . . .

George is a good guy. Please, God, give him a break . . .

I love him, dear God. Watch over him tonight.

Please, God — something's the matter with Daddy . . .

Franklin switches off prayers.

FRANKLIN
It's George Bailey. What day is it down there?

JOSEPH
Christmas Eve.

FRANKLIN
Hmmm. Tonight's his crucial night. Let's see what he's doing now.

(turns some knob; then they both peer into glass top desk as if they see something)

You're right. We must send someone down quick. Whose turn is it?

JOSEPH
That's why I came in to see you, sir. It's 1163–B's turn.

FRANKLIN
Oh — Clarence. We've passed him up right along, haven't we? Hasn't got his wings yet, has he?

JOSEPH
Well, you know, sir, he's got the I.Q. of a rabbit.

FRANKLIN
Yes, but he's got a good heart — high H.Q.

JOSEPH
You know what happened the only time we *did* send him down — he got lost. We finally found him on a merry-go-round in Coney Island.

FRANKLIN
(thinking)
But that was New York City. This is a small town. He's got the faith of a child — simple. Yes, that'll reach George quicker than a high I.Q. Joseph, let's take a chance. Send for Clarence.

JOSEPH
Poor George Bailey.
(toward door)
Johnny!

A young Page pops in at door.

JOSEPH (cont'd)
Ask 1163–B to come in. You'll probably find him flying his kite.

PAGE
Right away, Mr. Kearns . . . Call for 1163–B! . . . Call for 1163–B!

The Page exits.

JOSEPH
(to Franklin)
Of all the billions of people up here, George Bailey has to draw Clarence.

3   CLOSEUP — *parrot at entrance. A parrot is on a stand at entrance. It starts laughing and making funny noises.*

4   MED. SHOT — *entrance. Johnny and Clarence. Page is dressed like "Johnny" of Philip Morris fame, except that he is a colored boy.*

Clarence is a wide-eyed, childlike sort of man past fifty. He evidently belongs to the Seventeenth Century for he is dressed in the pre-Revolutionary American clothes of a moderately well-to-do shopkeeper.

As he comes in, he is nervous, eager and out of breath. He still has his thumb in a copy of "Tom Sawyer" which he has been reading. CAMERA STAYS WITH *him as he goes up to Joseph and Franklin.*

5   CLOSEUP — *Joseph and Franklin. Franklin looks Clarence over with thoughtful interest. Joseph makes a face as if he smelled something.*

6   CLOSEUP — *Clarence.*

CLARENCE
(breathing hard and tripping over something)
You sent for me, sir?

JOSEPH
(to Franklin)
See what I mean? He couldn't fight his way out of a paper bag.

FRANKLIN
Yes, Clarence, we sent for you. There's a man in trouble.

CLARENCE
(beaming)
Splendid! Why, that's fine!

FRANKLIN
(sternly)
I said *trouble.*

Franklin turns on speaker again. This time we hear George's voice, with a bar and juke-box background.

GEORGE'S VOICE
Dear Father in Heaven, I'm not a praying man . . .

FRANKLIN
Listen, it's George himself.

GEORGE'S VOICE
But if You're up there, God — and You can hear me — show me the way. I'm at the end of my rope, dear God. Show me the way.

Franklin shuts it off.

FRANKLIN
At exactly 10:45 tonight, earth-time, that man will be thinking seriously of throwing away God's greatest gift —

CLARENCE
Tch, tch, tch. His life.
(consults his watch)
Then I have only an hour to dress. What are they wearing now?

FRANKLIN
You will spend that time learning some of the details of George Bailey's life.

CLARENCE
Of course. Of course. I'm sure I can help him, sir. My friends used to say I was so gay I made them forget their troubles.

FRANKLIN
You're supposed to do more than entertain him. You're supposed to make him *understand* —

CLARENCE
(humble and moved)
Thank you, sir. I'll do my best. I appreciate your trust in me.

FRANKLIN
I'll leave you with Joseph. He'll give you the details. I promised to take a walk with that new man F.D.R.
(turns to go)
We mustn't fail George Bailey.

CLARENCE
He's alright in here.
(taps his chest)

JOSEPH
(going to desk and beginning to operate dials)
Poor George. If this works, I'm going to believe in fairies from now on.

CLARENCE
(to Franklin, who is leaving)
Sir.

Franklin turns.

CLARENCE *(cont'd)*
If I should accomplish this mission — do you think, sir — I mean — might I perhaps win my wings? I've been waiting for nearly two hundred years now, sir — and people *are* beginning to talk.

Joseph grimaces. Franklin muses thoughtfully.

FRANKLIN
Clarence, you do a good job of this, and you'll get your wings.

CLARENCE
Oh, thank you, sir — thank you.

FRANKLIN
What's that book you've got there?

CLARENCE
"The Adventures of Tom Sawyer."

FRANKLIN
Clarence, by golly, I think you're going to make it!

JOSEPH
(to himself)
Not for my dough.

Franklin leaves.

CLARENCE
(to Joseph)
It's been too humiliating, you know. I've sat there and watched young fellows who've been here only a hundred years being pushed up ahead of me. I've had some ugly thoughts on the subject. — Like I came to the wrong place or something.

JOSEPH
You've got to be smart to get in the other place.

Joseph turns some knobs and glass top table elevates to a vertical position.

CLARENCE
Where does this George Bailey live?

JOSEPH
Bedford Falls, New York State.
(picks up phone)

CLARENCE
Oh, then maybe I can go to Coney Island again.

JOSEPH
You do, and we leave you there this time.
(into phone)
Run JB X 23475, Series NN2. Start in the year 1919.

CLARENCE
What now?

JOSEPH
Sit down here. You're supposed to go down and help George Bailey, aren't you?

CLARENCE
Why, yes — I —

JOSEPH
Well, then you want to know what makes George tick, don't you?

CLARENCE
Well, naturally. I —

JOSEPH
Well, relax and look at the screen. It's coming on now. See the town?

CLARENCE
(squinting, but not seeing anything but glass table top)
Oh, yes, yes —
(honestly, turning to Joseph)
I don't see a thing — where?

JOSEPH
Right there in front of you.

CLARENCE
(seeing nothing)
Now, honestly — you see anything?

JOSEPH

You mean to tell me you don't — aw, I keep forgetting you haven't got your wings yet. Poor George. Now, look, take it easy, I'll help you out. Concentrate. Put your mind to it. All of it. Begin to see something?

CLARENCE
(in wonderment)

Yes, yes! I *do* see something! This is amazing.

JOSEPH

When you get your wings you'll see all by yourself.

CLARENCE

Oh, really? Wonderful! That's what it means to earn your wings.

JOSEPH

Look at the screen.

7   CLOSE SHOT — *The screen. The thing on the screen, fuzzy and obscure, comes into clear focus and is revealed as a soot-stained, snow-covered sign which reads:*

NO TRESPASSING
VIOLATORS WILL BE PROSECUTED
TO THE FULL EXTENT OF THE LAW

HENRY F. POTTER

CAMERA, PULLING BACK, *reveals the sign is on the edge of an empty, junk-filled lot. It is snowing.* CAMERA STARTS MOVING, PASSING BY *the most abject and squalid sort of houses. In the bitter desolation of winter, the hovels look more wretched than ever, and the glimpse we get of the people of the section, shivering in their shabby, inadequate garments, indicates we are definitely on the wrong side of the tracks. The scene is in striking contrast to the sunny vistas of Heaven we have been witnessing.*

The MOVING CAMERA PASSES *several* "TO RENT" *signs on the miserable dwellings, and each of the signs bears the name* HENRY F. POTTER. *The* PROGRESS *of* CAMERA *is leisurely, ruthless, in its exposition of this cold and bitter hell-on-earth.*

INT. PROJECTION ROOM — HEAVEN — MUSIC — DAY

8   TWO SHOT. *Clarence and Joseph.*

CLARENCE

Where in the world is that?

JOSEPH

Town called Bedford Falls.

CLARENCE

What an awful place!

JOSEPH

This is only the slum section. It's called Potter's Field.

CLARENCE

Why?

JOSEPH

It's owned by a man named Potter.

CLARENCE

Must be an awfully poor man.

JOSEPH

He's the richest man in town.

CLARENCE

Then why is the place so ugly and cheerless?

JOSEPH
(a bit impatiently)

If you'll only keep your eyes and ears open —

CLARENCE

Excuse me.

He relaxes into the chair and glues his eyes on screen.

9   CLOSE SHOT — *the screen. As* CAMERA MOVES UP CLOSE *to it,* FRAMING OUT *the screen itself, we are on:*

EXT. TOWN — ON RIGHT SIDE OF TRACKS — MUSIC — DAY

10   MOVING SHOT. *The* CAMERA NOW MOVES PAST *grounds enclosed within a tall, spiked, iron fence. As it* PROGRESSES TOWARD *the entrance, we get a glimpse of several signs:*

NO TRESPASSING
BEWARE OF THE DOGS
KEEP OUT

In the b.g., presently, we discern through the falling snow a gaunt and forbidding house, bleak in the winter landscape.

INT. PROJECTION ROOM

11 TWO SHOT — *Clarence and Joseph.*

CLARENCE
Is that a prison?

JOSEPH
It's the home of Henry F. Potter.

CLARENCE
Why have they got an iron fence all around it? Is he violent?

JOSEPH
(exasperated)
If you'll stop asking questions —

CLARENCE
(contritely)
I'm sorry.

He settles back in his seat again, watching.

INT. PROJECTION ROOM

12 MED. SHOT — *screen. As* CAMERA MOVES UP CLOSE *we are on:*

EXT. ROAD — OUTSIDE POTTER HOME — MUSIC — DAY

13 FULL SHOT. *The* MOVING CAMERA GOES UP TO *the house, looks in at a window, and* STOPS. *When* CAMERA STOPS, *the* MUSIC *stops also, right in the middle of a passage. The simultaneous stoppage of sound and motion is dramatic. Gradually we hear the pleasant distant shrieks of children at play.*

14 CLOSE SHOT — *Potter. Through the window we see a man of about fifty, clad in a dressing gown. His face is ravaged and bitter.*

INT. PROJECTION ROOM — DAY

15 TWO SHOT — *Joseph and Clarence.*

CLARENCE
Who is that? George Bailey?

JOSEPH
No. Henry F. Potter.

CLARENCE
I don't like him.

JOSEPH
You're not supposed to.

16 CLOSE SHOT — *Potter. His face reacts vengefully as he watches kids playing.*

EXT. RIVER

17 *Six boys, ages 9 to 12, are playing hockey with homemade hockey sticks and a tin can. They are playing on the frozen river just outside of Potter's picket fence. Later on we will see "No Trespassing" and "Beware of Dog" signs freely used here too.*
Just beyond is a bridge that spans the river. On the bridge is a little girl of eight, named Mary.

18 CLOSE SHOT — *George. George, a virile, happy boy of 12, is dribbling the puck on the ice, past the others.*

GEORGE
Gangway! Here comes the 20th century! Look out everybody!

19 INT. PROJECTION ROOM — DAY

CLARENCE
Hey, who's that? I like him.

JOSEPH
That's him, George Bailey.

CLARENCE
A boy?

JOSEPH
That's him when he was twelve. Something happens here you'll have to remember later on.

CLARENCE
Oh.

20 CLOSE SHOT — *Harry Bailey, George's younger brother.*

> HARRY
> Pass it to me, George — pass it to me!

> JOSEPH'S VOICE
> That's George's young brother, Harry. Keep your eye on him, too.

21 MED. SHOT — *game. Sam Wainwright intercepts shot.*

> SAM
> Hee haw! Not through me — Hee haw!

> MARY
> *(shouting on bridge)*
> Marty! Marty! Mamma wants you! Marty!

22 CLOSE SHOT — *Marty.*

> MARTY
> Oh, that sister of mine! Go home, will you!

23 FULL SHOT.

> MARY
> Marty, you come home this minute.

> GEORGE
> Mary — you wanna break up the game?

> SAM
> Hee-haw! Mary — hee haw!

He puts his hands to his ears and waggles them.

> MARY
> You're just a big jackass, Sam Wainwright! And you're a bigger jackass, George Bailey — twice as big. Marty!

> MARTY
> *(savagely)*
> Go home, will you?

Boys resume hockey game. George lets fly with a hefty swat which sends can over fence into Potter's yard, breaking a "No Trespassing" sign on the way. Boys stop dead in their tracks, and stare at can beyond the fence.

> MARY'S VOICE
> Marty! Marty!

EXT. POTTER HOUSE

24 CLOSE SHOT — *at window. Through the window we see Potter's malignant reaction to this invasion of his sacred property rights.*

25 MED. SHOT — *at picket fence. The kids have come up and are looking through the fence for the missing puck.*

> SAM
> *(points)*
> There it is!

> GEORGE
> Somebody better get it.

26 REVERSE ANGLE.

> SAM
> Hee-haw.

His eyes are fixed on:

27 INSERT — SIGN ON FENCE:

> BEWARE OF DOGS!

28 BACK TO SCENE: *The o.s.* SOUND *of vicious barking freezes the boys in their tracks.*

> MARY'S VOICE
> Marty! Marty!

29 MED. SHOT — *Kennels. The caretaker, a plug-ugly of a man, unleashes two straining vicious dogs. Dogs start for boys.*

30 MED. SHOT — *Boys at fence.* SHOOTING OVER *boys' heads, we* SEE *the vicious dogs come charging toward fence. Caretaker follows.*

> AD LIBS
> *(from kids)*
> Look out!
> Beat it!
> Potter's dogs!

A warning scream from Mary:

> MARY
> George!

The kids start running in all directions.

31 CLOSEUP — *Harry.*

HARRY
(looking back)
Run! He's opening the gate!

32 CLOSE SHOT — *Gardener opens gate and holds the two leaping barking dogs by the leash. A sadistic grin is on his cruel face.*

33 LONG SHOT — *River. Boys skating away as fast as they can.*

MARY'S VOICE
Marty!

Harry is going off by himself.

GEORGE
(calling)
Harry — not over there! This way, Harry!
(he stops with a look of terror)
Harry!

SAM
George! George! It's Harry! The ice broke!

34 MED. SHOT — *Harry and boys. Harry has broken through the ice. He tries to drag himself up on the edge, but the ice breaks each time. The other boys are hurrying up to the fringes of the break.*

GEORGE
Hang on, Harry. I'll get you. Watch it, watch it, fellers. It's a big crack. Watch it!

MARY'S VOICE
Marty! Marty!

George's eyes race over the situation. He pulls off his coat, drops down and begins to snake forward on his belly. Harry clutches at the fringe of the ice, and again it breaks, dropping him back.

SAM
Don't try it, George.

MARTY
Someone get a rope.

GEORGE
No. This is the way. I read it in a book.
(calling to Harry)
Hang on, Harry! I'm coming.

The standing boys inch up some distance behind George. He throws the coat for Harry to catch, but more ice cracks, and George is in the water. He catches Harry and holds him up.

GEORGE (cont'd)
(to the others)
Lay down on your belly. Make a chain . . . chain.

Sam pulls off his coat and drops down, calling to Marty.

SAM
Get down and grab my ankles.

The boys make a chain on the ice, headed by Sam, who throws out his coat toward George, holding on to one of the sleeves. George misses it, but a second try is successful.

GEORGE
(chattering)
Get Harry out. I'm awright.

MARY'S VOICE
Marty!

MARTY
(almost crying)
I'll kill her if she don't stop —

The boys slowly pull in Harry.

SAM
We got him okay! We got him!

MARY'S VOICE
Marty!

Harry drags himself along the ice, away from danger. The boys throw the coat again to George, and slowly start to drag him out.

QUICK DISSOLVE

EXT. RIVER ROAD

35 TRUCKING SHOT. *The group of five boys are trotting along, taking Harry home. Sam and Marty's mackinaws are over Harry's shoulders.*

George wears Ernie's coat over his. Harry is between George and Sam. They have him by the arm, urging him on. The other boys are carrying the skates, running and jumping to keep warm. Mary is running beside the boys, slipping and sliding in the snow, trying to keep up with them. As Harry begins to flag, George urges him on.

GEORGE
(to Harry)

Shake it up, Harry, like you were an Indian doing a war dance. We'll soon be home.

George prances to show him. Harry feebly follows suit. Mary pulls off her coat and runs up to George, trying to throw it over his shoulders.

GEORGE (cont'd)
(roughly)

Get out of here, will you?

He shakes the coat off his shoulders.

MARY

Your ear's bleeding, George.

GEORGE

Will you put your coat back on and let me alone!

He throws her coat to the ground. Mary picks it up and stands looking after them, in tears.

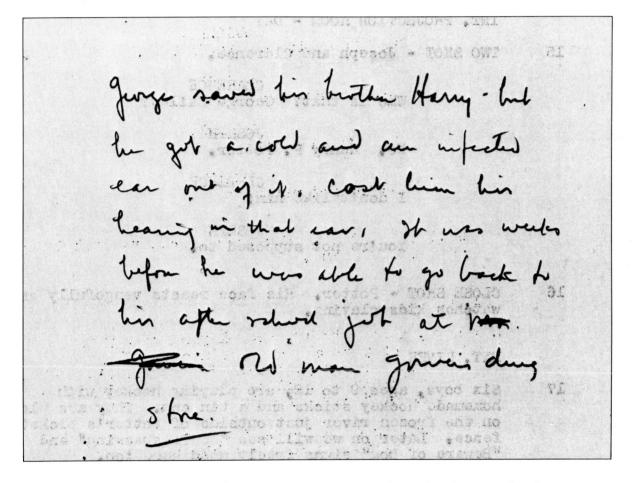

George saved his brother Harry — but he got a cold and an infected ear out of it. Cost him his hearing in that ear. It was weeks before he was able to go back to his after school job at old man Gower's drug store.

Capra's Dialogue Changes

apra's handwritten notes on the estimating script show how he constantly played with dialogue, changing wording to a simpler, more naturalistic state. With every change Capra strove to make things more specific (as in his note to establish the date of 1919 in Bailey's office), warmly human, realistic, and individual. His tendency was to shorten speeches, to use more colloquialisms, and to provide a unique line of dialogue for even the most insignificant bit player. These reprints of notes he penciled opposite the script pages show his style.

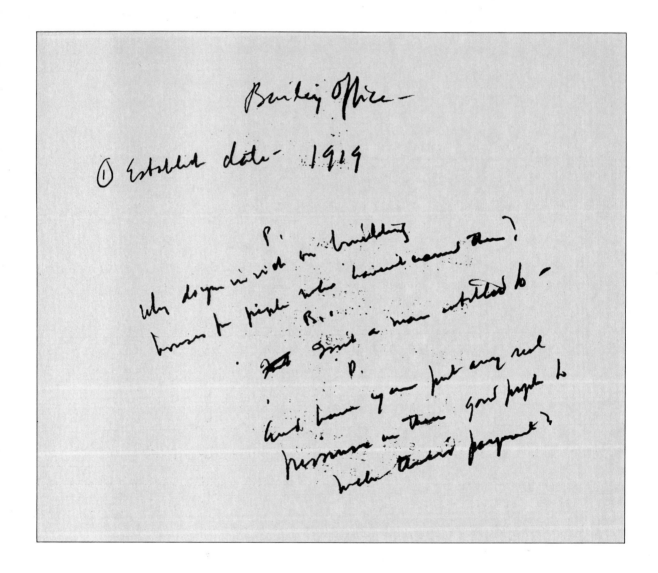

Bailey's Office

1 Establish date — 1919

P [Potter]: Why do you insist on building houses for people who haven't earned them?

B [Bailey]: Isn't a man entitled to —

P: And have you put any real pressure on these good people to make their payments?

334

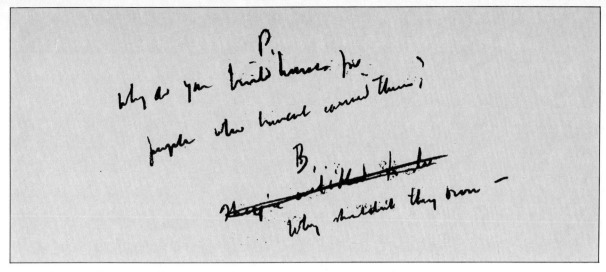

[or]

P: Why do you build houses for people who haven't earned them?

B: Why shouldn't they own —

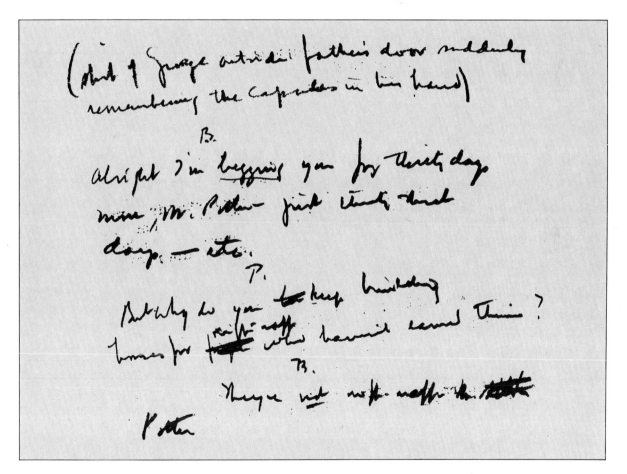

(shot of George outside father's door suddenly remembering the capsules in his hand)

B: Alright I'm *begging* you for thirty days more, Mr. Potter — just thirty short days — etc.

P: But why do you keep building homes for riff-raff who haven't earned them?

B: They're *not* riff-raff Mr. Potter.

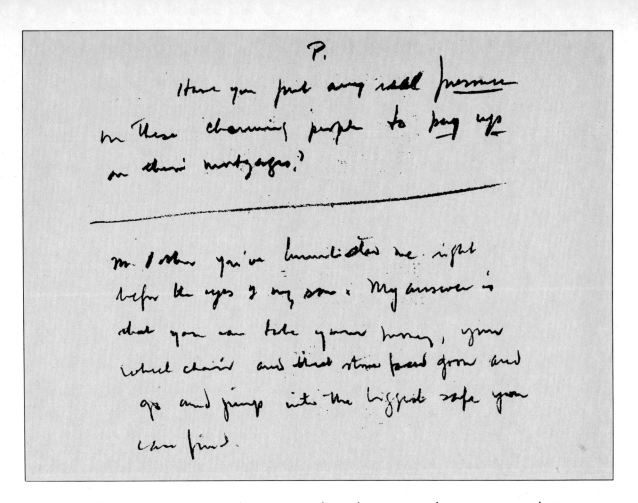

P: Have you put any real *pressure* on these charming people to *pay up* on their mortgages?

Mr. Potter, you've humiliated me right before the eyes of my son. My answer is that you can take your money, your wheel chair and that stone faced goon and go and jump into the biggest safe you can find.

for me — listen you — whatever you are — where's Mary — tell me where's Mary —
Clarence: You won't like it George —
G: Where is she?

C: She's an old maid — unmarried —

G: Where is she before I strangle you —

C: She's about to close up the library — since there was no Bailey Park they continued to live in Potters Field. Fire burnt down several houses that year. Mr. Martini saved the baby but he died next day — nice people they were —

You see George you really had a wonderful life — *

G: I've got one chance left. If I could only find Mary — she'll get me out of this — Mother always said she'd have the right answer.

* The line "You see, George, you really had a wonderful life" occurs in the final script, but *before* the discussion of Mary.

Capra's Planning Method

Capra often wrote out his mental image of the scene, as if it were a story being told, but a visual story of fluid action to be viewed. An ex-ample is this notation for the famous swimming-pool sequence at the school dance reproduced here.

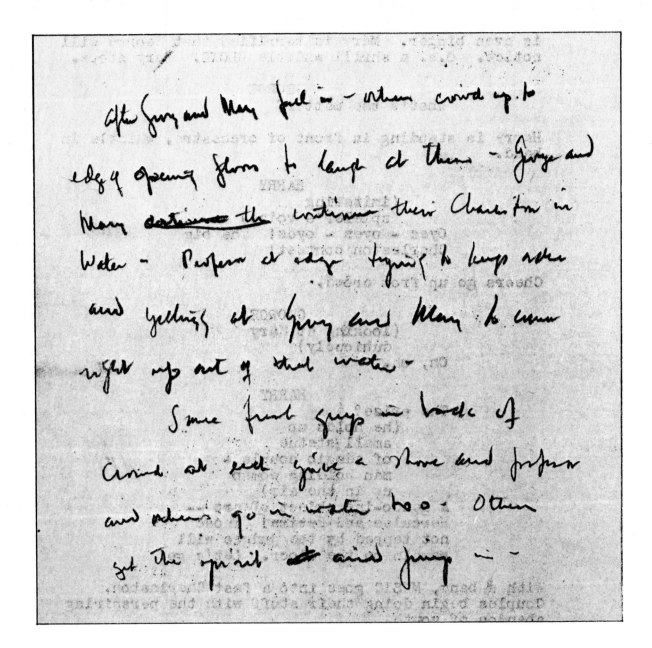

After George and Mary fall in — others crowd up to edge of opening floor to laugh at them — George and Mary continue their Charleston in water — Professor at edge trying to keep order and yelling at George and Mary to come right up out of that water.

Some fresh guys in back of crowd at end give a shove and professor and others go in water too. Others get the spirit and jump in.

The swimming-pool scene is one of the highlights of *It's a Wonderful Life*. It is here that George and Mary first became involved with one another and find the motivation for their walking home together in bizarre costumes due to their wet clothes. It existed clearly in Frank Capra's mind as he worked on the estimating script. As the original scene appears there, George and Mary "whirl to the edge of opening in floor and fall in. Others follow them in — some being pushed — some, getting the spirit, jump in. At the top of the excitement FADE OUT."

The difference is small, subtle, but it definitely illustrates Capra's directorial style. A good idea is made better through two things — having George and Mary keep on dancing in the water, and having the final moment be the principal (not "the Professor") himself abandoning order and diving in (the latter an on-the-set inspiration). Capra always found a way to deepen characterization within any comic moment, so that the laughs were there, but more involvement with and knowledge of the characters happened, too. In a minor moment in the film, the principal becomes a real human being, an unforgettable character. The wild joy of George and Mary, and their ability to be together inside a disaster without losing either their humor or their ability to press on — these qualities make the scene a comic metaphor of their entire life together in Bedford Falls. With the addition of these small touches, the pace of the scene is quickened, the humor expanded. The forward motion of the film is enhanced by a "capper" on the scene, instead of a fizzling out with a lot of unidentified people just jumping in. A very great difference.

Capra's Personal Script Changes

There are two kinds of differences between Capra's estimating script and the final script as shot: minor changes which tighten dialogue and action, and major changes which eliminate entire sections and scenes that, in fact, would have utterly altered the final presentation had they been included. Throughout the estimating script, Capra is always cutting dialogue, streamlining action, and generally tightening the progress of events.

To illustrate major scripting changes made by Capra during the shooting of the film, these sequences are included:

1. The honeymoon evening at the old Granville House
2. The downtown street scene between Violet and George
3. The final sequence, in which the Baileys' friends bring money.

A dramatic example of Frank Capra's changes for the actual shooting of the film is illustrated by the honeymoon evening at the old Granville House. In the final script, Bert and Ernie are involved in the preparations, not only lending a sense of how George's life is deeply touched by these very loyal friends (the film's motif) but also illustrating how Capra uses humor even in his most romantic scenes. There is a brief but very funny exchange between Bert and a friend as they hang posters out in the rain. What could have been overly sentimental, routine, emptily romantic became funny as well as touching and romantic — and again, the scene flowed out toward the next on a "capper" that brought a laugh without spoiling the emotion. As originally planned, the sequence ends with the predictable honeymoon kiss between George and Mary. The revised version has Bert and Ernie standing in the rain singing their heads off, and Ernie provides a capper by kissing Bert's head — an ending that's funnier, more human, and more representative of what the film is ultimately about.

The original scene was followed by a discussion between Clarence and Joseph. Capra understood that a discussion between two nonhumans, charming and comic as it was, would not be as appropriate or as meaningful for the film as the scene between Bert and Ernie. The shift of emphasis is toward reality, humor, and friendship.

Here is the original scene from the estimating script:

115 EXT. GRANVILLE HOUSE

An old-fashioned, run-down house, unpainted and warped by the weather. It once had class but has not been lived in for years. This is the house George and Mary will live in from now on. The rain is coming down. A faint glow of light shines out from bottom windows. George hurries into scene. He stops to make sure it is the right number before going up steps. He goes up to the old-fashioned ornate door. A large bronze knocker is on the door. Within the knocker, a typewritten card is tacked on, reading:

"BRIDAL SUITE"

George knocks with the knocker.

A small port-hole panel opens, revealing Ernie's face topped by a high hat.

ERNIE

Ah, the groom! Entray, entray!

Ernie opens door, revealing himself as a home-made butler. This he has accomplished by rolling up his pants, and putting on an old coachman's hat. George enters.

116 LIVING ROOM

George enters. The house is carpetless, empty — the rain and wind cause funny noises upstairs. A huge fire is burning in the fireplace. Near the fireplace a collection of packing boxes are heaped together in the shape of a small table and covered with a checkered oil cloth. It is set for two. A bucket with ice and a champagne bottle sit on the table as well as a bowl of caviar. Two small chickens are impaled on a spit over the fire. A phonograph is playing on a box. It is playing "The Wedding March." In front of phonograph is a sign reading, "Guy Lombardo." Mary is standing near the fireplace looking as pretty as any bride ever looked. She is smiling at George, who has been slowly taking in the whole set-up. Through a door he sees the end of a cheap bed, over the back of which is a pair of pajamas and a nightie.

ERNIE

Master, if you want me, just ring. I'll be in the music room. Sweet dreams.

Ernie exits and closes door. George looks at Mary. Without taking her eyes off him, she turns off phonograph.

GEORGE

(overcome)

Mary!

They rush into each other's arms, and hold each other in ecstasy.

A male duet starts singing "Oh Promise Me."

Ernie and Bert, the cop, standing in the rain outside window, singing.

117 *Back to George and Mary. They remain embraced.*

GEORGE

Mary, how —

MARY

I cashed in our railroad tickets. You're not too angry?

GEORGE

Darling, you're wonderful — just wonderful — just wonderful.

Their lips meet. "Oh Promise Me" continues.

DISSOLVE

118 CLARENCE AND JOSEPH — *Clarence is continuing the last few bars of "Oh Promise Me." Joseph looks at him with infinite boredom.*

CLARENCE

They sang that at my wedding, you know.

(Check date of song to see if that old)

I was so excited I tried to put the ring on Parson Tuttle's finger — my wife said I never got over it. What a honeymoon we had!

JOSEPH

Must have made history.

CLARENCE

Just like George wanted to go away to build things I wanted to go away to study music, but my wife — she wore the pants you know — she says, "Clarence you get to work in my father's clock shop." And you know what?

JOSEPH
Couldn't guess.

CLARENCE
I went to work in her father's clock shop.
And you know what else?

JOSEPH
I'm not very bright.

CLARENCE
I hated 'em. Tick tock — tick tock —
tick — tock. I hated 'em just like George
hated what he was doing. But I con-
quered it believe me. You see I put my
musical soul right *into* those confounded
clocks. You know, the chimes —
    (musically)
Ding dong — ding dong. Yeah, that was
me, you see. Today all over the world my
chimes are ringing. Ding dong — ding
dong! Ding dong — ding dong!

JOSEPH
Hate to bring up clocks, but it's ten
twenty.

CLARENCE
Yes, yes, knuckle down to work, of
course. What's next?

DISSOLVE

This original scene between Violet and George is
longer than that which appears in the final film.
The changes at first may seem minor, but on ex-
amination they reflect careful consideration of both
George's and Violet's character, as well as of the
elements of pacing and dramatic tension. First of
all, the cuts focus the scene on Violet's not understanding the poetic side of George Bailey, a change
that not only makes her a more specific type of
character — one wrong for George — but also defines George more clearly as the special man he is,
the man who yearns for something grand, romantic, special. By implication, this scene thus defines
in absentia the character of Mary, who will become
George's wife — a more innocent, poetic woman
who can respond to this quality in George.

Secondly, the cuts tighten the overall screenplay and thus the final film. The scene as shot eliminates a third character — the man Violet is with,
whom George socks — the sort of "faceless" char-

acter that weak films often drag in simply to make
a point. Capra accomplishes his dramatic goal
without this minor character, by keeping the action
between Violet and George and, most importantly,
by keeping viewers aware of the town, itself such
an important character in *It's a Wonderful Life*.
This scene demonstrates Capra's mastery of screenwriting and his subtle understanding of how to delineate character with the minimum of event and
dialogue.

MED. SHOT — *Front of Violet Bick's Beauty
Shop. It looks like a new shop. A sign on it
reads:*

VI'S BEAUTY SHOPPE

*Violet is locking up for the night. A couple of
men — apparently her last two customers —
are crowding around her, each one bent on taking her out. There is laughter, kidding and
pawing.*

MEN
(ad lib)
Vi, you promised me tonight —
I called you this morning, Honey —
I got a table waiting, Vi —
Now look, who got it for you wholesale,
huh?

VIOLET
(ad lib)
Now wait a minute — take it easy — one
at a time — and no hands, please —

She sees George walking alone.

VIOLET (cont'd)
Oh-oh. Excuse me, boys — I think I've
got a date — but hang around, fellows,
just in case —

She exits in George's direction.

90A CLOSE SHOT — *George and Violet. Violet
comes up and takes George's arm.*

VIOLET
Why, Georgie-Porgie!

GEORGE
Hi, Vi.

*He looks her over. Violet takes her beauty shop
seriously and she's an eyeful. She senses the fact*

that George is far from immune to her attractions. She links her arm in his and continues on down the street with him.

90B CLOSE (MOVING) SHOT — *George and Violet. Behind them, the two men follow.*

> GEORGE
>
> How's ye old-fashioned permanent wave shoppe?

> VIOLET
>
> Well, it's not a tidal wave yet, but I'm getting some of the city mothers in — thanks to you. Got the fish-eye when I tried to put an ad in the paper though.

> GEORGE
>
> Censorship, huh? We'll see about that.

> VIOLET
>
> The old geezer said I should call it a barbershop. Georgie, can I help it if they hang around?

> GEORGE
>
> You can't help it — and they can't help it either. After all, it's the vernal equinox, when the sap rises in the trees.

He becomes aware of the two men walking behind them.

> GEORGE (cont'd)
>
> Who are those saps?

> VIOLET
> *(carelessly)*
>
> Oh, a couple of vernal equinoxes. Where you heading?

> GEORGE
>
> Oh, going to the library, I guess.

> VIOLET
>
> Georgie, don't you ever get tired of just reading about things?

Her eyes are seductive and guileful as she looks up at him. He is silent for a moment, then blurts out:

> GEORGE
>
> What are you doing tonight?

> VIOLET
> *(feigned surprise)*
>
> Why, Georgie-Porgie!

One of the men comes up and gets into step alongside of Violet, familiarly taking her arm. She stops. He glares truculently at George.

> THE MAN
> *(to Violet)*
>
> Look, dream-puss, is this guy annoying you?

> VIOLET
>
> Did you hear me scream for help?
> *(amiably she introduces them)*
> Georgie, this is Mr. Judson. He sells cold cream.

> GEORGE
>
> Hi.

> THE MAN
>
> Hi.

Holding onto Violet's arm, he starts away. George bars his progress.

> GEORGE
>
> Wait a minute.

> THE MAN
>
> Beat it, stringbean, this one's on me.

> GEORGE
>
> I'm glad to know you, Mr. Judson. I've been looking for you all night.

> THE MAN
> *(surprised)*
>
> Me?

Violet is as much surprised as Judson. An astonishing change has come over George. He suddenly seems to have gained an inch in height. And although he speaks quietly there's a certain tenseness in his voice.

> GEORGE
>
> All night I've been wanting to hit somebody. Practically anybody. Now I'm taller than you are, but you're heavier. Put up your dukes.

Something in George's eyes makes the man let go of Violet's arm and back away a step.

GEORGE (cont'd)
Come on, I'll give you the first sock.

THE MAN
(backing up)
Look now, hey, this is all in fun.

With his left hand George reaches for the man's coat collar and pulls his right back for a hay-maker. The man jerks loose and runs. With a frustrated expression George's right hand comes down.

GEORGE
Cold cream.
(despondently)
It's not my night.

Violet is looking at him with a new and wor-shipful respect.

GEORGE (cont'd)
Excuse me, Vi, the way I feel tonight I'm looking for either a fight, or a —

He stops, then with a sudden impulse he takes Violet's hands.

GEORGE (cont'd)
Are you game, Vi? Let's make a night of it — I've got to talk to somebody. Let's go out in the fields. We'll take off our shoes and walk through the grass. Then we'll go to the falls — they're beautiful in the moonlight — there's a pool there — a green pool —
(looking around to see that nobody is listening)
— and we can swim in it. Then we'll climb Mt. Bedford — and smell the pines — and watch the sunrise hit the peaks. What do you say, Vi? We'll stay out the whole night, and everybody'll talk — and there'll be a terrific scandal — What do you say?

VIOLET
Oh, Georgie — I was out all night last night. Besides — walk in the *grass* in my bare feet?

She makes a face at this. George unconsciously imitates her face in a sickly way. She continues, seductively:

VIOLET (cont'd)
Can't we go to a dance, or something?

GEORGE
(deflated)
Yeah, yeah, dance. Guess it was a silly idea — kinda crude, too. Kinda forgot you were a lady . . . Forgive me, Vi — be seeing you —

He leaves her more perplexed than ever.

VIOLET
You're a funny guy — what's the matter with you?

She looks after him greatly disturbed. Somehow he has made her feel cheap and common. The second man, Judson's companion, who has been waiting in the background, now comes up to her.

MAN
Come on, Vi — how about it? Let's go over and shake a leg. I've got a table waiting.

VIOLET
(still in a daze)
You know what he wanted me to do?
(with rising force)
Do you like to walk through the grass in your bare feet? No! Do you ask me to swim in the moonlight? No! Do you want me to smell the pines and watch the sunrise hit the peaks? No! All you want me to do is dance and to drink and to neck!
(kicking violently at his shin)
Well, get out! Beat it! Let me alone! This is one night I'm going home.

She starts up the street in a determined walk, leaving the wolf nursing his shin.

DISSOLVE OUT

The final sequence of *It's a Wonderful Life* in the estimating script is subtly different from the ending of the movie. The "Lord's Prayer" sequence is not used in the final film. Appropriately, Capra let the healing action of the friends' arrival to help George make its own statement, without any obvious official endorsement from religion. The gathering of friends, the song, the Christmas tree, the parade of characters we've met and grown to love — this is finale enough. Capra has carefully written a line for each bit player, turning them from a generalized group of "friends" into a warm and funny group of specific human beings who directly link themselves to prior events of the film. This changes the scene from a deus-ex-machina event to a real payoff to what has happened. Instead of a solution one finds a resolution. Instead of simply feeling relieved, one feels uplifted. Instead of tacking an ending onto a good movie, the scene brings every event, every character in George's life back to him at this crucial moment.

In the estimating script, even Potter makes an appearance at George's house. But the final version eliminates him: George has triumphed over self-doubt, and there is no need for a spelled-out victory over one mere mortal villain.

Throughout, Capra's notes and changes in the estimating script show his ability to work both ways — to tighten or to expand where needed. In the final scene, he chose to expand by adding specific lines of dialogue and action — one for each individual who enters the room and drops money into George's laundry basket.

The magnificent triumph — the joyously high emotion — the sort of relieved laughter an audience can *feel* — these were added into the script by Capra as he shot this finale.

INT. LIVING ROOM

Uncle Billy, Mary and crowd come into living room. A table stands in front of George. George picks up Zuzu to protect her. Uncle Billy dumps basketful of money on table. It overflows and falls all over.

UNCLE BILLY
George, where've you been? — you never saw anything like it — you never saw anything like it!

The rest of the crowd all greet George with greetings and smiles. Each one comes forward with money. In their pockets, in shoe boxes, in coffee pots. Money pours on the table — pennies, dimes, quarters, dollar bills — small money, but lots of it. Mrs. Bailey and Mrs.

Hatch push toward George. More people come in. The place becomes a bedlam. Shouts of "Gangway — gangway" as a new bunch comes in and pours out its money. Gower comes in with an apothecary jar full. Annie comes in. Martini comes in. Mrs. Martini. All the people we've met. Violet Bick comes in with the money George loaned her. The house fills up. Throughout this there is ad lib chatter directed to George.

AD LIBS
Glad to do it, George.
If it wasn't for you I'd have no roof over my head.
Any old time, for you, George.

Mary stands next to George watching him. George stands there overcome and speechless as he holds Zuzu. As he sees the familiar faces, he gives them sick grins. Tears course down his face. His lips frame their names as he greets them.

UNCLE BILLY
(emotionally at the breaking point)
Isn't this wonderful? You never saw anything like it, George! Mary did it — she told a few people you were in trouble and then — you never saw anything like it. Like a prairie fire, George. People scattered through the town collecting money. No questions asked, George — all they said was, "if George's in trouble, count on me." Nickels, dimes, dollars — you never saw anything like it —
(he breaks)
— a miracle — all these friends — We're saved, George — we're saved.

Without premeditation Uncle Billy sinks down on his knees and starts audibly to say the Lord's Prayer.

UNCLE BILLY (cont'd)
Our Father Who art in Heaven —

George sinks down on his knees. Mary and Mrs. Bailey join in. Gradually the whole roomful takes up the prayer. Even Carter and the D.A. man. The prayer gains in volume. At the line, "For Thine is the Kingdom — " the mantel clock strikes.

CLOSEUP — *Mantel clock registering and strik-ing twelve.*

MED. SHOT — *As the people finish the bells of the town begin tolling. George rises. He man-ages to stammer a couple of words.*

> GEORGE
> Friends — Merry Christmas.

The cry is taken up. Everybody wishes every-body else, "Merry Christmas." Mary comes to life.

> MARY
> Janie — the piano. We've got punch, everybody! Mother, Annie — glasses. Mr. Martini, how about the wine!

Janie hops to the piano and begins playing the Christmas carol she had been practicing. Some-body starts singing — soon all are singing. Mary, Mrs. Bailey, Annie and Mrs. Martini are busy passing out punch.

EXT. GEORGE'S HOUSE — CLOSE SHOT — AT DOOR.

It is still snowing. Potter, muffled in a heavy overcoat, is standing at door. He looks at an en-velope in his hand. It is Uncle Billy's money. From inside comes the Christmas carol. Potter is about to knock, but he can't. Something tells him he is unworthy to be with those inside. He sits on step fingering money — a lonely beaten man. Potter and his money count for nothing at this moment.

INT. LIVING ROOM

CLOSE SHOT. *George, still holding Zuzu, glances down at pile of presents under tree. His eye catches something on top of pile. He reaches down for it. It is Clarence's copy of "Tom Saw-yer." George recognizes it. He opens it and finds an inscription written in it.*

CLOSEUP — *fly leaf of book.*

> "Dear George — This is to remember me by, and to remember this: no man is a failure who has friends. Thanks for the wings. Love, Clarence."

MED. SHOT — *as George stares at inscription. Mary comes into shot.*

> MARY
> What's that, darling?

> GEORGE
> Present. A Christmas present from a very dear friend.

Mary takes it and reads it. Perhaps it is the jos-tling by some of the people on the other side of the Christmas tree, but a little bell on one of the limbs next to George's head begins to tinkle as it swings to and fro.

> ZUZU
> Look, daddy —
> (*she points to bell*)
> Teacher says every time a bell rings some angel gets his wings.

George nods vigorously. Then he looks up, and shaking a congratulatory fist, his eyes and his smile say, "atta boy, Clarence." The voices of the people singing swell into a final crescendo for the

FADE OUT

THE END

AN INTERVIEW
WITH FRANK CAPRA

On November 2, 1968, Frank Capra appeared at the Academy of Motion Picture Arts and Sciences theater as part of a seminar called "Directors' Choice." A distinguished group of Hollywood directors were each asked to select one of their own films that was a personal favorite, attend an audience screening of it, and answer questions about the movie afterward. Although Mr. Capra's remarks have appeared in part in his autobiography and some of this information appears elsewhere in this book, the transcript represents an important milestone in his thinking about *It's a Wonderful Life*. Responding to a packed and deeply appreciative audience — people who were articulate about the film and their responses to it — Capra was able to look backward more than twenty years to the film that was his personal favorite, and perhaps the final high point of his work, and to place his feelings and thoughts in clear perspective. We are grateful to the Academy for allowing us to use this edited transcript.

CAPRA: Thank you very much, ladies and gentlemen. I suppose I ought to tell you why this is my choice to show you as a picture. Primarily because it was the first picture I made after a hiatus in service in the army for about five years, during which I had not looked in the eyepiece of a camera or seen actors. I was very frightened. I really had stage fright because I'd been away for so long. Mr. Charlie Kerner — he was running RKO Studio — said to me, "Frank, I've got an idea that's just made for you." And of course everybody had an idea just made for me, you know. This is another one. So he said, "But you must read this thing." I said, "What is it?" He says, "Well, it's a story. We've had three scripts on it, one by Marc Connelly, one by Dalton Trumbo, and one by Clifford Odets." I said, "Well why three scripts? Why didn't you make the picture?" He says, "Well, because it's not as good as

the original idea of it." I said, "What was the original idea?" He said, "It was a Christmas card." I thought he was pulling my leg about a Christmas card. "The idea came from a Christmas card?" He says, "Yes, we bought it. A man with four names," he said, "wrote it in New York and this was just made for you." I said, "Well, let me read the Christmas card." So I read the Christmas card, and the whole idea of this picture was right in that little Christmas card which he had written and had printed and sent to his friends. I said, "How much did you pay for this Christmas card?" He says, "You can have everything — if you just pay us the original price for the Christmas card we'll throw in the three scripts." So there must have been half a million dollars in those three scripts, you see. So I read the three scripts and as far as I was concerned none of them had the spirit of the original Christmas card. So we started all over again and finally came out with this picture. Well, that was one reason I chose this. Another one is about a year after it was released I got an enormous package, in butcher paper almost — enormous big package, rope — in the mail, and it was addressed from San Quentin. In it was a letter from the warden of San Quentin saying, "My dear Mr. Capra, I've had these letters here for almost a year. It's about a year ago we ran your film at the prison here, as we do on Sundays, and I heard there was so much talk about it that I asked in the middle of the week over the loudspeaker that if anybody wanted to write me a letter about the picture they saw, why, they could. Fifteen hundred letters came in." And they were written on everything from toilet paper to beautiful typewritten paper and everything else and all different kinds of English. But they all expressed one thing. They all just suddenly realized that there was a reason for them being alive. They all said, "Well, if I hadn't been around my Aunt Tillie wouldn't have done so-and-so." And they all expressed themselves in these various ways which made the fact that they were living something very meaningful to them as individuals. It gave them a great lift. I assure you that you couldn't read ten of these letters without choking up, because these are human beings telling their own story. So that's those two reasons that I chose this film outside of the fact that I like it myself too. Now we'll open up the questions.

STUDENT: I couldn't help but be overtaken by the humor in this picture. I was amazed at the detail, and what I'd like to know is, were you as the director responsible for such minute detail as when the policeman was shooting at the man? I noticed when he fired one of his shots a letter in a distant sign went out simultaneously and to me this was hilarious. Who catches such minute detail? Who puts it in? That's what I would like to know.

C: That was an accident. (*Laughter*) And sometimes accidents are very fortuitous, you know.

S: I see. Well, it went along with some of the humor that was planned, I'm sure, and set up in the movie.

C: But that particular one was an accident. That was Clarence working for us.

S: I'd like to know where you found those Christmas cards. Are any more available? I think it's a wonderful picture, and this is the type of picture that Hollywood should make more of. (*Applause*)

S: You made many pictures like this, Mr. Capra. Which was your favorite of all the stories that you made?

C: Of all the stories I think this is my favorite because I think it's a very unusual story. The idea of bringing a man back into the world and showing him what the world would have been like had he not been born. It's a very unusual idea, for me, the most unusual idea that I ever had as a script theme.

S: One has this theme over and over again in your work of a man going back to Shangri-La, the man goes back in time to the town tonight, the man goes back at the end of *State of the Union*. It's as if this theme of a second life is dotted throughout your films, and it's something that you enjoy or like going back to. Is it an accident that the same theme appears over and over again?

C: When you have a right to select your material and you do select your material, it probably is not a total accident, no. Probably something inside of you that is attracted to that particular kind of an idea. You may have something. I never thought of it in that light at all.

S: Mr. Capra, I come from a small town and I feel that you have captured the mood quite well in this film — the way it is in a small town, and the way people live and know each other. People from a city like Los Angeles wouldn't know that. However, my question is, the set of the town seems so large, with the snow and the buildings — did you utilize a number of sound stages, or how did you set up the town?

C: That street was set up at the RKO ranch in the San Fernando Valley. That was a set, exterior set.

S: Mr. Capra, of the other three scripts that were written and the fourth one that you completed, were the endings in the other three scripts any different than the ending that we saw? Was the Lionel Barrymore character handled any differently in the other three scripts?

C: The Lionel Barrymore character was not in any of the other three scripts. They were three scripts that went completely tangential to one another. They had no common denominator at all. One was about politics. The other was about commerce. And the other one was about the small town. Odets' was about the small town. And the character of the druggist and the little scene with the boy — that little scene where the boy saves him from sending out those pills — that was in Clifford Odets' script. And that's about all we used out of the three scripts. The other two scripts were completely different, completely different tales. This idea, but not in a small town like this.

S: Had you any idea of dealing with the Lionel Barrymore character in the film at all? Or were there any other scenes written that were cut out, or did you decide just to leave it as we saw it, feeling that he may have gained the money but he lost what the other people in the town had?

C: What to do with Lionel Barrymore really came up at the time we were shooting it, at the time we were writing the script. How do you handle a guy like that? Well, we just left him alone. We just let him go on about his business. He was the kind of guy who wouldn't change, couldn't change. So we just left him and our main interest was what happened to George Bailey. This Lionel Barrymore character was too crusty, too old, too happy with what he was doing to change. So we just left him as he was.

S: Mr. Capra, this is a question that's being asked each week for purposes of comparison of the directors' approach. What is your approach as you approach the script and cast to create the chemistry, workability among the cast? Would you just go through this in a brief . . . your approach.

C: Well, my approach to a script of course is that I'm completely involved in the script at all times. Actually, even if somebody else likes the scenes I rewrite them, even word by word, so that they are mine finally. I see them as mine. When I start making a picture I don't need the script. I know everything in there that has to be known plus everything else that I do. So it becomes a complete self-expression even though somebody else wrote it, because I have to tell it in film. I have to tell it in scenes. I have to tell it in terms of actors. And when I cast actors, the principal actors of course I usually have in mind to begin with. But say all the bit people. When I cast them I don't make screen tests. I never made a screen test in my life that I can remember. First of all I think they're very unfair to the actors. Secondly I don't think they tell you anything because the tension under which the poor actor's making that test just denies all he's got. So I just interview them, talk to them. And if something says that's the person, I say that's the person, and then I say thank you and good-bye. Casting is completely by hunch. In other words I have to see that man not as an actor but see him as part of the story that I'm telling. If I think that's the man, something tells me that's the man, that's the man, and I couldn't tell you why. And he may be not too good an actor, but I don't particularly care, because there are no bad actors. There are only bad directors. Does that answer your question, or part of it?

S: Part of it. One step further would be, to what extent do you do pre-production rehearsal, and then what is your approach to create the chemistry that you want between the players?

C: Well, I can tell you more about the first part of that than I can tell you anything about the second. Very little pre-production rehearsal. In fact practically none. You want to know about the chemistry between the actors and the story or between me and the actors or the actors and the story? I could talk for hours on this and say absolutely nothing because it's very difficult to describe chemistry. That's part of directing. Part of the directing is to know when that chemistry occurs. It's very difficult to say — to do this, punch this and punch this, and say that'll produce the chemistry. But it's not too difficult to know when it occurs if you are a director. And a director is the only audience a film actor has. You are the sole audience the film director plays to. And you have to know when that chemistry happens, when that scene becomes real. I use this method. I used it once as a trick to circumvent Harry Cohn. He would only let us print one take of each scene. Well, sometimes you take three takes or four takes, and it's very difficult to keep three takes in your mind and at the end of the day you circle the one take to be printed and then you only see one print in your rushes. You wonder if the other two scenes might not have been better. You're always worried that the best scene is in the film vault. So in order to circumvent him on this one-take business and the one take is the slates — the slate number on each take — well, I'd take one and let the actors go through the scene and then when they were through I'd call them right back in again and do it over again, and then call them right back in again to do it over again, three or four times. This gave me three or four scenes with one take. (*Laughter and applause*) He was satisfied. Only one take was circled. So it was fine with him. But in being a little cagey about this take business I found out that usually the second or third take or even the fourth take that actors did, they forgot the tension. In the excitement of doing it over, they forgot cue marks, they forgot some of their lines, they forgot this, they began to sweat, their hair began to come down. They turned into human beings rather than actors saying lines. In other words the actors were just excited out of them and the human beings came in, came together. And I used this method of upsetting actors, getting them out of their routine. Long after I didn't have to put three scenes on one take to get them printed I used it as a method of directing, as a method of easing up, as a method of arriving at that chemistry that you speak of. That was my particular way and other directors have their own way. But this is one way that I achieved a scene where I thought a scene was real, felt real to me. If it didn't feel real to me I would work until it did feel real to me. And that is the chemistry you talk about and that's a pretty difficult thing to explain, but directors have various ways of arriving at it in their own peculiar way. It wouldn't fit somebody else. But my way was to upset the actors, change the lines, change their routines, change their set lines. Any actor came in knowing his whole speech, I'd cut out lines in the middle or put new ones in right at the last minute. They had been rehearsing it. They'd been doing it in front of a mirror. So they had a little set mechanical way of doing that scene. Well, I'd trip them up on that. I'd make them forget the way they did it, and get them excited in the way to do it with the other actors together. And a lot of actors didn't like that because they'd rehearsed a whole lot by themselves. But they did give better performances because of it. That's all I have on the question of chemistry, although mechanical engineering I could tell you a lot more about. (*Laughter*)

S: I'm curious about one detail about the angel carrying the Mark Twain book because this story is, so to speak, the reverse of Mark Twain's "Mysterious Stranger," where the boy dies, and in the story you discover that if he had lived he would have created all kinds of mischief so it was better that he died. He died also by falling through and drowning. And I wondered whether this was in Van Doren Stern's story or how it came to be that he carried a Mark Twain book.

C: No, it wasn't in Van Doren Stern's original. It's a detail we thought of. I've always liked Mark Twain and I thought I'd give him a plug. (*Laughter*) It wasn't in connection with a Mark Twain story. It was not in answer or in any way connected with his.

S: Mr. Capra, were you able to shoot large portions of that picture in sequence, or did you have to go in and out?

C: You know the ideal way of course would be to shoot in sequence. That's to do one scene after another. But then there are many reasons why you can't. The most important one is the budget. If you shot from beginning to end and carried actors on salary that appeared maybe a little at the beginning and a little at the end it just would be too expensive. But wherever possible I tried to shoot in sequence. Wherever possible. And certainly I tried to shoot one sequence, one whole small act or one small portion of the thing in sequence. Even if it is just a master shot I tried to shoot it in sequence without a break. Take all the closeups and everything before going on to something else. That's one of the most difficult parts of directing. You see you've got a thousand scenes, and they're all beads strung on a string, and they must be like a matched string of pearls, and you maybe shoot scene two and then scene fifty and then scene one hundred and fifty, and you must know the growth factor from one scene — from scene two to scene fifty, and you've got to figure that out. Only the director can do that. And this growth factor in characters and plot is what the director has to carry in his head when shooting these various scenes out of sequence. And that's very difficult to do. And when you see a director walk out in back of the set and smoke his pipe and wonder, and pace, or Leo McCarey used to go to his piano and play or George Stevens go out and smoke his pipe and never say anything, then come back and just say, "Let's take it over again," what he was doing was matching those scenes up — each character there — how far has he gone, how far has he grown in this story, which is the part of directing that is very, very seldom talked about and this keeping of this story in mind, matching these beads together, but shooting the beads in nonsequential order. Wherever possible everything should be done in sequence. Wherever it isn't possible at least shoot one sequence from beginning to end before you tackle another one.

S: Mr. Capra, I loved this movie. I really appreciate it. I've seen it a couple of times before and I really liked it. One thing that really disappointed me was that the man Lionel Barrymore played — Mr. Potter, I think it was — I was disappointed to see that he didn't get bawled out enough. I mean, you know, it really seems bad because, you know, I guess it's because in most pictures the bad man really gets defeated. Well, Mr. Potter didn't and that sort of made me mad. He should have really gotten whomped on. (*Laughter*)

C: I think I told you before that we did discuss that and we did try to find out some way in which we could get this old crusty guy to suffer a little. But the only way to make him suffer was to take his money away, and we couldn't find a way to take his money away.

S: The story of our film today is certainly the complete antithesis of today's theme of playing it cool — character-wise. I don't think I've seen a film recently, an American film, that had an outcry, for instance, as was the one of the druggist with young George, done so beautifully and so very well, and so moving. I saw the film, I remember now, when I was very young, probably six or seven. I feel sorry for kids today. They don't have this kind of film to look at and to kind of ponder about.

C: Well, thank you very much. (*Applause*)

S: The kind of story that you seem drawn to and do very, very well. There aren't very many people who do that kind of picture anymore.

C: Well, I hope some of these students here that are thinking in terms of stories might think in terms of such stories. You will notice how much more there is in a picture like this than maybe in a picture you get today. First of all it's longer so it's got more in it. But I mean it's pretty packed. There's an awful lot going on, a lot of comedy, an awful lot of drama, an awful lot of excitement and an awful lot of melodrama. In other words it's a lot for your money. A lot going on here. It's a complete emotional experience. You're up and down. You're up and down. You're up and down. It's not one key. Now these stories are very difficult to make. It's very difficult to make your audience cry and then make them laugh and then make them cry and control them like that. It takes quite a bit of experience, but if you think that pictures like this should be made, go see them and go make them.

S: I was wondering if you could explain perhaps what was the most significant thing about your previous experience in the "Why We Fight" series as it correlates maybe to this picture, which I enjoyed very much, and maybe other pictures that you made since that time. In other words, what experience within the "Why We Fight" series as a filmmaker was most important for you?

C: Well, probably two. One was that it made me more conscious of reality. The reality, the brutality of war . . . it's pretty real. It loses its glamour. It loses its gallantness and heroic stuff. It becomes pretty rugged, and you know here in Hollywood we tended then, and probably tend today, to make pictures for each other, to make pictures like other pictures thinking that that's real life, whereas it's only real life as we see it here . . . I mean real life as you see it in somebody else's picture. So the experiences and all that just let me know that there was much more to the world than what we did here for each other in Hollywood. And that was one thing. It made me think of reality. And another thing, it gave me enormous experience in film editing and how very, very important film editing was and what you could do with film editing, how you could get effects — with the same pieces of film you could get far different effects by the method of putting them together, by their construction and by their juxtaposition and by their filmic flow. And that played a part in my later films. My other films I think are better edited film-wise than the earlier ones. Those two, reality and editing, came out of the "Why We Fight" series.

S: Mr. Capra, I've noticed from many of your other films that you seem to have struck onto a formula that's very successful for you . . . the personification of just plain folks caught up in a moving emotional drama. And it's kind of glossed over, but it's very emotional and very grabbing, and I want to know *why* . . . or first *how* you hit upon this formula and why you used it and became known for it so closely?

C: Perhaps because of my own experiences I knew that part of life better than I did any other. I think every man's picture's in a sense an autobiography. You put them all together and you've got the man's autobiography pretty well there somewhere if he's the filmmaker and not just an employee. And so this feeling to make pictures about the common people was just my answer. As an immigrant kid coming over here I liked the common people, and you know, I wanted to sing their songs.

S: I think your films have a quality of three time periods — the obvious time you're filming, say in the 1919 series when the little brother fell in the pool, and the time you were filming it in 1947 it had that flavor, and yet the overall film has kind of a universal message that still gets people and I like that very much.

C: Thank you very much. If you can relate the temporal in some way to the eternal when you make a film, then you have something out of which greatness is possible. Relating the temporal to the eternal is an ingredient that is . . . there's possible greatness in that duality.

S: Mr. Capra, do you feel that the emphasis on advanced technology in films today has lessened the emphasis on fine acting or the era of fine acting of the thirties?

C: Yes I do. I really think that there's too much emphasis on camera movement, on techniques and on tricks. Unnecessarily so, because the greatest director in the world can't tell a story completely with his camera in terms of human beings. His best tools are his actors.

S: Do you feel that when you made your movies you wanted your actors to come prepared with a creative spirit, an advance idea of what they wanted, or did you want them to come very open and let you fill them with what you wanted?

C: Very open. Very open. I wanted to tell them what the story was about, then from there on they could take it but I didn't want somebody else telling them about the story. I didn't want them to get their own interpretation of the story. About your other question about the technique and the actors, the most important tools are the actors. Everything else must be subjected to the actors. The story is told through the actors. The audiences you make these pictures for equate with the actors and not with the camera. When they notice the machinery your story is out the window. The trick is not to let them notice the machinery. Notice only human beings — don't even notice they're actors. Just notice that they're human beings playing a story up there.

S: You spoke about the mechanics of a film being unnoticeable in a good film. I noticed on this program that Tiomkin got credit for the score but I wasn't conscious of a score at all. I think it probably was a very great job but I was conscious of one thing — that the various levels of the dialogue throughout the picture were almost like an orchestration. Was this consciously done on your part — the height of volume and the low peaks of volume in the different scenes?

C: I don't remember any real attempt to achieve that effect except as it was achieved . . . as the actors looked natural . . . whether they were screaming or whispering or whether they were shouting or speaking normally. I doubt there was any attempt to orchestrate the dialogue. And if you didn't notice the score, which by the way is excellent, that's the best thing I've heard about the picture. (*Laughter*)

S: We've been sort of discussing in the center your depiction and finesse in dealing with reality. Now Negro characters are generally used as stereotypes but I noticed that in the last few scenes you had a Negro woman who was contributing money and also a Negro male in that scene. I wonder if this was an obvious intention on your part to depict reality — I mean, after all, we do see them in real life — and if this was fairly standard procedure in filmmaking of the . . . of that time. I know Stanley Kramer sort of likes to take the credit for having brought Negroes into films but I wonder what you would say?

C: Well, I don't want to take any credit for having Negroes in films because, you know, Negroes to me are like anybody else. They're just people. There was no . . . I guess it was just part of the scene. That's why whenever I thought Negroes should be used or not . . . they're just part of the scene. There was no conscious attempt to be conscious of the black people or unconscious of them. My favorite actor was Clarence Muse. I had him in every show because he was a surefire laugh-getter. I doubt if I ever thought of him as a Negro, actually. I thought he was a fine actor. No, there was no conscious intent in that particular scene as to why these characters were black.

S: Sir, if you were doing the picture again what changes would you make?

C: If I were doing this picture again what changes would I make? I wouldn't do the picture again, that's all. That's one change I'd make. Never repeat yourself. Go on to something new. (*Applause*) It's gone. That's why I hate to take retakes after a picture is over. Dread them. I was unwound. That picture was finished. I'd gotten out of that shell. I'd gotten out of that cocoon. It just was difficult for me and for the actors too. All the scenes looked terrible and it didn't seem to fit. So I retook my scenes that I thought needed to be retaken when shooting, not afterwards, because it was gone — yesterday's newspaper.

S: Sir, when you walk onto a set are your scenes pre-blocked with the camera movements? And if they aren't, what criteria do you use to determine which is best for the action?

C: When I walk onto the set, I have in mind pretty much what I'm going to do the whole day. You've got to keep ahead of the actors and keep ahead of the crew and everything else. I rehearse the whole sequence with the actors and this is just walking through. Could change the whole thing around in the rehearsal or change part of it or do it a different way or not or do it all in one shot or cut it up into close-ups in that rehearsal. Now once I get a rehearsal in which the action of the actors seems pretty good and seems to be interesting from a camera angle, then I rehearse the camera — how to shoot this and then we block it out. Then we send the actors off the set and the crew gets in there — they were the stand-ins — and we lay it out camera-wise, all the movements. Then we light it, light it down almost to the last detail. Then bring in the actors again. Let them walk through it once. Then the crew . . . Then that part is over. Then the taking of the scene. I take it when I think the actors are ready. I get the technical work over with first. Once the actors are keyed up to take a scene I don't want somebody coming in and moving things. I want that all over with. Then the stage is taken by the actors and when I think they're ready then we do the scene. When I don't think they're ready we don't do the scene, and I don't try to bother the actors once they're in a mood to make a scene. It's their show from that time on.

S: Is this mostly from feeling, sir? I mean, you don't have any criteria as such that determine where the camera goes for composition and blocking? Is it mostly feeling that determines?

C: Yes, just by instinct. This is how you'd like to do it. Just like playing violin. That technique kind of comes to you. You find it's your own pretty soon and you visualize it on the screen. Then you try to reproduce it as you visualize it.

S: Would you please comment on your reasons for handling the prologue in just the manner that you did — the beginning of the film in the cosmos?

C: Yes, very interesting because for a long time we were going to show heaven. Well, I can tell you that but how will I show it to you? How am I going to film it? Heaven is never the same to any two people and my heaven wouldn't be your heaven or somebody else's. So it just became ridiculous because I knew we wouldn't please everybody and I knew probably we'd get some laughs with the thing, some laughs we didn't want. So rather than getting laughs we didn't want I used laughs we did want. So in dealing with heaven — I knew it was a ticklish subject — I did it in a humorous way. The little method of dealing with the stars — cartoons — came up after many, many sessions in which we tried to figure out how to shoot the scene between these angels and this little angel. You accepted them as something incarnate. He grew flesh when he came down but up there how do you show him? Now this was a way out of the difficulty. When something gets tough try to make it funny. Then it'll go over. Like Mae West with sex. You know sex is very terrible but not when you make it funny. You can get away with murder but it's got to be humorous. So I had heaven as humorous this way and didn't offend anybody.

S: Mr. Capra, how long was your shooting schedule and what was the most difficult scene to direct?

C: I suppose the most difficult scene and I think one of the best scenes in the picture — actually the most difficult — is the little scene where he comes in and raises hell with his kids there while she's playing and just before he runs out and tries to throw himself in the river. That whole little scene in there with the kid playing the piano — it's a very dramatic scene and yet it can get laughs. The action . . . that little girl pounding on the piano is funny and the little kid asking those silly questions is funny. Here you're playing with dynamite. You're playing with laughs in a dramatic scene. Which do you want them to do? So that particular scene is probably one of the most difficult to stage because if it becomes too funny then the drama will not come over and they'll laugh at the drama too, and the audiences will think they have to laugh at everything. I suppose that was the hardest scene to stage.

S: And how long was your shooting schedule?

C: I suppose around twelve weeks. There was a great deal of exterior shooting — exterior night shooting on that. Well, I want to thank you for sitting here and listening to these silly answers to very intelligent questions.

APPENDIXES

APPENDIXES

Appendix A: The Archive Scripts

Although most people assume that the name on the screenwriting credit is that of the author of the movie, it may also be true that many other people worked on it. This was particularly true of Hollywood in the 1930s and 1940s. Although the Screen Writers Guild effectively protected the writer's on-screen credit, many writers were under contract to studios and made valuable contributions to scripts as part of their working day. They did not always do enough to earn a screen credit. In other cases, writers produced entire scripts that were discarded when newer versions were produced. This is the case with *It's a Wonderful Life* (officially known as "Project 1838" in the RKO files), for which the Archives contain the following:

A story report by David Robison, on the original story "The Greatest Gift" by Philip Van Doren Stern. Dated March 6, 1944. (2 pages)

A story outline by Marc Connelly, entitled "The Greatest Gift." Dated June 3, 1944. (31 pages)

First rough-draft screenplay, marked "Incomplete," by Marc Connelly. Dated August 18, 1944. (90 pages)

First draft revised screenplay by Marc Connelly, still entitled "The Greatest Gift." (Dated October 12, 1944. (186 pages)

Story report by Virginia Denman, identified as covering the October 12, 1944 version by Connelly but referring to it as "a 133-page screenplay." Actually covers the December 19, 1944 version. Dated January 9, 1945. (11 pages)*

A complete screenplay with no identifying name, still entitled "The Greatest Gift." Dated December 19, 1944. (134 pages)

A story report by David Robison, identified as covering the December 19, 1944 unsigned "Screenplay — 186 pp." Actually covers the October 12, 1944 version. Dated January 9, 1945. (15 pages)*

A screenplay/estimating script by Clifford Odets, still entitled "The Greatest Gift." Dated February 12, 1945. (217 pages)

A revised estimating script, incomplete, by Clifford Odets. Dated February 26, 1945. (106 pages)

A story report on the original Odets (2/12/45) by Lewis Clay. Dated June 28, 1945. (14 pages)

An unidentified script, now entitled *It's a Wonderful Life* (with "The Greatest Gift" penciled in over the new, typed title). First-draft continuity. (Believed to be the first script by Albert Hackett and Frances Goodrich for Frank Capra.) Dated January 3, 1946. (200 pages)

Frank Capra's estimating script. Dated March 20, 1946. Contains pages marked "Swerling-Capra," dated April 18, 1946.

The final script as shot. Dated March 4, 1947. (167 pages)

A story report by Norah Gibbons, on the 167-page final script (3/4/47). Dated July 25, 1947. Film was already in production. Brief one-page synopsis, possibly for publicity use.

---

*Confusion arises in analyzing the script chronology because of an error made in identifying the story reports. Virginia Denman, who is said to have written up the October 12 version by Connelly, actually wrote up the unidentified script of December 19. David Robison, who is said to have written up the December 19 script, actually wrote up the October 12 version. This leads to a question: Did Connelly actually write the unidentified version too, or was this script the alleged Dalton Trumbo version? The scripts are a potential area for further study.

Appendix B

Form C-34-A

Typed March 25, 1946

IT'S A WONDERFUL LIFE
NAME OF CAST AND NUMBER

NUMBER	CHARACTER	NAME	Days Work	Days Idle	Days	DATE START	DATE FINISH
#1	George	James Stewart	69	14	83 2 Hol.	4/15	7/22
#2	Mary	Donna Reed	30	40	70 2 Hol.	4/15	7/6
#3	Harry	Tod Karns	11	12	23	4/15	5/10
#4	Uncle Billy	Thos. Mitchell	24	24	48 1 Hol.	4/24	6/19
#5	Potter	Lionel Barrymore	18	32	50 1 Hol.	4/24	6/21
#6	Gower	H. B. Warner	12	48	60 1 Hol.	4/18	6/27
#7	Ernie	Frank Faylen	17	38	55 2 Hol.	5/2	7/6
#8	Bert	Ward Bond	11	45	56 2 Hol.	5/2	7/8
#9	Joseph		5	0	5	7/13	7/18
#10	Clarence	Henry Travers	20	7	27 1 Hol.	6/20	7/22
#11	Violet Bick	Gloria Grahame	14	52	66 1 Hol.	4/15	7/2
#12	Mrs. Bailey	Beulah Bondi	10	46	56 1 Hol.	4/29	7/3
#13	Mrs. Hatch	Sara Edwards	6	24	30 1 Hol.	5/15	6/19
#14	Mr. Martini	Bill Edmonds	6	16	22 1 Hol.	5/29	6/24
#15	Bailey Kids:						
	a. Peter		6	0	6	6/13	6/19
	b. Jane		6	0	6	6/13	6/19
	c. Zuzu		6	0	6	6/13	6/19
	d. Tommy		6	0	6	6/13	6/19
#16	Annie	Lillian Randolph	7	37	44 1 Hol.	4/29	6/19
#17	Pop Bailey	Sam. S. Hinds	3	3	6	4/24	4/30
#18	Cousin Tillie Miss Brackett	Mary Treen	10	29	39 1 Hol.	4/24	6/8
#19	Ruth Dakin		5	8	13	5/4	5/18
#23	Marty	Hal Landon	3	0	3	4/15	4/17
#24	Sam Wainwright	Frank Albertson	7	33	40 1 Hol.	4/15	5/31
#25	Mrs. Martini	Argentina Brunetti	4	14	18 1 Hol.	5/29	6/19
#26	Eddie	Chas. Williams	10	29	39 1 Hol.	4/24	6/8
#27	Freddie	Alfalfa Switzer	3	0	3	4/15	4/17
#28	Nick		8	24	32 1 Hol.	5/21	6/27
	Ben Franklin		5	0	5	7/13	7/18

Code	Role	Actor				Start	End
	Page Boy		2	0	2	7/13	7/15
KIDS - #1A	Little George	Bobbie Anderson	6	0	6	4/18	4/24
			3	1	4	7/19	7/23
3A	Little Harry		1	0	1	4/22	4/22
			3	1	4	7/19	7/23
23A	Little Marty		1	0	1	4/22	4/22
			3	1	4	7/19	7/23
24A	Little Sam	Ronnie Ralph	1	0	1	4/22	4/22
			3	1	4	7/19'	7/23
	6 Boys (Play hockey)		3	1	4	7/19	7/23
2A	Little Mary	Jean Gale	3	0	3	4/18	4/20
			3	1	4	7/19	7/23
11A	Little Violet	Jeanine Roose	2	0	2	4/18	4/19
	Caretaker at Potters		2	0	2	7/19	7/20
	Joe Kepner (Luggage shop owner)		1	0	1	5/1	5/1
	Man Bit (Ext. " ")		1	0	1	5/1	5/1
	School Principal	Harry Holman	3	0	3	4/15	4/17
	Grumpy Old Man		2	0	2	5/19	5/20
	Dr. Campbell & 6 Men Bits		2	0	2	4/25	4/26
	6 Bit Men & 6 Bit Women (Bank Run)		5	0	5	5/20	5/24
	4 Martini Kids		2	0	2	5/29	5/31
	Sam's Wife-Jane		2	0	2	5/29	5/31
	Lester Raineman (Potter's real estate man)		1	0	1	5/25	5/25
	Mr. Schultz		1	0	1	5/29	5/29
	Carter (Bank Examiner)		6	7	13	6/5	6/19
	Bank Teller		1	0	1	6/4	6/4
	Miss Lester (Potter's Secy.)		1	0	1	6/4	6/4
	Mr. Welch		2	0	2	6/28	6/29
	Home Owner (at tree)		2	0	2	6/28	6/29
	Truck Driver		1	0	1	7/9	7/9
	Toll Keeper		2	0	2	7/10	7/11
	Policeman Bit (Sc. 541)		1	0	1	7/1	7/1
	Cemetary Caretaker		1	0	1	7/22	7/22
	Man from Dis't Atty's. Off.		2	0	2	6/18	6/19
	Dbl. Ernie (go thru window)		1	0	1	7/6	7/6
	Dbl. George (fell in pool)		2	0	2	4/16	4/17
	Dbl. Mary (" " ")		2	0	2	4/16	4/17
	Dbl. George (in river)		1	0	1	7/19	7/19
	Dbl. Clarence (in river)		1	0	1	7/19	7/19

Appendix C

BIT & EXTRA BUDGET   3/29/46

IT'S A WONDERFUL LIFE

SET NO. & DATE	SET & DESCRIPTION	NO. OF DAYS	RATE	AMOUNT
#20 4/15 16 17	INT. HIGH SCHOOL GYM-1928			
	Bit man - Freddie	3	100.00	300.00
	" " - School Principal	3	75.00	225.00
	6 Bit boys	3	35.00	630.00
	6 Bit Girls	3	35.00	630.00
	Double - George	1	50.00	50.00
	" - Mary	1	50.00	50.00
	" - Harry	1	50.00	50.00
	" - Violet	1	50.00	50.00
	8 pc. Orchestra	3	18.00	432.00
	1 Leader	3	27.00	81.00
	30 Boys-Extras-Dancers	6	13.75	1475.00
	30 Girls " "	6	13.75	1475.00
	(3 days rehearsal - 3 shooting)			
	20 Boys - extras	3	10.50	630.00
	20 Girls - "	3	10.50	630.00
	20 Extras - Adults	3	10.50	630.00
	4 " - Attendants	3	10.50	126.00
	6 Life Guards	1	35.00	210.00
#15-20 4/18 19 20	INT. GOWER DRUG STORE AND BACK ROOM - 1919			
	20 Extras	2	10.50	420.00
	6 " (with cars @ $5.00)	2	10.50) 5.00)	186.00
	4 Extras - children	2	10.50	84.00
	Welfare Worker	3	13.50	40.50
#15-20 22 23	INT. GOWER DRUG STORE-1919 Same as above EXT. GOWER DRUG & BLDG. & LOAN			
	35 Extras	1	10.50	367.50
	1 Western Union Boy	1	10.50	10.50
	1 Policeman	1	10.50	10.50
	2 Bus Drivers	1	10.50	21.00
	2 Truck Drivers	1	10.50	21.00
	1 Junk man	1	10.50	10.50
	1 Vegetable Vendor	1	10.50	10.50
	15 Kids	1	10.50	157.50
	1 Welfare Worker	1	13.50	13.50
#16 4/24	INT. OUTER OFFICE B.& L.-1919 INT. BAILEY'S OFFICE B.& L.			
	4 Extras	1	10.50	42.00
#16 4/25 4/26	INT. BAILEY'S PRIVATE OFFICE (1928)			
	4 Bit Men	2	75.00	600.00
	4 " "	2	35.00	280.00
	Dr. Campbell	2	150.00	300.00
	4 Extras	2	10.50	84.00
4/27	INT. OUTER OFFICE B.& L.-1928			
	Dr. Campbell	1	150.00	150.00
	3 Extras	1	10.50	31.50
#15-12 4/29 4/30	INT. BAILEY DINING RM. - 1928 No Extras			
#15-15A 5/1	INT.& EXT. LUGGAGE SHOP-1928			
	Joe Kepner	1	150.00	150.00
	1 Bit man	1	50.00	50.00
	30 Extras	1	10.50	315.00
	10 Kids	1	10.50	105.00
	Welfare Worker	1	13.50	13.50
	2 Truck Drivers	1	10.50	21.00
	1 Bus Driver	1	10.50	10.50
	1 Street sweeper	1	10.50	10.50
	8 Extras (with cars @ $5.00)	1	10.50) 5.00)	124.00
#15-20 5/2 5/3	INT.& EXT. GOWER DRUG - 1928			
	4 Bit Kids	2	35.00	280.00
	3 Soda Jerks kids	2	35.00	210.00
	12 Kids	2	10.50	252.00
	2 Welfare Workers	2	13.50	54.00
	20 Extras	2	10.50	420.00
	10 Extras (with cars at $5.00)	2	10.50) 5.00)	310.00

SET NO. & DATE	SET & DESCRIPTION	NO. OF DAYS	RATE	AMOUNT
5/3	2 Truck Drivers	2	10.50	42.00
	2 Bus Drivers	2	10.50	42.00
	1 Western Union Boy	2	10.50	21.00
#21 5/4	EXT. RAILROAD STATION-1932			
	30 Extras (10 with cars at $5.00)	2	10.50) 5.00)	680.00
5/6	5 Train crew	2	10.50	105.00
	3 Pullman Porters	2	10.50	63.00
	3 Red Caps	2	10.50	63.00
	2 Baggage men	2	10.50	42.00
	4 Misc. Vendors	2	10.50	84.00
#15-12 5/7 5/8	EXT. FRONT PORCH BAILEY HOME - 1932			
	6 Boys to dance	2	10.50	126.00
	6 Girls to dance	2	10.50	126.00
	4 Extras (with cars at $5.00)	2	10.50) 5.00)	184.00
	8 Extras (guests)	2	10.50	168.00
#15-4 5/9 5/10	EXT. SYCAMORE ST. - 1928			
	1 Bit man (Grumpy man)	1	75.00	75.00
	3 Extras (with cars at $5.00)	1	10.50) 5.00)	93.00
#15-22 5/11	EXT. MAIN ST. B.& L.-1932			
	25 Extras (8 with cars at $5.00)	1	10.50) 5.00)	302.50
	1 Bus Driver	1	10.50	10.50
#15-3 5/13	4 of above extras (with cars at $5.00)	1	10.50) 5.00)	62.00
#15-4 5/14	EXT. GRANVILLE HOME			
	1 Bit man - Billposter	1	100.00	100.00
	4 Extras (with cars at $5.00)	1	10.50) 5.00)	62.00
#22 #23 5/15 5/16 5/17	INT. HATCH HOME INT. SAM'S N.Y. OFFICE No extras			
#15-12 5/18	INT. BAILEY HOME - 1932			
	6 Bit Men	1	35.00	210.00
	6 Bit Women	1	35.00	210.00
	1 Bit Man - Preacher	1	35.00	35.00
	2 pc. Orch. (Organist, Chello & Violin)	1	18.00	36.00
	1 Orchestra Leader	1	27.00	27.00
	12 Extras - adults (6 with cars at $5.00)	1	10.50) 5.00)	186.00
#15-49 #15-22 5/20	EXT. MAIN ST. BANK & B.& L. (1932 - Bank Run)			
	12 Bit Men	1	75.00	900.00
	12 " Women	1	75.00	900.00
	2 " Policemen	1	35.00	70.00
	60 Extras - Men	1	10.50	630.00
	60 " - Women	1	10.50	630.00
	3 Bus Drivers	1	10.50	31.50
	4 Truck Drivers	1	10.50	42.00
	2 Vegetable Vendors	1	10.50	21.00
	1 Junk Peddler	1	10.50	10.50
	1 Street sweeper	1	10.50	10.50
	1 Garbage Collector	1	10.50	10.50
	12 Storekeepers - Merchants	1	10.50	126.00
	10 Kids	1	10.50	105.00
	Welfare Worker	1	13.50	13.50
	15 Extras (with cars @ $5.00)	1	10.50) 5.00)	232.50
#16 5/21 5/22 5/23	INT. OUTER OFFICE B.& L.-1932 (Bank Run)			
	12 Bit Men as above	3	75.00	2700.00
	12 " Women as above	3	75.00	2700.00
	6 Kids as above	2	10.50	126.00
	Welfare Worker	2	13.50	27.00
	40 Extras as above (10 with cars @ $5.00)	2	10.50) 5.00)	940.00

SET NO. & DATE	SET & DESCRIPTION	NO. OF DAYS	RATE	AMOUNT
5/24	INT. POTTER'S OFF. AT HOME (1932)			
	1 Bit man	1	100.00	100.00
#15-49 5/25	INT. POTTER'S OFF.IN BANK (1934)			
	1 Bit man - Reineman	2	150.00	300.00
	1 Secretary	1	35.00	35.00
#18 5/28	INT. ERNIE'S TAXI - 1928 / 1932			
	No Extras			
#15-59 5/29	EXT. MARTINI HOME-SLUMS (1934)			
	3 Bit Men	1	50.00	150.00
	3 " Women	1	35.00	105.00
	Bit Man - Schultz	1	75.00	75.00
	1 Truck Driver	1	35.00	35.00
	4 Martini Children	1	35.00	140.00
	8 Neighbor "	1	10.50	84.00
	6 Extras - Neighbors (3 with cars @ $5.00)	1	10.50	78.00
	Sam's Wife - Jane	1	150.00	150.00
	Welfare Worker	1	13.50	13.50
#24 5/31	EXT.MARTINI NEW HOME-1934			
	4 Martini Children	1	35.00	140.00
	Sam's Wife - Jane	1	150.00	150.00
	3 Bits - neighbors	1	35.00	105.00
	1 Truck Driver	1	35.00	35.00
	Bit Man - Schultz	1	75.00	75.00
	4 Extras - Kids	1	10.50	42.00
	Welfare Worker	1	13.50	13.50
#40 6/1 3	INT. GEORGE'S LIVING RM.-1934 AND KITCHEN			
	No Extras			
#15-49 6/4	INT. BANK & TELLER'S WINDOW (1946)			
	3 Bit Men	1	35.00	105.00
	20 Extras (8 with cars @ $5.00)	1	10.50 / 5.00)	250.00
#16 6/5 thru 6/8	INT.GEORGE'S OFF. B.& L.-1946 / INT. OUTER OFFICE B.& L.			
	6 Extras	2	10.50	126.00
#38 6/10	INT. UNCLE BILLY'S LIVING ROOM - 1946			
	No Extras			
#15 6/11 6/12	EXT. MAIN STREET - 1946			
	45 Extras (15 with cars @ $5.00)	2	10.50 / 5.00)	1095.00
	2 Bus Drivers	2	10.50	42.00
	2 Truck Drivers	2	10.50	42.00
	1 Street sweeper	2	10.50	21.00
	6 pc. Salvation Army Band	2	18.00	216.00
	1 " " Leader	2	27.00	54.00
	1 Newsboy	2	10.50	21.00
	1 Santa Claus	2	10.50	21.00
	10 Kids	2	10.50	210.00
	Welfare Worker	2	13.50	27.00
#40 6/13 thru 6/17	INT. GEORGE'S HOME			
	3 Bailey kids -(Peter, Jane, Tommy)	4	50.00	600.00
#40 6/18 19	INT. GEORGE'S LIVING RM. (1946 - FINALE)			
	12 Bit Men	2	50.00	1200.00
	12 Bit Women	2	35.00	840.00
	20 Extras (15 with cars @ $5.00)	2	10.50 / 5.00)	495.00
	16 Children (9-16)	2	10.50	336.00
	2 Welfare Workers	2	13.50	54.00
	4 Martini Kids	2	35.00	280.00
	Schultz	2	75.00	150.00
	4 Bailey Kids -(Peter, Jane, Zuzu & Tommy)	2	50.00	400.00
#15-49 6/20 6/21	INT. POTTER'S OFFICE BANK (1946)			
	25 Extras (10 with cars @ $5.00)	2	10.50 / 5.00)	575.00
	2 Bus Drivers	2	10.50	42.00
#27 6/22 6/24	INT. & EXT. MARTINI'S ROADHOUSE - 1946			
	Bit man - Welch	2	150.00	300.00
	2 Bit Waiters	2	35.00	140.00
	Bit Man-Piano Player-Charac.	2	250.00	500.00
	4 Bar Flys (women)	2	35.00	280.00
	4 Bit men - bar types	2	35.00	280.00
	12 Extras - (6 with cars @ $3.50)	2	10.50 / 3.50)	273.00
#27 6/25 6/26 6/27	INT. & EXT. NICK'S PLACE (1946 - Unborn seq.)			
	2 Bit Bartenders	3	35.00	210.00
	4 Bit men - "Types"	3	35.00	420.00
	4 Bit Women - "Types"	3	35.00	420.00
	20 Extras - (6 with cars @ $3.50)	3	10.50 / 3.50)	651.00
	3 Waiters	3	10.50	94.50
#15 6/28	EXT. RESIDENTIAL ST. NEAR BRIDGE - 1946 / EXT. ST.- NEAR RIVER - 1946			
	Bit man - Home Owner	2	100.00	200.00
	" " - Truck Driver	1	35.00	35.00
#15 7/1	EXT.MAIN ST. POTTERSVILLE-1946			
	45 Extras (15 with cars @ $5.00)	1	10.50 / 5.00)	547.50
	2 Bus Drivers	1	10.50	21.00
	1 News boy	1	10.50	10.50
	1 Santa Claus	1	10.50	10.50
	4 Kids	1	10.50	42.00
	Welfare Worker	1	13.50	13.50
#15-4 7/2	EXT. GEORGE'S HOME (GRANVILLE HOME) / INT. HALLWAY - Unborn seq.			
	No Extras			
#15-12 7/3	EXT. MA BAILEY'S BOARDING HOUSE - 1946 - Unborn seq.			
	No extras			
#15-45 7/5	EXT. LIBRARY & STREET - 1946 - Unborn seq.			
	2 Bit men	1	100.00	200.00
	10 Extras (4 with cars @ $5.00)	1	10.50 / 5.00)	125.00
#15-47 7/6	INT.& EXT. BEER PARLOR - 1946 (Unborn Seq.)			
	Bit Negro Porter	1	75.00	75.00
	5 Bit Men	1	75.00	375.00
	5 Bit Women	1	50.00	250.00
	1 Piano Player - Character	1	27.00	27.00
	1 Drummer	1	18.00	18.00
	1 Saxaphone	1	18.00	18.00
	15 Extras	1	10.50	157.50
	2 Bartenders	1	10.50	21.00
	Dbl. Ernie - go thru window	1	50.00	50.00
#30 7/8	EXT. BRIDGE - 1946			
	No Extras			
#29 & #35 7/9	EXT. BRIDGE - 1946 / EXT. RIVER IN WATER			
	Dbl. George	1	35.00	35.00
	Dbl. Clarence	1	35.00	35.00
#36 7/10 7/11	INT. TOLL HOUSE			
	Bit Man - Toll keeper	2	250.00	500.00
#40 7/12	INT. ZUZU'S BEDROOM			
	Bit Kid - Zuzu	1	75.00	75.00
#1 7/13 15 16 17 18	INT. BEN FRANKLIN'S OFFICE (1946)			
	Bit Pageboy - colored	2	75.00	150.00
	Bit Man - Ben Franklin	5(1 wk.)	750.00	750.00
	1 Extra Page	2	10.50	21.00
#11 7/19 20	EXT. POTTER'S HOME & RIVER / ICE RINK - 1919			
	Bit Caretaker	1	100.00	100.00

SET NO. & DATE	SET & DESCRIPTION	NO. OF DAYS	RATE	AMOUNT	SET NO. & DATE	SET & DESCRIPTION	NO. OF DAYS	RATE	AMOUNT
7/20	10 Kids - (Ice skaters & Hockey players - 9-12)	2	10.50	210.00	7/23	10 kids extras as above	1	10.50	105.00
	3 Bit boys (9-12)	2	50.00	300.00		Dbl. Harry	1	35.00	35.00

TOTAL BITS & EXTRAS $43,465.00

#11 7/22	EXT. CEMETARY - ICE RINK (1946 - Unborn seq.)			
	1 Caretaker	1	75.00	75.00

Allowance for raise ($1.00 per day)   1420.00
Allowance for overtime (½ cks.at Ranch)   6519.00
6 Standins @ 84 days   5196.25
Standin for George - weekly - 14 wks.   1190.00

$14,325.25

#11 7/23	EXT. RIVER - BROKEN ICE			
	3 Bit boys - as above	1	50.00	150.00

GRAND TOTAL...............$57,790.25

Appendix D

Form No. C-34

RKO Radio Pictures, Inc.   SHOOTING SCHEDULE   DATE May 24, 1946

PICT. No. 541   TITLE IT'S A WONDERFUL LIFE   DIRECTOR FRANK CAPRA

	ESTIMATED		ACTUAL	
	DATE	DAYS	DATE	DAYS
Start Rehearsal		84		88
Start Photography	4/15/46	2 Hol	4/15/46	2 HO
Finish Photography	7/23/46	86	7/27/46	90

Holidays 2

DAY	DATE	DESCRIPTION OF SET OR LOCATION	ACTOR'S NUMBER	SET No.	LOCATION OR STUDIO	DAY OR NITE	PAGES
MON	5/27	INT. POTTER'S OFFICE IN HOME (Oct. 1932) RAIN Syn.: Run on B. & L.	5-B		STAGE 14	D	1
& TUES	5/28	INT. Hatch Home INT. Sam's New York Office (June - 1932) Syn.: Geo. & Mary talk to Sam on phone. (THESE SCENES TO BE SHOT AT SAME TIME).	1-2-13-24	22 23	STAGE 14 "	N N	8 3/4
WED	5/29	INT. Granville Home and INT. Bailey Home. (Oct. 1932) MIST - RAIN Syn.: Wedding seq. Large crane.	1-2-7- 1-2-7-12-13-16 19-B-X	15-4 15- 12 "	RANCH RANCH "	N D D	6-½D 6-½D
THURS	5/30	HOLIDAY		15-			
FRI & SAT	5/31 6/1	INT. Potter's Off. in bank (June - 1934) Syn.: Reineman talks to Potter about Geo. Potter offers George position.	1-5-B	49	RANCH	D	5¼
MON	6/3	EXT. Martini Home - Slums (June - 1934) Syn.: Martini family move out.	1-2-14-25-B-X	15- 59	RANCH	D	2 3/4
TUES	6/4	EXT. Martini new home. (June - 1934) Syn.: Martini's move in. Sam & Wife appear.	1-2-14-24-25-B-X	24	LOC.	D	2¼
WED & THURS	6/5 6/6	INT. George's living rm. & (June - 1934) kitchen. Syn.: George tells Mary he refused Potter. Mary tells him of blessed event.	1-2	40	PATHE 14	N	6
FRI	6/7	INT. Bank & Teller's window INT. Potter's Off. - Bank (Xmas-1946) SNOW Syn.: Potter picks up Uncle Billy's money.	4-5-B-X	15- 49 "	RANCH "	D D	2 1¼
SAT MON TUE WED	6/8 6/10 6/11 6/12	INT. Geo. Off. B. & L. INT. Outer Off. B. & L. INT. Uncle Billy's Off. B & L (Xmas-1946) SNOW Syn.: Violet borrows money from George. George brings in papers about Harry. Uncle Billy & George frantically search for money.	1-4-11-18-26-B-X	16 " " "	STAGE 5 " " " " " "	D D D D	1½ 4½ 4½
THUR	6/13	INT. Uncle Billy's Liv. Rm. (Xmas - 1946) SNOW Syn.: Uncle Billy & George continue search.	1-4	38	STAGE	N	3¼

DAY	DATE	DESCRIPTION OF SET OR LOCATION	ACTOR'S NUMBER	SET No.	LOCATION OR STUDIO	DAY OR NITE	PAGES
FRI	6/14	Ext. Main St. (Xmas-1946) SNOW	1-4-B-X	15	Ranch	D	1
SAT	6/15	Syn.: Geo. reading paper passes Uncle Billy.					
		Ext. Bldg. & Loan (SNOW)	1-4-X	15-22	Ranch	D	$\frac{1}{4}$
		Syn.: Uncle Billy & Geo. look for money					
		Ext. Main Street (SNOW)	1-12-X	15	Ranch	N*	$\frac{1}{2}$
		Syn.: Geo. driving his car, passes Mother, does not see her.					
		Ext. Main Street (FALLING SNOW)	1-X	15		N*	3/4
		Syn.: End of unborn seq. Geo. runs down St.					
		Ext. Potter's window - Bank (FALLING SNOW)	1-5-X	15-49	Ranch	N*	$\frac{1}{4}$
		Syn.: Potter sees George running.					
		Ext. Lincoln Ave. Uncle Billy's Home - (SNOW)	1-4-X	15-12B	Ranch	D	$\frac{1}{4}$
		Syn.: Uncle Billy & Geo. continue search.			(*NIGHT SHOOTING)	(at end of day)	
SUNDAY							
MON	6/17	Int. George's Home	1-2-15	40	Pathe 14	N	8$\frac{1}{2}$
TUE	6/18	Ext. George's Front Porch		"	"	N	1
WED	6/19	(Xmas-1946 - SNOW)					
THUR	6/20	Syn.: George comes home after money search, is cross with Mary and kids. Bawls out school teacher and husband on phone. He kisses Mary and leaves.					
		Ext. George's home (FALLING SNOW)	1	40	Pathe 14	N	$\frac{1}{4}$
		Syn: George runs home.					
FRI	6/21	Int. George's Living Rm.	1-2-4-5-6-7-8-				
SAT	6/22	(Xmas-1946 - FALLING SNOW)	11-12-13-14-15-				
		Syn.: FINALE	16-25-B-X	40	Pathe 14	N	6-3/4
SUNDAY							
MON	6/24	Int. Potter's Off. Bank	1-5	15-49	Ranch	N	3$\frac{1}{4}$
TUE	6/25	(Xmas 1946 - SNOW)					
		Syn.: George goes to Potter for help.					
		Int. Potter's Off. Bank (FALLING SNOW)	5-10	15-49	Ranch	N	3/4
		Syn: Clarence tells Potter off.					
		Ext. Window Potter's Home (1919 - SNOW)	5		Ranch	D	$\frac{1}{2}$
		Syn.: Potter watches kids play ice hockey (Project ice hockey game on window).					
WED	6/26	Int. & Ext. Martini's	1-14-B-X	27	Stage	N	3$\frac{1}{4}$
THUR	6/27	Roadhouse (Xmas 1946 - SNOW)					
		Syn.: George gets drunk; fight with Welch.					
'RI	6/28	Int. & Ext. Nick's Place	1-6-10-28-B-X	27	Stage	N	6-3/4
AT	6/29	(Redress Martini's) Pottersville					
ON	7/1	Syn.: UNBORN SEQ.					
UE	7/2	Ext. Residential St. near	1-B-X	15	Ranch	N	$\frac{1}{4}$
ED	7/3	Bridge. FALLING SNOW					
		Ext. Residential St. near River. (1946 - SNOW)	1-10-B-X	15	Ranch NIGHT SHOOTING	N	3$\frac{1}{2}$
		Syn.: George finds wrecked car at tree. George crashes car into tree; Returns					
FRI	7/5	Ext. Main St. Pottersville (1946 - SNOW - Unborn seq.)	1-8-10-11-B-X	15	Ranch NIGHT SHOOTING	N	2$\frac{1}{2}$
		(MAKES PLATES FOR SC.545)					
SAT	7/6	Ext. George's Home (Old Granville)	1-7-8-10	15-4	Ranch	N	2$\frac{1}{4}$
		Int. Hallway		"	"	N	1
		(1946 - SNOW - Unborn seq.)	Pottersville		NIGHT SHOOTING		
MON	7/8	Ext. Ma Bailey's Boarding House - Pottersville. (1946 - SNOW - Unborn seq.)	1-10-12	15-12	Ranch NIGHT SHOOTING	N	2-3/4